MW01033394

BIBLE DOCTRINES

Beliefs That Matter

by
MARK G. CAMBRON, D.D.

Introduction by HERBERT LOCKYER, D.D.

OF THE ZONDERVAN CORPORATION | GRAND RAPIDS, MICHIGAN 49506

BIBLE DOCTRINES

Nineteenth printing December 1979
ISBN 0-310-22260-5

Printed in the United States of America

FOREWORD

Paul distinguished between the simplicities of the Word and its more profound truths. When writing to the Corinthians he said, "I have fed you with milk, and not with meat" (I Cor. 3:2). Certainly, newborn babes in Christ thrive on the sincere milk of the Word. With spiritual development, however, the meat of Scripture is masticated.

One wonders whether the prevalent carnality among religious people would have been prevented if only they had consistently listened to doctrinal preaching in their churches. We fear that much of the present-day preaching is not only simple but superficial. The surface of the Bible is skimmed, but its depths are ignored.

How grateful to the Lord we are for fundamental seminaries and Bible institutes all over the land, in which young people are taught to handle the great doctrines of the Word! The Tennessee Temple Bible School is one of the outstanding training schools of this kind in the land, and is fortunate in having a gifted teacher like Dr. Mark G. Cambron as its Dean. Dr. Cambron's monumental work, *Bible Doctrines,* reveals how he has launched out into the deep of God's Word, and is able to present, in a clear and concise manner, those glorious doctrines of which God in Christ is Author, Matter and End.

We bespeak for *Bible Doctrines* a wide circulation among pastors, students and Christian workers in this and other lands!

DR. HERBERT LOCKYER, D.D., LL.D.

PREFACE

"God be thanked, that ye were the servants of sin, but ye have obeyed from the heart that form of doctrine which was delivered you" (Rom. 6:17). "All scripture is given by inspiration of God, and is profitable for doctrine, for reproof, for correction, for instruction in righteousness: that the man of God may be perfect, throughly furnished unto all good works" (II Tim. 3:16, 17).

The crying need of the Church today is the knowledge of the Word of God. The Church is cold, indifferent to the one purpose for which God has left it here – and that purpose is to win the lost to Christ. But it seems that some of God's choicest leaders are falling into the different isms of today; the cause: the lack of the knowledge of the *doctrines* of God's Word. God's children are backsliding into sin; the cause: the lack of the knowledge of the *doctrines* of the Word of God. Christians must feed upon the Word of God to grow thereby. Thus, the Truth of God will act upon Christian lives and conduct. The fact that man will not heed sound doctrine is a sign of the times – a sign that Christ is soon coming. "Now the Spirit speaketh expressly, that in the latter times some shall depart from the faith, giving heed to seducing spirits, and doctrines of devils" (I Tim. 4:1).

There is not a field of service anywhere but which demands of its pastors and ministers the right dividing of the Word of Truth. Souls are saved, yet these souls depend upon the Word for growth. The *Truth* will shape them, and *error* will misshape them. There is a vast difference between a person holding the Truth, and the Truth holding the person. Therefore, in the study of the doctrines of the Scripture, may the student pray that not only shall he *know* the doctrines, but that they shall become a reality to his soul and spirit.

TABLE OF CONTENTS

THEOLOGY
(The Doctrine of God)

Outline for Chapter I

THEOLOGY

I. The Names and Titles of God.
   A. Elohim.
   B. Jehovah.
   C. Adonai.
   D. Jehovistic Combinations.
   E. Eloistic Combinations.

II. The Existence of God.
   A. False and True Systems of Theology.
   B. Evidence of the Existence of God.

III. The Nature of God.
   A. Definitions of God.
   B. Spirituality of God.
   C. Personality of God.
   D. The Trinity of God.
   E. The Self-existence of God.
   F. The Infinity of God.

IV. The Attributes of God.
   A. Omnipotence.
   B. Omniscience.
   C. Omni-sapience.
   D. Omnipresence.
   E. Eternity.
   F. Immutability.
   G. Love.
   H. Mercy.
   I. Grace.
   J. Faithfulness.
   K. Holiness.

V. The Fatherhood of God.
   A. Old Testament Teaching.
   B. New Testament Teaching.

Chapter I

THEOLOGY

The word "theology" comes from the Greek word *theos,* meaning God. Thus, theology is the doctrine of God. To begin the study of the many Bible doctrines we must begin with the Source of all things – God! We must begin with God – there is no one, nothing, before Him. Before anything came into being, He *was*: "in the beginning *God* . . ." (Gen. 1:1); "*God,* who at sundry times and in divers manners . . ." (Heb. 1:1); "In the beginning was the Word, and the Word was with *God,* and the Word was *God*" (John 1:1).

The first things we shall study are:

I. The Names and Titles of God

The name of a person, place, or thing is that by which it is known. The names of God are those by which He is known. They denote His character. Yes, the names of the Lord are those by which He is known to His people; "Save me, O God, by thy *name*" (Ps. 54:1a); "They that know thy *name* will put their trust in thee" (Ps: 9:10).

The King James Version distinguishes the names of God by the use of printer's type. Thus, when you read in the Bible the word "God," you know that it is translated from the Hebrew word *Elohim;* the words "Lord," "God," "Lord God," "Lord God" are from the Hebrew word *Jehovah;* and the word "lord" is from the word *Adonai.* Each of these words, *Elohim, Jehovah and Adonai,* describes the character of God and of His actions toward mankind, distinguishing between the saint and the sinner.

A. Elohim.

The word *Elohim,* which is translated as "God," is found more than twenty-three hundred times in Scripture. Yet this is not a personal name of God, but it is God's official title – what He is, God! – *Elohim!* The word *Elohim* is not only used for God, but for men ("I have said, Ye are *gods;* and all of you are children of the most High" – Ps. 82:6 with John 10:34, 35) and for idols ("Thou shalt make thee no molten *gods*" – Ex. 34:17). It is the title of God just as the word "president" is the title of an office. The President is the official title of the chief executive of the United States. It is not his name, but his title. And likewise, there are many kinds of presidents: of companies, missionary societies, etc. God's *official* name is *Elohim* – His office.

Elohim is a plural noun. At once we say plural means two or more. This is true in English, but not so in the Hebrew language. We have two numbers in English: singular, meaning one; plural, two or more. In the Hebrew, however, we have three numbers: singular, meaning one; dual, equaling two; plural, denoting three or more. Thus, *Elohim* is a plural noun – three or more. Genesis 1:1 states: "In the beginning God [three or more] created the heaven and the earth." Another suggestion of the Trinity is found in Genesis 1:26, 27: "And God *[Elohim]* said, "Let *us* make man in *our* image."

The literal meaning of *Elohim* is The Putter-forth of Power, The Strong One. And in the first chapter of Genesis, *Elohim* is described as putting forth His power in these ten words: created, made (fashioned), moved, said, saw, called, divided, set, ended and blessed.

No creature has power but that which God has given him. Power belongeth unto God. Man has to work for his power in all phases of life; God only has to speak, and it is done. God not only creates, but *keeps* what He brings forth out of nothing.

Elohim (God) has power in government. Daniel pointed this out, and Nebuchadnezzar had to experience it "that the living may know that the most High ruleth in the kingdom of men, and giveth it to whomsoever he will, and setteth up over it the basest of men" (Dan. 4:17). With pride filling his heart, Nebuchadnezzar was struck with madness until he acknowledged that the Most High *did* rule. Then only did his reason return unto him, and he became a firm believer in this truth.

Elohim (God) has power in judgment, whether upon man or nation. When He smites, none can resist Him.

El is the singular form of *Elohim.* It is found two hundred and fifty times in Scripture. It is used in the proper names of men, such as Samu*el* (asked of God) and *Eli*jah (Jehovah is my God).

B. Jehovah.

Remember, the words God and Lord (all capital letters) in the King James version are best translated *Jehovah. Jehovah* is the *personal* name of God. It is that Name which is above every other name. The meaning of the word is Redeemer. Every time it is used in the Scriptures it is connected with deliverance by God: "And it came to pass, when the captains of the chariots saw Jehoshaphat, that they said, It is the king of Israel. Therefore they compassed about him to fight: but Jehoshaphat cried out and the Lord *[Jehovah]* helped him; and God moved them to depart from him" (II Chron. 18:31).

While the personal name of God, *Jehovah,* was written, it was never pronounced. The Jews considered that name too sacred to be spoken by human lips. It is a possibility that this pronunciation is not correct even today, for the Hebrew language is written without any vowels. The name *Jehovah,* in the Hebrew, is spelled *JHVH*. We trust that we are pronouncing it correctly: It could be pronounced *Jeheveh,* or *Jihivih,* or *Jahavah,* or many other different ways. When the scribes came to this name *Jehovah* to copy, they washed their bodies, and the pens with which they spelled this name were cleansed. Even in public, when readers of sacred Scriptures came to this word they would not pronounce it, fearing they would take it in vain, but would substitute the word *Elohim* or *Adonai* in its place. One reason why the word *Jehovah* was suppressed was to impress its sacredness upon the minds of the people.

When the Lord *[Jehovah]* appeared unto Moses in the burning bush, and commissioned him to lead the children of Israel out of Egypt into the Promised Land, Moses asked, "When I come unto the children of Israel, and say unto them, The God of your fathers hath sent me unto you; and they shall say to me, What is his name? what shall I say unto them?" God said unto him, "I AM THAT I AM . . . I AM hath sent me unto you" (Ex. 3:13, 14). *Jehovah* is the eternal *I AM*. There is no past nor future with *Jehovah;* He is the Eternal Present, the self-existent One — One that made Himself known.

In Exodus 20:2 we read: "I am the Lord thy God. . . ." "I

am Jehovah thy Elohim." There were many different Elohims, but there was only one *Jehovah.* You read in the Word, the "Elohim of Israel"; but never, the "*Jehovah* of Israel"; for there were no more Jehovahs. When Elijah and the prophets of Baal had a contest, it was to determine which was Elohim (God), *Jehovah* or Baal.

Yes, *Jehovah* was always related in a redemptive way with His own people, but His relationship to His creatures (this includes unregenerated men) was always as Elohim. The same today. God is God of all the unsaved, but He is *Jehovah,* the Father, of all who are saved. The Book of Jonah illustrates this. In chapters three and four the people called upon Elohim, but Jonah called upon *Jehovah!* They were lost; he was saved. They became saved, and could, after their salvation, call God *Jehovah.* See other Scriptures: Judges 7:14, 15; II Chronicles 19:6-9; Genesis 7:16; I Samuel 17:46.

We have another name for God, and that is *JAH.* It is found only once in the King James version, but it occurs forty-eight other times in the corrected translations. Some Bible scholars believe that *JAH* is an abbreviation of Jehovah. The meaning is the same. "Sing unto God, sing praises to his name: extol him that rideth upon the heavens by his name *JAH,* and rejoice before him" (Ps. 68:4). The name *JAH* is always connected with praise, and is first found in Exodus 15:2.

We believe that the word "God" (Elohim), being plural in Genesis 1:1, definitely suggests that the Trinity created the heavens and the earth. Yet we find that modern thought interprets this differently. Modern thought says that this portion of the Word should read, "In the beginning *Gods* created the heavens and the earth." And the reason for this, they say, is that Israel, to begin with, believed in many gods, but that their religion evolved into monotheism. This form of reasoning has proved difficult to many college students. Is there any Scripture which will refute this? Absolutely. Turn to Deuteronomy 6:4 – "Hear, O Israel: the Lord our God is one Lord." Now, put the correct words of *Elohim* and *Jehovah* in this passage and you will see that the Word plainly reveals the Trinity of Genesis 1:1: "Hear, O Israel, JEHOVAH our ELOHIM *[three or more persons]* is one JEHOVAH." Therefore, man began with a belief in *one* God and later degenerated into the depths "and changed the glory of the uncorruptible God into an image made like to corruptible man, and to birds, and fourfooted beasts, and creeping things" (Rom. 1:23).

C. Adonai.

The term *Adonai* really means master, or owner; one who owns, one who rules, one who blessed his own. It is found first in Genesis 15:1, 2: "After these things the word of the LORD came unto Abram in a vision, saying, Fear not, Abram: I am thy shield, and thy exceeding great reward. And Abram said, Lord GOD, what wilt thou give me, seeing I go childless, and the steward of my house is this Eliezer of Damascus?"

Adonai can always be known by the word "Lord," or "lord" in the Old Testament of the King James Version. There are two different forms of this word: *Adon,* which is singular, and *Adonai,* which is plural.

Adonai is used two ways in the Scriptures when related to man and his earthly relationships: As a *master* of his slaves – "And the servant put his hand under the thigh of Abraham his *master,* and sware to him concerning that matter. And the servant took ten camels of the camels of his *master,* and departed; for all the goods of his *master* . . ." (Gen. 24:9, 10a); and as a *husband* to his wife – "Even as Sarah obeyed Abraham, calling him *lord* [Adonai] . . . (I Peter 3:6a). See also Genesis 18:12.

A Hebrew could sell himself to another Hebrew, who became his master. But he could not sell himself forever; for at the Sabbatical Year, or the Year of Jubilee, all slaves were freed. Yet, there was a way by which a slave could become a slave forever, and that was by *choice*: "And if the servant shall plainly say, I love my master, my wife, and my children; I will not go out free: then his master shall bring him unto the judges; he shall also bring him to the door, or unto the door post; and his master shall bore his ear through with an aul; and he shall serve him for ever" (Ex. 21:5, 6). Paul said that he was a bond slave (servant) of Jesus Christ, bought by blood and bound by Love! Every time you use the name Lord Jesus Christ, you say, "He is my Master." "Ye call me *Master* and *Lord*: and ye say well; for so I am" (John 13:13).

D. Jehovistic Combinations.

1. *Jehovah-jireh* – "the Lord will provide." "Abraham called the name of that place *Jehovah-jireh*: as it is said to this day, In the mount of the LORD it shall be seen" (Gen. 22:14). This was the occasion when Abraham led his son, his only be-

gotten son, Isaac, to the mount. Isaac carried the wood; Abraham carried the knife and the fire. His son asked the whereabouts of the sacrifice. To this Father Abraham replied, "God will *provide* himself a lamb for a burnt-offering." And God did! Before Abraham could kill his son as a sacrifice demanded by God, the angel of the LORD stayed his hand; his eyes looked upon the thicket and saw the ram which the LORD had provided. Nearly two thousand years ago the Son of God carried, Himself, a wooden burden, the Cross; and the Father held the fire (which speaks of judgment), and the knife (which speaks of death), and God *did* provide *Himself* a Sacrifice for our sins – His Son, our Lord and Saviour, Jesus Christ. Have you found Him to be your *Jehovah-jireh?* Whatever may come, remember, He is *Jehovah-jireh* – "the LORD will provide."

2. *Jehovah-Rapha* – "the Lord that healeth." ["The LORD] said, If thou wilt diligently hearken to the voice of the LORD thy God, and wilt do that which is right in his sight, and wilt give ear to his commandments, and keep all his statutes, I will put none of these diseases upon thee, which I have brought upon the Egyptians: for I am the LORD *[Jehovah-Rapha]* that healeth thee" (Ex. 15:26). He is LORD, The Physician. The way this is used is not, "I will *cure* your diseases"; but, "I won't *put* sickness upon you."

The world is called the "sick world"; Livingstone called Africa the "open sore"; and the reason for this is the deep wound of *sin!* The word "heal" is an interesting word and means to repair, mend, cure. And there is perfect cure in *Jehovah-Rapha,* for "by his stripes we are healed" (I Peter 2:24). See also Psalm 41:4.

3. *Jehovah-nissi* – "the Lord our Banner." "Moses built an altar, and called the name of it *Jehovah-nissi*" (Ex. 17:15). The LORD is our Victory. Christ crucified is our Banner of Victory!

4. *Jehovah-Qadash* – "the LORD that doth sanctify." "Ye shall keep my statutes, and do them: I am the LORD *[Jehovah-Qadash]* which sanctify you" (Lev. 20:8). And God is the same LORD of the Christian as of the Hebrew: "Then said he, Lo, I come to do thy will, O God. . . . By the which will we are sanctified through the offering of the body of Jesus Christ once for all" (Heb. 10:9, 10). See also Hebrews 10:14, and Exodus 31:13.

5. *Jehovah-shalom* – "the LORD our Peace." "Then Gideon built an altar there unto the LORD, and called it *Jehovah-shalom*: unto this day it is yet in Ophrah of the Abiezrites" (Judg. 6:24). There is only one way to secure peace today, and that is through the Lord Jesus Christ. He is our Peace: "For he is our peace, who hath made both one, and hath broken down the middle wall of partition between us" (Eph. 2:14). See also Romans 5:1.

6. *Jehovah-Tsidkenu* – "the LORD our Righteousness." "In his days Judah shall be saved, and Israel shall dwell safely: and this is his name whereby he shall be called, THE LORD OUR RIGHTEOUSNESS" (Jer. 23:6). Israel shall be restored to the Land of Promise once again, and during the Millennium Jehovah shall be called *Jehovah-Tsidkenu* – "the LORD our Righteousness." The LORD did come, the only righteous one, yet they crucified Him. But one day He shall come the second time, and Israel shall claim the Lord Jesus Christ as their own Righteousness. Christ Jesus is the only Righteousness that any can claim.

7. *Jehovah-Shammah* – "the LORD is There." "It was round about eighteen thousand measures: and the name of the city from that day shall be, The LORD *[Jehovah-Shammah]* is there" (Ezek. 48:35). When Israel is restored to the land, and the earth shall be full of knowledge of the LORD, Jerusalem shall be called *Jehovah-Shammah* – "the LORD is There.'

8. *Jehovah-Sabaoth* – "the LORD of Host." "This man went up out of his city yearly to worship and to sacrifice unto the LORD of hosts *[Jehovah-Sabaoth]* in Shiloh" (I Sam. 1:3a). Israel is the Host; the LORD is the LORD of Hosts. See also Exodus 12:41; II Kings 6:14-23; Romans 9:29; James 5:4.

9. *Jehovah Ra-ah* – "the LORD my Shepherd." "The LORD *[Jehovah Ra-ah]* is my shepherd; I shall not want." (Ps. 23:1). One time a little girl was quoting this verse, and this is the way she said it: "The LORD is my Shepherd, why should I worry?" Have you found that Source of Strength? Have you found perfect peace by following the Saviour wherever He leads? Fears will not annoy; darkness cannot distress; poverty is not able to destroy if Jesus is your *Jehovah Ra-ah* – your Shepherd.

E. Eloistic Combinations.

As there are the Jehovistic combinations, so are there the *Eloistic* combinations.

1. *El Elyon* – "Most High God." "Melchizedek king of Salem brought forth bread and wine: and he was the priest of the most high God *[El Elyon]*" (Gen. 14:18). Here in the King James Version the name is translated "most high God." *Elyon* means highest; with *El* it means the most high God. See also Deuteronomy 32:8; Daniel 4:34, 35. Jesus Christ is our *El Elyon* – "All power *[authority]* is given unto me in heaven and in earth" (Matt. 28:18b).

2. *El Olam* – *"Everlasting God."* "Abraham planted a grove in Beer-sheba, and called there on the name of the LORD, the everlasting *[El Olam]* God" (Gen. 21:33). Yes, God is the "Everlasting God" – "the God of All Ages."

3. *El Shaddai* – "Almighty God." This is first found in Genesis 17:1: "When Abram was ninety years old and nine, the LORD appeared to Abram, and said unto him, I am the Almighty God *[El Shaddai]*; walk before me, and be thou perfect." "El" means the Strong One. *Shaddai* comes from the word *shad*, meaning a breast, a woman's breast. This is illustrated by that portion found in Isaiah 28:9. *El Shaddai*, therefore, means the Breast of God, the Nourisher, Strength-giver, the Satisfier.

One of the most cherished names of God held by Bible students everywhere is this one – the Breast of God, the Strength-giver, the All-Sufficient God, the All-Bountiful God, the God Who is Enough! the God Who is Able. "He is *able* also to save them to the uttermost" (Heb. 7:25). Why? Because Jesus Christ our Lord is our *El Shaddai* – "The God Who is Able."

II. THE EXISTENCE OF GOD

A. False and True Systems of Theology.

1. *Deism.* This system acknowledges that there is a God, but denies that God sustains the creation. "God is the Maker, but not the Keeper."

2. *Atheism.* Those who hold to this belief – so called – exclude God altogether.

3. *Skepticism and Infidelity.* Skeptics and infidels are full of doubt and disbelief with regard to God, especially the God of Revelation.

4. *Agnosticism.* This school of thought does not deny God, but denies that God can be *known.*

5. *Pantheism.* Everything is God, and God is everything. Everything you see is God. God is *in* everything. God and creation are synonymous.

6. *Polytheism.* This is belief in many Gods. There are various gods over us; these in turn have gods over them; and these have gods over them, and so on.

7. *Tritheism.* This is the doctrine of *three* Gods.

8. *Dualism.* This is the belief in *two* Gods: a God that is Good, and a God that is Bad. They are both equal in power and persuasion.

9. *Theism.* The belief in the existence of a personal God is known as theism. Should one boast in this, his boasting is vain, for one must know *who* God is, *what* His name is, in order to trust Him.

10. *Monotheism.* This is the doctrine of one God. We are monotheists. Jews and Mohammedans are monotheists. If that is true, are they saved? No! "Thou believest that there is *one* God; thou doest well: the devils also believe, and tremble" (Jas. 2:19). Believing in one God is not sufficient, but "if thou shalt confess with thy mouth the Lord Jesus, and shalt believe in thine heart that God hath raised him from the dead, thou shalt be saved" (Rom. 10:9).

B. Evidence of the Existence of God.

May the student realize that the Bible never tries to prove there is a God. It assumes that man knows that there is a God, and states, "The *fool* hath said in his heart, There is no God" (Ps. 14:1).

There are many evidences of the existence of God, the first being:

1. *From Reason.* (The Intellectual).

a. *The Intuitional Argument:* That which is in man, sometimes called the "first-truths"; that belief that knows that there is a God without anyone revealing that fact. A child knows there is a God. Who has told him? All races of the world know there is a God, though they are not worshiping the One and Only and True God. There is no such thing as a true atheist. The evidence of the existence of God is in man — born in him.

b. *The Cosmological Argument*: This is the argument

from cause and effect. Here is the world – how did it come to be? There is a Cause or Power behind everything. There must be a Maker or Creator. It is easy to think that back of the Creation is God, but it is impossible to think back of God.

c. *The Teleological Argument*: By this we mean design. There is perfect design and order in the universe. The snowflake is a beautiful pattern that man could never duplicate. Why does ice rise to the top of the water and not to the bottom when it freezes? Should this not be so, then all water would eventually freeze, and the fish would perish. How is it possible that spring, summer, fall and winter all come in order, and have been doing so for millenniums? Why is it that the sun comes no closer to the earth (*melting it*) nor goes further away from it (freezing it)? There *must* be a Designer behind all creation – and that Designer is God!

d. *The Anthropological Argument*: This argument is based upon the moral and intellectual qualities of man. Man is a direct result of the creation of God, as other creatures are, yet these creatures do not possess the moral and intellectual qualities of man. Why? If man could create them, so could animals. But man has the capacity to know, to reason. If man did not get these qualities from some One, where did he get them?

2. *From History*. Truly, history is His story! History verifies the fact that there is a God. History has proved the fact of God against those who have repudiated His law. Thus, Christians should never worry over world conditions. God is on His throne. Nothing can happen, but by His will. Someone has said, "Prophecy is the mould of history." God speaks, and years later what He spoke is fulfilled to the letter. History only fulfills what God has said would happen. History *proves* there is a God!

3. *From Experience*. This is one of the greatest proofs yet for the existence of God. Men have been transformed by the power of God. There is no explanation other than God! Prayers which have been answered attest to the existence of God.

4. *From Scripture*.

a. *Biblical Assumption*. The Bible is the only Book that is God-inspired. The Bible is the standard for all right conduct in the world. If the Bible is not the Word of God, then we have no God; we can never know God.

b. *Christological Revelation.* In Jesus Christ, God came down to man to tell us what God is like. If Jesus is not God, then there is no God. God can never be known. "No man hath seen God at any time; the only begotten Son, which is in the bosom of the Father, he hath declared him" (John 1:18). But Jesus Christ is the Son of God, and He and His life prove the existence of God!

c. *Prophetical Declaration.* God forecast the future. Anyone who can do this is more than man. Man cannot always tell the past, much less the future. It is said that when Christ was crucified there were twenty-five distinct prophecies fulfilled – prophecies written centuries before.

III. The Nature of God.

A. *Definitions of God.*

1. *Scriptural Definitions.*

a. *God is Spirit* – "God is a spirit: and they that worship him must worship him in spirit and in truth" (John 4:24).

b. *God is Light* – "This then is the message which we have heard of him, and declare unto you, that God is light, and in him is no darkness at all" (I John 1:5).

c. *God is Love* – "He that loveth not knoweth not God; for God is love" (I John 4:8).

d. *God is a Consuming Fire* – "For our God is a consuming fire" (Heb. 12:29).

2. *Theological Definitions.*

a. *Westminster Catechism*: – "God is a Spirit, Infinite, Eternal, and Unchangeable in His Being, Wisdom, Power, Holiness, Justice, Goodness and Truth."

b. *Dr. Strong*: – "God is the Infinite and Perfect Spirit. The Source of all things, the Support of all things, the End of all things."

c. *Andrew Fuller;* – "God is the First Cause and Last End of all things."

d. *Ebrards*: – "God is the Eternal Source of all that is temporal."

B. *Spirituality of God.*

1. *His Essence.* He is a Spiritual Being ("God is a

Spirit"—John 4:24), invisible ("Who is the image of the invisible God"—Col. 1:15a). What is a spirit? A spirit is a being without flesh and bones. "Behold my hands and my feet, that it is I myself: handle me, and see; for a spirit hath not flesh and bones, as ye see me have" (Luke 24:39). A spirit has a body, a spirit-body; but it has no natural body, no material body. God cannot be seen by human eye; God, in His pure essence, has never been seen. "No man hath seen God at any time; the only begotten Son, which is in the bosom of the Father, he hath declared him" (John 1:18).

2. *His Manifestations.* While God, in His true essence, has never been seen, yet He hath shown Himself, revealed His Person to man in different forms. The Scriptures ask, "To whom then will ye liken me, or shall I be equal? saith the Holy One" (Is. 40:25). Man cannot know God but in the way He has revealed Himself. Are we not glad that God has revealed Himself in His Son? Where Christ is the image of God, the Anti-christ shall be an imitation.

There *seems* to be some contradictions in the Word; in some places it says that people saw God: "The LORD spake unto Moses face to face" (Ex. 33:11); "Then went up Moses, and Aaron, Nadab, and Abihu, and seventy of the elders of Israel: and they saw the God of Israel . . ." (Ex. 24:9, 10). In other places the Word says that it is impossible to see God: "He said, Thou canst not see my face: for there shall no man see me, and live" (Ex. 33:20). The truth is, man has never looked upon the face of God in His true essence, but has looked upon His face and spoken mouth to mouth with God when God manifested Himself in some form other than His true essence. "With him will I speak mouth to mouth . . ." (Num. 12:8a).

We do know this, that the Spirit (Holy Spirit) can manifest Himself in a visible form. "John bare record, saying, I saw the Spirit descending from heaven like a dove, and it abode upon him" (John 1:32). It was at the Lord Jesus' baptism that John saw the form, but not the Spirit; yet the Spirit was manifested.

God has manifested Himself in many forms; among them are the following:

a. *In Creature Forms.* By this we do not mean that the LORD appeared in the form of animals, but rather in the form of human beings. Genesis 3:8 and 12:7 illustrate this fully:

"They heard the voice of the LORD God walking in the garden in the cool of the day: and Adam and his wife hid themselves from the *presence* of the LORD God amongst the trees of the garden" (Gen. 3:8); "The LORD *appeared* unto Abram, and said, Unto thy seed will I give this land: and there builded he an altar unto the LORD, who *appeared* unto him" (Gen. 12:7). See also Genesis 16:7, 10, 13; Exodus 24:9-11; Genesis 18:1-16; Judges 13:22, 23; Genesis 32:24-30.

God also manifested Himself as the Angel of the LORD — "The angel of the LORD encampeth round about them that fear him, and delivereth them" (Ps. 34:7); "The angel of the LORD said unto her, Behold, thou art with child, and shalt bear a son, and shall call his name Ishmael; because the LORD hath heard thy affliction" (Gen. 16:11). It is agreed among most Bible scholars that the Angel of the LORD is no other than the Lord Jesus Himself.

b. *In Material Forms.* Man could not see God; therefore, God manifested Himself in forms from which He spoke to and led him. One such form was the Burning Bush: "When the LORD saw that he turned aside to see, God called unto him out of the midst of the bush, and said, Moses, Moses. And he said, Here am I" (Ex. 3:4); Another form was the Pillar of a Cloud and a Pillar of Fire: "The LORD went before them by day in a pillar of a cloud, to lead them the way; and by night in a pillar of fire, to give them light; to go by day and night" (Ex. 13:21).

c. *In The Person of Christ Jesus.* Again we state that we are rejoicing that God does not choose today to reveal Himself other than in His Son, Jesus Christ! God does not choose to manifest Himself in a vapor, but rather in *human* form: "In the beginning was the Word, and the Word was with God, and the Word was God. . . . And the Word was made flesh, and dwelt among us (and we beheld his glory, the glory as of the only begotten of the Father,) full of grace and truth" (John 1:1, 14). See also I Timothy 3:16; Hebrews 1:3.

C. Personality of God.

God is a Person, One possessing Self-consciousness, Self-determination, and Power.

People have many vague ideas of God as a force, a power, an influence. But it is impossible to have fellowship with a force or an influence. The Words of our Lord as He was in the Garden suggest fellowship with God: "Now come I to thee; and these things I speak in the world, that they might have my joy fulfilled in themselves" (John 17:13). See also Exodus 3:14; I Corinthians 2:11.

Never confuse personality with visibility. Substance has nothing to do with personality. The personality of God can be seen:

1. *In Names.* "God said unto Moses, I AM THAT I AM: and he said, Thus shalt thou say unto the children of Israel, I AM hath sent me unto you" (Ex. 3:14). The words "I AM THAT I AM" suggest personality.

2. *In Contrasts.* By this we mean that the Scriptures contrast the only wise God with the gods of the pagans: "Ye turned to God from idols to serve the living and true God" (I Thess. 1:9). See also Jeremiah 10:16; Acts 14:15.

3. *In Attributes.* That which is characteristic of God is called an attribute. That which He *does,* denotes personality, such as:

a. *God Grieves.* Only a person can grieve: "It repented the LORD that he had made man on the earth, and it *grieved* him at his heart" (Gen. 6:6).

b. *God Repents.* In the above Scripture (Gen. 6:6) we note that God repents. I Samuel 15:29 says: "The Strength of Israel will not lie nor repent: for he is not a man, that he should repent." Here one portion of the Scriptures states that God repents, another declares that He does not repent. What is the answer? When man repents, he repents of some moral deed; when God repents, He repents of some judicial act. God's attitude toward sin never changes. Take the case of Jonah and Nineveh. Nineveh repented; it changed its mind; it changed its character. God, however, did not change His mind; He did not change His attitude toward sin. But inasmuch as Nineveh had repented, there was no need of judgment against sin. Its sin had been confessed and forgiven.

c. *God Loves.* "God so loved the world, that he gave his only begotten Son, that whosoever believeth in him should not perish, but have everlasting life" (John 3:16). "As many as I love, I rebuke and chasten: be zealous therefore, and repent" (Rev. 3:19). Only a personality can love.

d. *God Hates.* "These six things doth the LORD hate: yea, seven are an abomination unto him" (Prov. 6:16).

e. *God Hears.* "He that planted the ear, shall he not hear? he that formed the eye, shall he not see? He that chastiseth the heathen, shall not he correct? he that teacheth man knowledge, shall not he know" (Ps. 94:9, 10)?

4. *In Acts.*

a. *God Creates.* "In the beginning God *created* the heaven and the earth" (Gen. 1:1). See also Isaiah 45:18.

b. *God Provides.* "These wait all upon thee; that thou mayest give them their meat in due season. That thou givest them they gather: thou openest thine hand, they are filled with good. Thou hidest thy face, they are troubled: thou takest away their breath, they die, and return to their dust. Thou sendest forth thy spirit, they are created: and thou renewest the face of the earth" (Ps. 104:27-30). The material needs of this entire world are met and supplied by God.

c. *God Promotes.* Some people seemingly are pushed ahead of others. The world has a name for this – luck. But the correct answer is the LORD! Kings receive their power from Him; pastors receive their charges from Him; husbands receive their wives from Him. All promotions are from the Lord. "*Promotion* cometh neither from the east nor from the west, nor from the south. But God is the judge: he putteth down one, and setteth up another" (Ps. 75:6, 7).

d. *God Cares.* God has a heart; only a person has a heart. God has concern: "Humble yourselves . . . casting all your care upon him; for he careth for you" (I Peter 5:6, 7).

D. The Trinity of God.

1. *Trinity in Personality.* By this, of course, we mean that God is Three in One. There are some errors concerning the Trinity; some have been proposed ignorantly, and others deliberately.

We know that the Bible is the Word of God, if for no other reason than that we have the Trinity in it. If man had written the Bible, he would have left the Trinity out of it; for the Trinity is too hard to understand – the mind of man cannot comprehend it. The only thing that the Child of God can do is to accept it by faith and stand upon what God says about it. Just because we cannot seem to understand all about it is no sign that it is not true.

There is one error which proposes that there are three Individuals in the Godhead. But remember, God is not a Triad.

Another error is that the Trinity is just one Person, manifesting Himself in three. That is, there are three essences in one Person, Jesus Christ. The Father and the Holy Spirit are only manifestations.

Still another, and damnable, denies the Trinity altogether, and consequently makes the Son and Holy Spirit creatures of God, those who came into existence after God. In other words, they who hold to this erroneous theory declare that there was a time when the Son was not; that there was a time when the Son of God never existed. They use this sort of reasoning: "A son cannot be as old as his father – a father always has to exist before his son in order to beget him; God is the Father of the Son of God; therefore, the Father had to exist before the Son in order to beget Him." To this we reply: "If a person should declare that he is a father, and has been one for ten years, then we know that he has had a child for ten years. A man cannot be a father without having a child. Yes, a man who has been a father for ten years has had a child for ten years. Even so in the Godhead – if God is the *Eternal* Father, then He must have had an *Eternal* Son!"

The doctrine of the Trinity is a doctrine of pure revelation from God. And remember, we worship not three Gods, but One – God: the Father, Son and Holy Ghost.

It is practically impossible to give examples of the Trinity. Some have offered the three-leaved clover as an example; others have suggested water: in its natural state, liquid; when heated, vapor; when frozen, solid. Still, this is not clear. For God is Three in One! Therefore, we propose that the best illustration is man himself: body, soul and spirit. He is not three persons, but a three-in-one person. And there are three things which pertain to each separately: food to the body, music to the soul, and worship to the spirit – yet all three of these things appeal to the one man.

Rays from the sun may be used as a further type. When the sunshine breaks upon the earth it is composed of three elements: heat rays, which can be felt but not seen; light rays, which can be seen, but not felt; chemical rays, which cannot be seen, nor felt, but do have effects. All together make sunshine. We cannot understand light – three rays and yet one light.

Without one of these elements there would be no light; without one part of man, man would cease to be; and without one Person of the Godhead, God would not be God!

a. *Old Testament Names*

(1) *Plural Nouns* "In the beginning *[Elohim]* created the heaven and earth" (Gen. 1:1). Elohim is the plural noun, meaning three or more. This, of course, suggests the Trinity in creation. See also Genesis 3:5; Exodus 20:3; Deuteronomy 13:2, 3. Many times Elohim is translated (in English) in the singular and the plural.

(2) *Plural Pronouns.* "The LORD God said, Behold, the man is become as one of *us*, to know good and evil: and now, lest he put forth his hand, and take also of the tree of life, and eat, and live for ever . . ." (Gen. 3:22). See also Genesis 1:26; Isaiah 6:8. This is God speaking to God – thus the Trinity.

(3) *Scriptural Statements.* The Scriptures state that God anointed God, and how could this be if God be not a Trinity? "Thy throne, O God, is for ever and ever: the sceptre of thy kingdom is a right sceptre. Thou lovest righteousness, and hatest wickedness: therefore God, thy God, hath anointed thee with the oil of gladness above thy fellows" (Ps. 45:6, 7). See also Hebrews 1:8-12; Psalm 110:1.

(4) *Scriptural Designations.* That is, in Genesis 1:1 God declares that He created the heavens and the earth, and in verse 2, the Holy Spirit, the Third Person of the Trinity, is singled out: "The Spirit of God moved upon the face of the waters." (See also Job 24:13). And elements of personality are accounted for by reference to the Holy Spirit: "There shall come forth a rod out of the stem of Jesse, and a Branch shall grow out of his roots: and the spirit of the LORD shall rest upon him, the spirit of wisdom and understanding, the spirit of counsel and might, the spirit of knowledge and of the fear of the LORD" (Is. 11:1, 2).

The Son, the Second Person of the Trinity is singled out also: "I will declare the decree: the LORD hath said unto me, Thou art my Son; this day have I begotten thee. . . . Kiss the Son, lest he be angry, and ye perish from the way . . ." (Ps. 2:7, 12a). The Angel of the LORD of the Old Testament is no other than Jesus Christ Himself, and in the following portion of Scriptures He is declared as being separate from God the

Father and Holy Spirit: "The angel of the LORD found her by a fountain of water . . . in the way to Shur" (Gen. 16:7).

The following Scriptures plainly reveal the Trinity of the Godhead: Genesis 18:1, 2, 33; Isaiah 48:16; 63:8-10.

(5) *Triple Expressions.* Whenever the Scriptures express praise or benediction of the Godhead, a triple exclamation is declared which points to the fact that as God is the Three-In-One God these expressions must also be three: "The Lord bless thee, and keep thee: the Lord make his face shine upon thee, and be gracious unto thee: the Lord lift up his countenance upon thee, and give thee peace" (Num. 6:24-26). "And the four beasts had each of them six wings about him; and they were full of eyes within: and they rest not day and night, saying, *Holy, holy, holy,* Lord God Almighty, which was, and is, and is to come" (Rev. 4:8).

b. *New Testament Disclosures.*

(1) *Baptism of Christ.* The baptism of Christ is one of the best illustrations which prove the Trinity: "Jesus, when he was baptized, went up straightway out of the water: and lo, the heavens were opened unto him, and he saw the Spirit descending like a dove, and lighting upon him: and lo a voice from heaven, saying, This is my beloved Son, in whom I am well pleased" (Matt. 3:16, 17). Here there is presented the Father in heaven, the Son in the water, and the Holy Spirit descending as a dove.

(2) *Baptismal Formula.* The Church of God in Christ Jesus has always used that formula laid down by its Founder Himself, Jesus Christ: "Go ye therefore, and teach all nations, baptizing them in the name of the Father, and of the Son, and of the Holy Ghost . . ." (Matt. 28:19, 20). Note that the Scriptures do not say, "in the names of"; but, "in the name of." One in Three; one *name,* but three Persons: Father, Son and Holy Spirit.

(3) *Apostolic Benediction.* The Church has used this benediction (which was first used by the Apostle Paul by inspiration of the Holy Spirit) for the last nineteen hundred years: "The grace of the Lord Jesus Christ, and the love of God, and the communion of the Holy Ghost, be with you all. Amen" (II Cor. 13:14).

(4) *Other Scripture.* The following verse plainly reveals the fact of the Trinity: "The Comforter, which is the Holy

Ghost, whom the Father will send in my name, he shall teach you all things, and bring all things to your remembrance, whatsoever I have said unto you" (John 14:26).

2. *Unity of Being: Undivided and Invisible.* There is *one* God; He is the one and only God: "Thou art great, O LORD God: for there is none like thee, neither is there any God beside thee, according to all that we have heard with our ears" (II Sam. 7:22); "Who hath wrought and done it, calling the generations from the beginning? I the LORD, the first, and with the last; I am he" (Is. 41:4). See also Isaiah 43:10, 11; 44:6; Deuteronomy 6:4.

God – Elohim – is a compound unity; that is, the noun, God (which is plural), is used always with a singular verb: "In the beginning God [plural] created [singular] the heaven and the earth" (Gen. 1:1); "The LORD [singular] God [plural] of gods, the LORD [singular] God [plural] of gods, he knoweth, and Israel he shall know; if it be in rebellion, or if in transgression against the LORD [*singular*], (save us not this day,) . . ." (Josh. 22:22). See also Genesis 1:5, 8, 13; 33:20.

3. *A Scriptural Summary.*

a. *Three Are Recognized as God.*

(1) *The Father is Recognized as God.* "To all that be in Rome, beloved of God, called to be saints: Grace to you and peace from God our Father, and the Lord Jesus Christ" (Rom. 1:7). See also John 6:27; I Peter 1:2.

(2) *The Son is Recognized as God.* "Unto the Son he saith, Thy Throne, O God, is for ever and ever: a sceptre of righteousness is the sceptre of thy kingdom" (Heb. 1:8); "We should live soberly, righteously, and godly . . . looking for that blessed hope, and the glorious appearing of the great God and our Saviour Jesus Christ" (Titus 2:12, 13).

(3) *The Holy Spirit is Recognized as God.* "Peter said, Ananias, why hath Satan filled thine heart to lie to the Holy Ghost, and to keep back part of the price of the land? Whiles it remained, was it not thine own? and after it was sold, was it not in thine own power? why hast thou conceived this thing in thine heart? thou hast not lied unto men, but unto God" (Acts 5:3, 4).

b. *Three Are Described as Distinct Persons.*

(1) *Father and Son Are Persons Distinct From Each Other.*

(a) *Christ Distinguishes the Father From Himself.* "As the Father hath life in himself; so hath he given to the Son to have life in himself; and hath given him authority to execute judgment also, because he is the Son of man" (John 5:26, 27). See also John 5:32.

(b) *Father and Son are Distinguished as the Begetter and the Begotten.* See John 3:16.

(c) *Father and Son are Distinguished as the Sender and the Sent.* "When the fulness of the time was come, God sent forth his Son, made of a woman, made under the law" (Gal. 4:4). See also John 10:36.

(2) *Father and Son Are Persons Distinguished from the Holy Spirit.*

(a) *The Son Distinguishes the Holy Spirit From Himself and the Father.* "I will pray the Father, and he shall give you another Comforter, that he may abide with you for ever; even the Spirit of truth; whom the world cannot receive, because it seeth him not, neither knoweth him: but ye know him; for he dwelleth with you, and shall be in you" (John 14:16, 17).

(b) *The Spirit Proceeds From the Father.* "When the Comforter is come, whom I will send unto you from the Father, even the Spirit of truth, which proceedeth from the Father, he shall testify of me" (John 15:26).

(c) *The Spirit Is Sent by the Father and the Son.* "The Comforter, which is the Holy Ghost, whom the Father will send in my name, he shall teach you all things, and bring all things to your remembrance, whatsoever I have said unto you" (John 14:26); "When the Comforter is come, whom I will send unto you from the Father, even the Spirit of truth, which proceedeth from the Father, he shall testify of me" (John 15:26).

c. *These Three Persons Are Equal.*

(1) The Father is not God as such, for God is Father, Son and Holy Ghost (Holy Spirit).

(2) The Son is not God as such, for God is Father, Son and Holy Ghost (Holy Spirit).

(3) The Holy Spirit is not God as such, for God is Father, Son and Holy Ghost (Holy Spirit).

E. The Self-existence of God.

Existence of God is within Himself. We are dependent upon Him; He is not dependent upon anything. Something caused us to be; nothing caused Him to be; He always was; God does not exist because He brought Himself into existence. God exists because it is His nature to be.

Our lives come from an external source; there was a time when we began. "I have greater witness than that of John: for the works which the Father hath given me to finish, the same works that I do, bear witness of me, that the Father hath sent me" (John 5:36). We cannot say this.

F. The Infinity of God.

Divine nature has no limit or bound. "Great is our Lord, and of great power: his understanding is infinite" (Ps. 147:5); "Canst thou by searching find out God? canst thou find out the Almighty unto perfection? It is as high as heaven; what canst thou do? deeper than hell; what canst thou know? The measure thereof is longer than the earth, and broader than the sea" (Job 11:7-9); "Will God indeed dwell on the earth? behold, the heaven and heaven of heavens cannot contain thee; how much less this house that I have builded?" (I Kings 8:27); "O the depth of the riches both of the wisdom and knowledge of God! how unsearchable are his judgments, and his ways past finding out!" (Rom. 11:33). See also Isaiah 66:1; Psalm 113:5, 6.

The world is a bud from His bower of beauty —
The sun is a spark from the light of His wisdom —
The sky is a bubble on the sea of His power.

IV. The Attributes of God

The attributes of God are the essential qualities of a perfect Being — the property of God.

A. The Omnipotence of God.

This means that God is all-powerful, all-mighty: "I heard as it were the voice of a great multitude, and as the voice of many waters, and as the voice of mighty thunderings, saying, Alleluia: for the Lord God omnipotent reigneth" (Rev. 19:6); "Jesus beheld them, and said unto them, With men this is impossible; but with God all things are possible" (Matt. 19:26); "Is anything too hard for the LORD?" (Gen. 18:14a).

There is only *one* thing which can limit God, and that is His own holy will. Some foolish person may propose II Timothy 2:13: "If we believe not, yet he abideth faithful: he cannot deny himself." This person says, "Here is something God cannot do." But this is not a question of what God *can* do, but what God *will* do.

1. *God Has Power Over Nature.* "By the word of the LORD were the heavens made; and all the host of them by the breath of his mouth. He gathereth the waters of the sea together as an heap: he layeth up the depth in storehouses. Let all the earth fear the LORD: let all the inhabitants of the world stand in awe of him. For he spake, and it was done; he commanded, and it stood fast" (Ps. 33:6-9); "Thus saith the LORD of hosts; Yet once, it is a little while, and I will shake the heavens, and the earth, and the sea, and the dry land" (Hag. 2:6). See also Genesis 1:1-3; Nahum 1:3-6. Man has to have tools to make things – God only has to speak, and it is done.

2. *God Has Power Over Men.* "There is one lawgiver, who is able to save and to destroy: who art thou that judgest another? Go to now, ye that say, To day or to morrow we will go into such a city, and continue there a year, and buy and sell, and get gain: whereas ye know not what shall be on the morrow. For what is your life? It is even a vapour, that appeareth for a little time, and then vanisheth away. For what ye ought to say, If the Lord will, we shall live, and do this, or that" (Jas. 4:12-15). See also Exodus 4:11.

3. *God Has Power Over Angels.* "All the inhabitants of the earth are reputed as nothing: and he doeth according to his will in the *army of heaven,* and among the inhabitants of the earth: and none can stay his hand, or say unto him, What doest thou?" (Dan. 4:35).

4. *God Has Power Over Satan.* In Job 1:12; 2:6 we notice that Satan is subjected to God; "The LORD said unto Satan, Behold, all that he hath is in thy power; only upon himself put not forth thine hand. So Satan went forth from the presence of the LORD. . . . And the LORD said unto Satan, Behold, he is in thine hand; but save his life." And we know of the end of Satan from the following Scriptures: "The God of

peace shall bruise Satan under your feet shortly . . ." (Rom. 16:20a); "He laid hold on the dragon, that old serpent, which is the Devil, and Satan, and bound him a thousand years. . . . And the devil that deceived them was cast into the lake of fire and brimstone, where the beast and the false prophet are, and shall be tormented day and night for ever and ever" (Rev. 20:2, 10). See also Luke 22:31, 32.

5. *God Has Power Over Death.* Paul prays that the Ephesians may know "what is the exceeding greatness of his power to usward who believe, according to the working of his mighty power, which he wrought in Christ when he raised him from the dead, and set him at his own right hand in the heavenly places, far above all principality, and power, and might, and dominion, and every name that is named, not only in this world, but also in that which is to come" (Eph. 1:19-21). Ultimately, death shall be destroyed: "Death and hell [hades] were cast into the lake of fire. This is the second death" (Rev. 20:14).

B. The Omniscience of God.

Omniscience means "all knowing." God is the "All-Knowing God" – He knows everything! "For if our heart condemn us, God is greater than our heart, and knoweth all things" (I John 3:20).

1. *Includes All Nature.* God, the Creator, knows everything concerning His creatures.

a. *Of His Inanimate Creatures.* "He telleth the number of the stars; he calleth them all by their names" (Ps. 147:4); "Hast thou not known? hast thou not heard, that the everlasting God, the LORD, the Creator of the ends of the earth, fainteth not, neither is weary? there is no searching of his understanding" (Is. 40:28).

b. *Of His Brute Creatures.* "Are not two sparrows sold for a farthing? and one of them shall not fall on the ground without your Father" (Matt. 10:29).

c. *Of His Human Creatures.* God has full knowledge of man: "Be not ye therefore like unto them: for your Father knoweth what things ye have need of, before ye ask him" (Matt. 6:8). He knows man's need; he has knowledge of the need of man. He knows the very *thoughts* of man: "Thou knowest my downsitting and mine uprising, thou understandest my thought afar off" (Ps. 139:2). "The LORD knoweth the thoughts of man, that they are vanity" (Ps. 94:11). See also I Chronicles 28:9 and Hebrews 4:13. God knows the *heart* of man: "Hear thou in heaven thy dwelling place, and forgive, and do, and give to every man according to his ways, whose heart thou knowest; (for thou, even thou only, knowest the hearts of all the children of men;)" (I Kings 8:39). See also Psalm 44:21 and Acts 1:24. God knows the *experiences* we have gone through: "The LORD said, I have surely seen the affliction of my people which are in Egypt, and have heard their cry by reason of their taskmasters; for I know their sorrows" (Ex. 3:7). How absurd for man to try to deceive God!

2. *Covers All Time.* "Known unto God are all his works from the beginning of the world" (Acts 15:18). And this covers the *past,* the *present* and the *future.* The past can God see, for He has given to us those things which have happened millenniums ago (Book of Genesis); the Present is an open book to Him: "Neither is there any creature that is not manifest in his sight: but all things are naked and opened unto the eyes of him with whom we have to do" (Heb. 4:13); and the future is known as the past and present is known. He knows the end from the beginning: "Who verily was foreordained before the foundation of the world, but was manifest in these last times for you" (I Peter 1:20). I Kings 13:2 is also a marvelous illustration of God knowing the future: a baby was named three hundred years before it was born, its name given, from what family it was to come and the things it was to do in later life: "And he cried against the altar in the word of the LORD, and said, O altar, altar, thus saith the LORD; Behold, a child shall be born unto the house of David, Josiah by name; and upon thee shall he offer the priests of the high places that burn incense upon thee, and men's bones shall be burnt upon thee." See also Isaiah 44:28; Jeremiah 1:5; Galatians 1:15, 16; Exodus 3:19; Daniel 2:8.

With God knowing the future, we must put ourselves in His hands.

3. *Includes All Possibilities.* Only God knows what would have happened if something had happened which did not happen. "Thou, Capernaum, which art exalted unto heaven, shalt be brought down to hell: for if the mighty works, which

have been done in thee, had been done in Sodom, it would have remained until this day" (Matt. 11:23). See also I Samuel 23:12; Isaiah 48:18.

C. The Omni-sapience of God.

By this we mean the "All-Wisdom of God"; that is, God has all wisdom. There is a vast difference in wisdom and knowledge. Knowledge is what one knows; wisdom is the perfect display of that knowledge. Wisdom includes discernment and judgment.

1. *Choice of The Highest End.* All things are chosen which will bring about the highest end for God's glory.

2. *Best Way of Securing That End.* Here wisdom asserts itself, not only choosing that which will bring about the highest end, but devising the best ways of securing that end. "O the depth of the riches both of the wisdom and knowledge of God! how unsearchable are his judgments, and his ways past finding out" (Rom. 11:33). See also Romans 16:27; I Corinthians 2:7; Ephesians 1:8; 3:10; I Timothy 1:17.

D. The Omnipresence of God.

There are many vague ideas concerning the omnipresence of God. "Omnipresent" simply means everywhere present. God is everywhere present. God is everywhere, but He is not *in* everything. The belief that He is in everything is Pantheism. If God were in everything, then all man would have to do would be to bow down to a stone, a tree, a desk, a table, or any object, and he would be worshiping God. God is not *in* everything, but He is everywhere! He is everywhere present. The best illustration of this is of a teacher before his class. The teacher is omnipresent to every student in that classroom; but he is not omnipresent to those on the outside, nor to those in the basement, nor even to those who are in the next room. Why? Because the walls, floors and space are barriers between him and those in other parts of the building. But God transcends *all* barriers – space, materials, all things.

We believe, however, that there is a certain place where He manifests Himself, where He is located – and from that locality He is present to everything of the universe. "Hearken thou to the supplication of thy servant, and of thy people Israel, when they shall pray toward this place: and hear thou *in heaven* thy dwelling place: and when thou hearest, forgive" (I Kings

8:30). See also Jeremiah 23:24; Ephesians 1:20; Revelation 21:2.

While God's dwelling place is in heaven, yet we do know that He has manifested Himself in other places: on *earth,* as when He dwelt in the burning bush (Ex. 3:4): "When the LORD saw that he turned aside to see, God called unto him out of the midst of the bush, and said, Moses, Moses. And he said, Here am I"; and in the *flesh,* in the incarnation of Jesus Christ: "Let this mind be in you, which was also in Christ Jesus: who, being in the form of God, thought it not robbery to be equal with God: but made himself of no reputation, and took upon him the form of a servant, and was made in the likeness of men: and being found in fashion as a man, he humbled himself, and became obedient unto death, even the death of the cross" (Phil. 2:5-8).

The Holy Spirit is everywhere. He is *in* believers: "I will pray the Father, and he shall give you another Comforter, that he may abide with you for ever; even the Spirit of truth; whom the world cannot receive, because it seeth him not, neither knoweth him: but ye know him; for he dwelleth with you, and shall be *in* you" (John 14:16, 17). He is *with* the unbelievers: "Nevertheless I tell you the truth; It is expedient for you that I go away: for if I go not away, the Comforter will not come unto you; but if I depart, I will send him unto you. And when he is come, he will reprove the world of sin, and of righteousness, and of judgment" (John 16:7, 8).

God is with us no matter where we are; He is omnipresent; He is everywhere present!

E. The Eternity of God.

This is one thing which has never been grasped by the human mind: God is without beginning and without ending. He is the Eternal Now. He is the only One who *is.* There is no past, and there is no future in eternity. God is eternal; therefore, there is no past nor future with God. "I said, O my God, take me not away in the midst of my days: thy years are throughout all generations. Of old hast thou laid the foundation of the earth: and the heavens are the work of thy hands. They shall perish, but thou shalt endure: yea, all of them shall wax old like a garment; as a vesture shalt thou change them, and they shall be changed. But thou art the same, and thy years shall have no end" (Ps. 102:24-27). See also Psalm 90:4.

Some one may ask, "What is the difference between Genesis 1:1 and John 1:1?" Genesis 1:1 says: "In the beginning God created the heaven and the earth." John 1:1 says: "In the beginning was the Word, and the Word was with God, and the Word was God." Are both "beginnings" the same? If so, then the Word, Jesus Christ, had a beginning! Both passages start at the same point – the beginning; Genesis 1:1 begins with the beginning and looks *forward* into eternity; while John 1:1 begins with the beginning and looks *backward* into eternity. Therefore, the Word, the Lord Jesus Christ, had no beginning.

F. The Immutability of God.

In other words, this means the "unchangeableness of God." His Being, attitude and acts are without change; "I am the LORD, I change not; therefore ye sons of Jacob are not consumed" (Mal. 3:6); "Every good gift and every perfect gift is from above, and cometh down from the Father of lights, with whom is no variableness, neither shadow of turning" (Jas. 1:17); "God, willing more abundantly to show unto the heirs of promise the immutability of his counsel, confirmed it by an oath" (Heb. 6:17).

For a discussion of the repentance of God see Chapter I, III, C, 3, b, p. 26.

G. The Love of God.

1. *Its Citation.* "He that loveth not knoweth not God; for God is love. . . . And we have known and believed the love that God hath to us. God is love; and he that dwelleth in love dwelleth in God, and God in him" (I John 4:8-16).

This is the *one* definition of God. There are many adjectives defining God, but a noun needs a noun. The love of God comes from revelation. It does not come by one's own knowledge. It cannot be seen in nature. Only from God's Word comes that knowledge that God is love. There are those who deny the inspiration of the Scriptures, but who still say that God is love. If the Scriptures are not the Word of God, how do we know that God is love? You can search the world over and never find a "God is love" among the heathen. They have their gods and idols, but a God that is "God is love" is unknown to them. The Bible *is* the Word of God – it, and it only, tells us that "God is love."

2. *Its Objects.* If God is love, then that love must be directed to someone. And it is, for we learn from the Scriptures that the objects of His love are:

a. *His Son.* God loves His Son more than man could ever love his own offspring. "Lo a voice from heaven, saying, This is my beloved Son, in whom I am well pleased" (Matt. 3:17). See also Matthew 17:5. God's love is a perfect love and transcends all bounds: "Father, I will that they also, whom thou hast given me, be with me where I am; that they may behold my glory, which thou hast given me: for thou lovedst me before the foundation of the world" (John 17:24).

b. *Believers.* All who believe in the Lord Jesus Christ are the objects of God's divine love. He manifests that love day by day. "The Father himself loveth you, because ye have loved me, and have believed that I came out from God" (John 16:27). "I in them, and thou in me, that they may be made perfect in one; and that the world may know that thou hast sent me, and hast loved them, as thou hast loved me" (John 17:23).

c. *Israel.* Be careful how you speak of the "lowly" Jew. He is the object of God's love, the same as we Christians: "The LORD hath appeared of old unto me, saying, Yea, I have loved thee with an everlasting love; therefore with lovingkindness have I drawn thee" (Jer. 31:3).

d. *Sinners.* God never changes concerning His attitude toward sin. God hates sin, but *loves* the sinner! "God, who is rich in mercy, for his great love wherewith he loved us, even when we were dead in sins, hath quickened us together with Christ, (by grace ye are saved;)" (Eph. 2:4, 5). "When we were yet without strength, in due time Christ died for the ungodly. For scarcely for a righteous man will one die: yet peradventure for a good man some would even dare to die. But God commendeth his love toward us, in that, while we were yet sinners, Christ died for us" (Rom. 5:6-8).

3. *Its Manifestations.*

a. *In the Gift of His Son for Sinful Man.* "In this was manifested the love of God toward us, because that God sent his only begotten Son into the world, that we might live through him" (I John 4:9). See also John 3:16; Romans 5:6-8.

Man cannot look upon Calvary and say, "God doesn't love me." One dear man told of the time when his own son was in the pangs of death. The hardest thing he ever had to do was to say, "Thy will be done. If thou wantest my son, thou canst have him." Oh, to give up an only son! But mankind gives up its sons to *God,* who takes care of them better than man ever could. But God gave His Only Son to sin – to pay for sin, to pay for the sins of sinners! Yes, we may see our children in the throes of death, but God saw His Son suffer as no man ever did. The dearest child on earth is only a stranger compared with the love of God toward His Son. God points toward Calvary and says, "See my Son! See Him mocked, smitten and bruised?" God saw Him. God saw sinners as they crucified His Son. God could have wiped them off the face of the earth, but He did not. The nails that pierced His Son pierced the heart of the Father. We can *never* understand it. "For God so loved the world, that He *gave. . . .*" The Father gave Him up to the hands of justice, to pay for our sins.

Many a murderer has had to pay with his life for his crime. Jesus was delivered up to pay for our crimes of sin.

b. *In Giving Life and Position In Christ.* To believers only is given that sacred position – in Christ; there is where we are – saved, and uncondemned. "Beloved, now are we the sons of God, and it doth not yet appear what we shall be: but we know that, when he shall appear, we shall be like him; for we shall see him as he is" (I John 3:2): "Even when we were dead in sins, hath quickened us together with Christ, (by grace ye are saved;) and hath raised us up together, and made us sit *together* in heavenly places *in Christ Jesus*" (Eph. 2:5, 6).

c. *In Granting That We Should Be Called the Children of God.* "Behold, what manner of love the Father hath bestowed upon us, that we should be called children of God; and such we are. For this cause the world knoweth us not, because it knew him not" (I John 3:1, R. V.).

d. *In Chastening of His Loved Ones.* "Whom the Lord *loveth* he chasteneth, and scourgeth every son whom he receiveth. If ye endure chastening, God dealeth with you as with sons; for what son is he whom the father chasteneth not? But if ye be without chastisement, whereof all are partakers, then are ye bastards, and not sons. Furthermore we have had fathers of our flesh which corrected us, and we gave them reverence: shall we not much rather be in subjection unto the Father of spirits, and live? For they verily for a few days chastened us after their own pleasure; but he for our profit, that we might be partakers of his holiness. Now no chastening for the present seemeth to be joyous, but grievous: nevertheless afterward it yieldeth the peaceable fruit of righteousness unto them which are exercised thereby" (Heb. 12:6-11). Remember, the chastening of the Lord is for *our* benefit – for *our* profit. We need chastisement; it is a must in the life of the Christian; and we receive it from our Father in Heaven.

e. *In Remembering His Children in All Circumstances of Life.* The question is asked and answered in the Word concerning the care of parents. Is there a love greater than mother love? Listen to what God says: "Can a woman forget her sucking child, that she should not have compassion on the son of her womb?" Is it possible that a mother could ever leave her child? The answer is, "Yea, they may forget." In our own lifetime we have witnessed the desertion of children by their parents. It is a shame that the United States and the separate States have to have laws which compel parents to take care of their children. However, this is the nature of the flesh; this is the Adamic nature, the sinful nature, that parents desert their offspring. You may know someone who has. You, yourself, may have been deserted by some one. But listen to the rest of God's Word: "Yet will I not forget thee" (Is. 49:15). There is One who will never desert *His* children!

f. *In Rejoicing Over the Return of the Prodigal Son.* This great story is found in Luke 15:11-24. It is the story of a *Son,* not a sinner. A sinner is not a son. Only a son is a son, and you cannot un-son a son. A son is born a son forever. But here was a son who sank so low that the testimony he might have had was lost. Remember, he was still a son, and as much so while feeding swine as he was in his Father's house. Relationship was still there, but fellowship was broken. You can lose fellowship, but you cannot lose sonship. He made up his mind what he would say to his father upon his return, but he did not get the chance. He did say, "I have sinned against heaven, and in thy sight, and am no more worthy to be called thy son"; but before he could add, "Make me as one of thy hired servants," the Father, holding his son in his arms, cried to the servants, "Bring forth the best robe, and put it on him; and put a ring on his hand, and shoes on his feet: and bring hither the fatted calf, and kill it; and let us eat, and be merry: for this my son was dead, and is alive again; he was lost, and is found" (Luke 15:21-24).

Let the prodigal know that if he has been once born from above he is still God's child. Only let him resolve to "arise and go" to his Father. The Father stands with open arms ready to plant His kiss upon the penitent lips of His wayward child. "Arise and go!"

4. *The Forms of God's Love.*

a. *In the Goodness of God.*

(1) *As Manifested in Creation.* "God saw . . . that it was good." This is characteristic of the first chapter of Genesis. God is good, and all things that He creates and makes are for the good of man.

(2) *As Manifested In His Care of Brute Creation.* "The eyes of all wait upon thee; and thou givest them their meat in due season. Thou openest thine hand, and satisfiest the desire of every living thing" (Ps. 145:15, 16).

(3) *As Manifested In the Variety of Pleasure for His Creatures.* Why all the beauty of nature, if not to be enjoyed by the eye of man?

(4) *As Manifested in the Gift of His Son.* This proves the goodness of God – that God is good.

(5) *As Manifested In Allowing Sinners to Repent.* "Despisest thou the riches of his goodness and forbearance and longsuffering; not knowing that the goodness of God leadeth thee to repentance?" (Rom. 2:4).

b. *In the Loving-kindness of God.* "He that spared not his own Son, but delivered him up for us all, how shall he not *with him* also freely give us all things?" (Rom. 8:32). Since God has given us the Greatest Gift – His Son – we can be assured that we shall be given "the wrappings" with it. The Son is the Gift, and the wrappings are "things" of His supply which make our souls happy.

c. *In the Long-suffering of God.* "The Lord is not slack concerning his promise, as some men count slackness; but is longsuffering to us-ward, not willing that any should perish, but that all should come to repentance" (II Peter 3:9). "The LORD passed by before him, and proclaimed, The LORD, the LORD God, merciful and gracious, longsuffering, and abundant in goodness and truth" (Ex. 34:6). See also Numbers 14:18.

How many of us praise the Lord that the Saviour gave us "time" in trusting Him for our salvation? Oh, the long-suffering of God which is manifested toward us, in that we were able to hear the Gospel twice, when there are millions who have never heard it once!

d. *In the Patience of God.* "Now the God of patience and consolation grant you to be like-minded one toward another according to Christ Jesus" (Rom. 15:5). Here we note that the patience of God is a divine title, for He is the God of patience! This is clearly manifested in:

(1) *His Dealings With Sinners: Those Before the Flood.* "Which sometime were disobedient, when once the longsuffering of God *waited* in the days of Noah, while the ark was a preparing, wherein few, that is, eight souls were saved by water" (I Peter 3:20). The Lord demonstrated His patience for at least a hundred years. As long as the ark was a preparing, the Gospel was preached – the people warned. His patience was exhausted, finally, and the flood carried the unbelievers away. It will be the same with the coming of the Son of Man at His revelation, at the end of the Tribulation. All those who are found not to be in the Ark, Jesus Christ, shall be destroyed.

(2) *His Dealings With Israel.* "And yet for all that [Israel's sin], when they be in the land of their enemies, I will not cast them away, neither will I abhor them, to destroy them utterly, and to break my covenant with them: for I am the LORD their God. But I will for their sakes remember the covenant of their ancestors, whom I brought forth out of the land of Egypt in the sight of the heathen, that I might be their God: I am the LORD" (Lev. 26:44, 45).

Israel today is Godless, and by this we do not mean that Israel is worse than any other nation, but simply that it is without God. Jehovah has sent prophets unto her, but she has stoned them. He sent even His Son, and Him they crucified. They have been driven unto the uttermost parts of the earth because of it. Yet, for all of this, God has shown His patience, and that patience shall be rewarded, for that nation shall be born anew in a day, and all Israel (those alive at the time of the Revelation of Jesus Christ) shall be saved!

(3) *His Dealings With the World Today.* Why does not God strike today? Why are men allowed to blaspheme the

God of heaven and His Son Jesus Christ? The answer is found in the patience of God.

H. The Mercy of God.

1. *As To Its Citation.* "(For the LORD thy God is a merciful God;) he will not forsake thee, neither destroy thee, nor forget the covenant of thy fathers which he sware unto them" (Deut. 4:31). "The LORD is merciful and gracious, slow to anger, and plenteous in mercy. . . . But the mercy of the LORD is from everlasting to everlasting upon them that fear him, and his righteousness unto children's children" (Ps. 103:8, 17). "God, who is rich in mercy, for his great love wherewith he loved us . . . hath quickened us together with Christ" (Eph. 2:4, 5). See also Psalms 130:7; 145:8; 136:1.

2. *As To Its Explanation.* There is very little difference in the meaning of mercy and grace. *Mercy,* generally speaking, is used in the Old Testament, and *grace* in the New Testament. Old Testament *mercy* and *loving-kindness* go together. Someone has said that mercy is negative, and loving-kindness is positive. Mercy is shown to the disobedient, and loving-kindness is showered upon the obedient – both together mean grace.

3. *As To Its Manifestation.*

a. *In Pardoning the Sinner.* "Who was before a blasphemer, and a persecutor, and injurious: but I obtained mercy, because I did it ignorantly in unbelief" (I Tim. 1:13).

b. *In Removing the Guilt and Penalty.* "He hath not dealt with us after our sins; nor rewarded us according to our iniquities. For as the heaven is high above the earth, so great is his mercy toward them that fear him. As far as the east is from the west, so far hath he removed our trangressions from us" (Ps. 103:10-12).

c. *In Delivering the Periled.* "Return, O Lord, deliver my soul: oh save me for thy mercies' sake" (Ps. 6:4).

d. *In Saving Its Object.* Luke 10:33-37 records the parable of the Good Samaritan. After He has told the parable Jesus asks, "Which now of these three, thinkest thou, was neighbour unto him that fell among the thieves?" And the answer comes: "He that shewed mercy on him." There can be no doubt but that Jesus Christ is typified by the good Samaritan, and it is He who saves, through His mercy, the objects of His concern.

I. *The Grace of God.*

1. *As To Its Citation.* "According to his mercy he saved us, by the washing of regeneration, and renewing of the Holy Ghost; which he shed on us abundantly through Jesus Christ our Saviour; that being justified by his grace, we should be made heirs according to the hope of eternal life" (Titus 3:5-7). "In whom we have redemption through his blood, the forgiveness of sins, according to the riches of his grace" (Eph. 1:7). "The God of all grace, who hath called us unto his eternal glory by Christ Jesus, after that ye have suffered a while, make you perfect, stablish, strengthen, settle you" (I Peter 5:10). See also I Corinthians 6:1.

2. *As To Its Explanation.* Grace is said to be undefinable. Grace always flows down. We might be able to love our equal, or one above our equal, or sometimes one below our equal, but look at the vast difference between God and us; there can be no comparison. The grace of God toward us is unmerited favor.

3. *As to Its Manifestation.*

a. *In That Grace Justifies.* Rather, grace *declares* the saint to be righteous: "All have sinned, and come short of the glory of God; being justified freely by his grace through the redemption that is in Christ Jesus" (Rom. 3:23, 24).

b. *In That Grace Imputes Righteousness.* This means, that by the act of God's grace, the righteousness of God is put to the account of the believing sinner, "Now to him that worketh is the reward not reckoned of grace, but of debt. But to him that worketh not, but believeth on him that justifieth the ungodly, his faith is counted for righteousness" (Rom. 4:4, 5).

c. *In That Grace Imparts a New Nature.* "By grace are ye saved through faith; and that not of yourselves: it is the gift of God: not of works, lest any man should boast. For *we are his workmanship,* created in Christ Jesus unto good works, which God hath before ordained that we should walk in them" (Eph. 2:8-10).

d. *In That Grace Saves.* Why should God save us? The only answer is *grace!* "By grace are ye saved through faith; and that not of yourselves: it is the gift of God" (Eph. 2:8).

e. *In That Grace Instructs.* "The grace of God that bringeth salvation hath appeared to all men, teaching us that, denying ungodliness and worldly lusts, we should live soberly, righteously, and godly, in this present world" (Titus 2:11, 12).

J. The Faithfulness of God.

Unfaithfulness is the greatest sin of today. This is true in every walk of life, whether in business, church, or state. But we have a God who is *faithful* at all times, under every circumstance. The Word bears out the faithfulness of God by the following:

1. *Citation.* Many Scriptures point out the faithfulness of God: "Know therefore that the LORD thy God, he is God, the faithful God, which keepeth covenant and mercy with them that love him and keep his commandments to a thousand generations" (Deut. 7:9); "God is faithful, by whom ye were called unto the fellowship of his Son Jesus Christ our Lord" (I Cor. 1:9); "There hath no temptation taken you but such as is common to man: but God is faithful, who will not suffer you to be tempted above that ye are able; but will with the temptation also make a way to escape, that ye may be able to bear it" (I Cor. 10:13). See also Deuteronomy 32:4 (R.V.); I Thessalonians 5:24; II Thessalonians 3:3; I John 1:9.

2. *Explanation.* The meaning of "faithfulness" is stay, lean, prop, support. God is our *support;* He it is upon whom we can lean; when we are faltering, He is our *Prop* – at *all* times!

3. *Manifestation.* How does God prove faithful?

a. *In Keeping His Promise.* "Let us hold fast the profession of our faith without wavering; (for he is faithful that promised;). . . . For ye have need of patience, that, after ye have done the will of God, ye might receive the promise. For yet a little while, and he that shall come will come, and will not tarry" (Heb. 10:23, 36, 37). The promise of the virgin-born son in Isaiah 7:9 is fulfilled in Luke 1:26-38; 2:7; the promise of God to Abraham in Genesis 15:13, that his seed would go to Egypt and stay there for four hundred years, is fulfilled in Exodus 12:41. See also these other Scriptures: Deuteronomy 7:9; I Kings 8:23, 24, 56.

b. *In Preserving His People.* Take Lamentations 3:22, 23 with Jeremiah 51:5 and you can see that once a people becomes God's people, they are His forever. That is because God is faithful: "It is of the LORD's mercies that we are not consumed, because his compassions fail not. They are new every morning: great is thy faithfulness" (Lam. 3:22, 23); "Israel hath not been forsaken, nor Judah of his God, of the LORD of hosts; though their land was filled with sin against the Holy One of Israel" (Jer. 51:5). Other Scripture bears out the faithfulness of God in preserving His people: "Let them that suffer according to the will of God commit the keeping of their souls to him in well doing, as unto a faithful Creator" (I Peter 4:19). See also Psalm 89:20-26; II Timothy 2:13 (R.V.).

c. *In Chastening His Children.* God is faithful in carrying out the "spankings" He has promised to His wayward children: "I know, O Lord, that thy judgments are right, and that thou in faithfulness hast afflicted me" (Ps. 119:75). Correction is needed when we disobey our Lord, and verily we can always count on the *faithfulness* of God to render the expression in this respect. "Whom the Lord loveth he chasteneth, and scourgeth every son whom he receiveth" (Heb. 12:6).

d. *In Forgiving Our Sins.* "If we confess our sins, he is faithful and just to forgive us our sins, and to cleanse us from all unrighteousness" (I John 1:9).

e. *In Answering Our Prayers.* How do we know that our prayers will be answered? God commands us to pray to Him without ceasing. How do we know that it will do any good? We know that God answers our prayers, because the faithfulness of God guarantees that His ears will always be opened to the cries of His children: "Hear my prayer, O Lord, give ear to my supplications: in thy faithfulness answer me, and in thy righteousness" (Ps. 143:1).

4. *Applications.*

a. *It will preserve us from worry.*

b. *It will check our murmuring.*

c. *It will increase confidence in God.*

K. *The Holiness of God.*

While we mention the holiness of God as the last of God's attributes, let us never forget that it is not the least at all. Consider first:

1. *Natural Holiness.* This is called the *fundamental* attribute, and is one attribute by which God wants His people to remember Him. Some Bible scholars declare that this is the most important of all of God's attributes. We know why they make such a statement. It is because holiness is named most often in the Scriptures. God is called holy more times in the Scriptures, and His holiness is mentioned more, than His might. Holiness is indeed the "attribute of attributes." When

we think not of God's holiness, we think light of sin. We are living in the day of compromise, when people hold "light views." It is hard to get people to consider their lost condition and the peril of hell ahead. They think lightly of salvation, because they have a light view of God's holiness: "Who is like unto thee, O LORD, among the gods? who is like thee, glorious in holiness, fearful in praises, doing wonders?" (Ex. 15:11); "I am the LORD your God: ye shall therefore sanctify yourselves, and ye shall be holy; for I am holy: neither shall defile yourselves with any manner of creeping thing that creepeth upon the earth. For I am the LORD that bringeth you up out of the land of Egypt, to be your God: ye shall therefore be holy, for I am holy" (Lev. 11:44, 45); "Above it stood the seraphims: each one had six wings; with twain he covered his face, and with twain he covered his feet, and with twain he did fly. And one cried unto another, and said, Holy, holy, holy, is the LORD of hosts: the whole earth is full of his glory" (Is. 6:2, 3); "Thus saith the high and lofty One that inhabiteth eternity, whose name is Holy; I dwell in the high and holy place, with him also that is of a contrite and humble spirit, to revive the spirit of the humble, and to revive the heart of the contrite ones" (Is. 57:15); "I am no more in the world, but these are in the world, and I come to thee. Holy Father, keep through thine own name those whom thou hast given me, that they may be one, as we are" (John 17:11); "Grieve not the holy Spirit of God, whereby ye are sealed unto the day of redemption" (Eph. 4:30). See also Leviticus 19:1, 2; Joshua 24:19; Psalms 22:1-3; 99:5, 9; I Peter 1:15, 16.

2. *Aspects of Holiness.* By this we mean the mien of holiness that of which holiness is composed.

a. *Purity.*

(1) *Its Citation.* "This then is the message which we have heard of him, and declare unto you, that God is light, and in him is no darkness at all" (I John 1:5).

(2) *Its Explanation.* In Him is light. In Him is no darkness ever. Light is always pure. There is no such thing as dirty light, nor can anyone make dirty light. God is Light – *pure,* free from defilement. There are two phases of purity: *negative,* free from all that defiles; *positive,* pure. God in His holiness is pure: free from all that defiles, and pure in essence.

b. *Righteousness.* This is another element of holiness.

(1) *Its Citation.* "He is the Rock, his work is perfect: for all his ways are judgment: a God of truth and without iniquity, just and right is he" (Deut. 32:4). "Righteous art thou, O LORD, when I plead with thee: yet let me talk with thee of thy judgments: Wherefore doth the way of the wicked prosper? wherefore are all they happy that deal very treacherously?" (Jer. 12:1); "O righteous Father, the world hath not known thee: but I have known thee, and these have known that thou has sent me" (John 17:25).

(2) *Its Explanation.* The formula for righteousness is found in Ezekiel 18:5, 9: "If a man be just, and do that which is lawful and right . . ." that is, do things right, in a right way, "he is just, he shall surely live, saith the Lord God." God is always right. He possesses character that makes Him do everything right. Righteousness always requires that which is right in character. God never asks anything that is not right. God never commands that which will make us do wrong.

c. *Justice.*

(1) *Its Citation.* "The just LORD is in the midst thereof; he will not do iniquity: every morning doth he bring his judgment to light, he faileth not; but the unjust knoweth no shame" (Zeph. 3:5). See also Deuteronomy 32:4.

(2) *Its Explanation.* The Greek and Hebrew words for justice mean the same. Righteousness is the legislative demand of God – the demand for holiness. *Justice* is judicial holiness – that judicial act of God which demands the penalty for those who have not measured up to the righteous commands of God. Justice, judicial holiness, governs those who are judged, and that brings about the execution of those who carry not out God's laws. Justice is the Executor of those who wrong God's holy commands. Man's justice is sometimes wrong, but God's justice is always right – thus holiness!

d. *Truth of God.*

(1) *Its Citation.* "Lead me in thy truth, and teach me: for thou art the God of my salvation; on thee do I wait all the day. . . . All the paths of the LORD are mercy and truth unto such as keep his covenant and his testimonies" (Ps. 25:5, 10); "God is not a man, that he should lie; neither the son of man, that he should repent: hath he said, and shall he not do it? or hath he spoken, and shall he not make it good?"

(Num. 23:19); "In hope of eternal life, which God, that cannot lie, promised before the world began" (Titus 1:2). See also the following Scriptures: Deuteronomy 32:4; Psalm 31:5; 86:15.

(2) *Its Explanation.* That which God has revealed to man in His Word is Eternal Truth. God never contradicts Himself. One portion of His Word never contradicts another. Are we not glad that the Word of God has not agreed with all the dead theories of the past? Certainly! Be not dismayed should the Bible not agree with any modern day theory concerning creation, man, etc. Man does not *know* apart from the Word of God. Anything apart from the revelation of God is mere supposition.

3. *Manifestation of God's Holiness.*

a. *By His Works.* Everything that God has created and made is perfect, holy. God did not create sin. God did not create a sinful nature which is in the unsaved man. God created man, who, has sinned. Man, by sinning, has passed on to man that perverted nature, that Adamic nature, or as we have called it, that "sinful" nature. Yes, God created man who was capable of sinning. If God had created man so that man could not have sinned, then He would have made a machine rather than a being with a free will. And if God had created man so that man could not sin and yet was not a machine, man would not only have been like God, but he would have been God Himself. God does not make God. Man is inferior to God. God cannot sin; that is His nature. Man would be God if he could not have sinned.

b. *By His Laws.* All the laws are right – they are truth. There is not a single untruth in the whole of God's laws. Thus God's laws manifest God's holiness.

c. *By His Hatred of Sin.* Do you know one reason why fellow Christians are tolerant toward the sins of another, or toward the sins of the unbelievers? It is because they do not hate sin as God hates it. Often we say that God hates sin, but He doesn't hate the sinner. That is not true. God *does* hate the sinner; "The foolish shall not stand in thy sight: thou hatest all workers of iniquity" (Ps. 5:5). This may be a revelation to some of us. God hates the sinner because of his sin, and not because of himself. God hates the sinner, but He loves him, too, because He knows that man is capable of holiness, although ruined by sin. Why does God punish the sinner? Because of the sinner's sins! God thus hates sin, no matter where it may be found, whether in the life of an unregenerated sinner, or in the life of His own believer! God's attitude and conduct toward sin reveal the holiness of God.

d. *By His Love of Righteousness.* God loves righteousness as much as He hates sin: "Hear thou in heaven, and do, and judge thy servants, condemning the wicked, to bring his way upon his head; and justifying the righteous, to give him according to his righteousness" (I Kings 8:32); "Thou hast loved righteousness, and hated iniquity; therefore God, even thy God, hath anointed thee with the oil of gladness above thy fellows. . . . For God is not unrighteous to forget your work and labour of love, which ye have shewed toward his name, in that ye have ministered to the saints, and do minister" (Heb. 1:9; 6:10).

e. *By His Justification of the Believing Sinner.* If man had his "rights," he would be in hell; but it is the mercy and grace of God which offers him the plan of salvation, which if he receives declares the believing sinner to be righteous: "God hath set [Christ Jesus] forth to be a propitiation through faith in his blood, to declare his righteousness for the remission of sins that are past, through the forbearance of God; to declare, I say, at this time his righteousness: that he might be just, and the justifier of him which believeth in Jesus" (Rom. 3:25, 26).

f. *By His Care of His Saints.* "The LORD executeth righteousness and judgment for all that are oppressed" (Ps. 103:6). "Many a time have they afflicted me from my youth, may Israel now say: many a time have they afflicted me from my youth: yet they have not prevailed against me. The plowers plowed upon my back: they made long their furrows. The LORD is righteous: he hath cut asunder the cords of the wicked" (Ps. 129:1-4). See also the following Scriptures: Psalm 98:1-3; 145:15-19; II Timothy 1:6-9.

g. *By His Cross.* "My God, my God, why hast thou forsaken me?" (Ps. 22:1). We can catch a glimpse of the Cross by reading the quoted verse and the remaining verses of Psalm 22. This Psalm is, of course, prophetical, spoken or written some nine hundred years before Christ actually died upon the Cross of Calvary. And Christ's death is a perfect manifestation of God's holiness. Some, no doubt, will ask how this could be. We know that God hates sin: therefore, when His Son was made "sin for us, who knew no sin," yea, when even God's Son became sin, God's attitude toward sin did not vary. God hated sin as much as ever, even when He made His Son sin. His Son did not change His view at all. Jesus, therefore, became hated of the Father because of sin. Jesus never became a sinner, but He became sin. And as God hated sin ("It pleased the LORD to bruise him" – Is. 53:10a), God forsook His Son, for God will always forsake sin. God's holiness did not change.

V. The Fatherhood of God

God is called the Father because of the association with Him. Popularity of the term "Father" is due to Christianity. There is no such thing as God being a Father in heathenism – this can be found only in Christianity. Today there are many fancies concerning the Fatherhood of God. The teaching of the Fatherhood of God and the Brotherhood of Man is nothing but Universalism: that which teaches that no one will ever be sent to hell. The Universalists reason that God will never send any of His children to hell – and that is true: He will not send any of His *children* to hell – but not all men are the children of God. The Scripture which the Universalists use to preach that God is the Father of all mankind is Ephesians 4:6: "One God and Father of all, who is above all, and through all, and in you all." But this means all Christians, all believers, *not* the unbelievers nor the unregenerated.

A. *Old Testament Teaching.*

"Doubtless thou art our father, though Abraham be ignorant of us, and Israel acknowledge us not: thou, O Lord, art our father, our redeemer; thy name is from everlasting. . . . Now, O Lord, thou art our father; we are the clay, and thou our potter; and we all are the work of thy hand." (Is. 63:16; 64:8).

God is mentioned in the Old Testament as a Father, but not the Father of the individual. Rather He is considered to be the Father of the nation Israel. You cannot find in the Old Testament where God is spoken of as a Father of a born-again sinner.

B. *New Testament Teaching.*

The Lord Jesus is the One who introduced God as the Father of the individual. He is the first to recognize that God is the Father of each separate Christian. The following Scriptures bear this out: "The Word was made flesh, and dwelt among us, (and we beheld his glory, the glory as of the only begotten of the Father,) full of grace and truth" (John 1:14); "Jesus answered them, My Father worketh hitherto, and I work. Therefore the Jews sought the more to kill him, because he not only had broken the sabbath, but said also that God was his Father, making himself equal with God" (John 5:17, 18); "My Father, which gave them me, is greater than all; and no man is able to pluck them out of my Father's hand. I and my *Father* are one. Then the Jews took up stones again to stone him. Jesus answered them, Many good works have I shewed you from my Father; for which of those works do ye stone me? The Jews answered him, saying, For a good work we stone thee not; but for blasphemy; and because that thou, being a man, makest thyself God" (John 10:29-33); "They took away the stone from the place where the dead was laid. And Jesus lifted up his eyes, and said, Father, I thank thee that thou hast heard me" (John 11:41).

1. *In That God is the Father of Our Lord Jesus Christ.* The expression, as we use it, "the Fatherhood of God," does not mean that God lived for a long time and then begat His Son. God, remember, is the eternal Father – and to be an eternal Father, He must have an eternal Son. The term "son" in Scripture does not always mean a son by generation; it may also mean a son by *relationship.* Take the Old Testament Scriptures: "Therefore the Lord himself shall give you a sign; Behold, a virgin shall conceive, and bear a son, and shall call his name Immanuel" (Is. 7:14); and: "For unto us a child is born, unto us a son is given: and the government shall be upon his shoulder: and his name shall be called Wonderful, Counsellor, The mighty God, The Everlasting Father, The Prince of Peace" (Is. 9:6). Notice the *child* and the *son.* The child is *born;* the Son is not born, but *given.* Yes, that Babe in Bethlehem was born, but that Life was the Son who has been forever. The Babe had a beginning; the Son had no beginning. He has existed always, from eternity, *with* the Father. Thus, Christ is the Son, not by generation (by birth), but by relation. He is related to the Father and the Holy Spirit; all together are related to each other, and thus compose the Godhead. God could never be God without all members of the Godhead being present from eternity throughout eternity.

In order for God to become flesh, He had to be born as any

other man; thus, He manifested Himself in His Son, who was conceived by the power of the Holy Spirit: "The angel answered and said unto her, The Holy Ghost shall come upon thee, and the power of the Highest shall overshadow thee: therefore also that holy thing which shall be born of thee shall be called the Son of God" (Luke 1:35); "When the fulness of the time was come, God sent forth his Son, made of a woman, made under the law" (Gal. 4:4).

a. *And the Father Recognizes Jesus as His Own Son.* "Lo a voice from heaven, saying, This is my beloved Son, in whom I am well pleased" (Matt. 3:17); "There came a voice out of the cloud, saying, This is my beloved Son: hear him" (Luke 9:35).

b. *And the Son Recognizes God as His Own Father.* "All things are delivered unto me of my Father: and no man knoweth the Son, but the Father; neither knoweth any man the Father, save the Son, and he to whomsoever the Son will reveal him" (Matt. 11:27); "I appoint unto you a kingdom, as my Father hath appointed unto me" (Luke 22:29); "These words spake Jesus, and lifted up his eyes to heaven, and said, Father, the hour is come; glorify thy Son, that thy Son also may glorify thee" (John 17:1).

c. *And Men Recognize Jesus as God's Own Son.* "Simon Peter answered and said, Thou art the Christ, the Son of the living God" (Matt. 16:16); "I saw, and bare record that this is the Son of God. . . . Nathanael answered and saith unto him, Rabbi, thou art the Son of God; thou art the King of Israel" (John 1:34, 49).

d. *And Demons Recognize Jesus as God's Own Son.* "Behold, they cried out, saying, What have we to do with thee, Jesus, thou Son of God? art thou come hither to torment us before the time?" (Matt. 8:29).

2. *In That God is the Father of Believers On the Lord Jesus Christ.* "There is . . . one God and Father of all, who is above all, and through all, and in you all" (Eph. 4:6).

We cannot emphasize too strongly the fact that God is not the Father of all mankind. He is only the Father of born-again children of God. All men are the creatures of God, but not all are children of God. Man is a creature of God by creation; he *becomes* a child by *re-creation*: "Grace and peace be multiplied unto you through the knowledge of God, and of

Jesus our Lord . . . whereby are given unto us exceeding great and precious promises: that by these ye might be partakers of the *divine nature,* having escaped the corruption that is in the world through lust" (II Peter 1:2, 4).

There can be no sonship apart from the spiritual re-birth. A child has, always, the nature of his father. Man, who is born of Adam, has Adam's nature, which is corrupt, which is perverted, which is sinful. And the *father* of Adam's sinful nature is Satan. Thus, the nature of our father (Adam) is the same nature as Adam's father's (Satan); therefore, our nature is the same as Satan's. All unregenerated sinners have Satan as their father: "Ye are of your father the devil, and the lusts of your father ye will do. He was a murderer from the beginning, and abode not in the truth, because there is no truth in him. When he speaketh a lie, he speaketh of his own: for he is a liar, and the father of it" (John 8:44). Summing it all up, if Satan is the father of the unsaved by the natural birth, we must have a supernatural birth in order for God to be our Father!

God does not have any fellowship with anything which is of Adam, for Adam is all that is of a sinful condition and nature. God only has to do with His Son. The world is divided into two divisions; in fact, there are only two men whom God recognizes: Adam and Christ; thus, sinners are divided as to their identity with these two men. The unsaved are identified with Adam; the saved are identified with Christ. All men are identified by the natural birth in Adam; born-again men are identified by the supernatural birth in Christ.

The unsaved man can only call God "God." The unsaved man cannot call God "Father." Only the child of God can call God "Father." When the Lord Jesus was hanging on the tree, He called out, "My God, my God, why hast thou forsaken me?" Notice that Christ did not cry, "My Father, my Father." but "My God, my God." Why? Why did He not call God "Father"? Because He was taking the sinner's place there in death, dying – the Just for the unjust. And as He was taking the sinner's place (a sinner can not call God "Father," but only "God"), He could only call God "God."

Where are we? In Adam or in Christ? "As in Adam all die, even so in Christ shall all be made alive" (I Cor. 15:22).

CHRISTOLOGY
(The Doctrine of Christ)

Outline for Chapter II

CHRISTOLOGY

I. Names and Titles of Christ.
   A. Jesus.
   B. Christ.
   C. Messiah.
   D. Lord.
   E. Jesus Christ.
   F. Christ Jesus.
   G. The Lord Jesus Christ.
   H. I Am.
   I. The Son of God.
   J. The Son of Man.
   K. The Son of Abraham.
   L. The Son of David.
   M. The Son of the Highest.
   N. Second Man.
   O. Last Adam.
   P. The Word.
   Q. Emmanuel.
   R. Saviour.
   S. Rabbi.
   T. Rabboni.
   U. Master.

II. The Incarnation of Christ.
   A. The Fact of the Incarnation.
   B. The Manner of the Incarnation.
   C. The Objections to the Incarnation.
   D. The Objects of the Incarnation.
   E. The Perpetuity of the Incarnation.
   F. The Proofs of the Incarnation.

III. The Two Natures of Christ.
   A. The Humanity of Christ.
   B. The Deity of Christ.
   C. The Blending of the Two Natures Into One Person.
   D. The Errors Concerning the Two Natures.

IV. The Death of Christ.
   A. The Fact of the Death.
   B. The Form of the Death.
   C. The Unscriptural Theories Concerning the Death.
   D. The Scriptural Names of the Death.
   E. The Objectives of the Death.
   F. The Extent of the Death.
   G. The Results of the Death.

V. The Resurrection of Christ.
   A. The Importance of the Resurrection.
   B. The Meaning of the Resurrection.
   C. The Unscriptural Theories Concerning the Resurrection.
   D. The Proofs of the Resurrection.
   E. The Result of the Resurrection.

VI. The Ascension and Enthronement of Jesus Christ.
   A. The Meaning of the Ascension and Enthronement.
   B. The Message of the Ascension and Enthronement.
   C. The Nature of the Ascension and Enthronement.
   D. The Necessity of the Ascension and Enthronement.
   E. The Purpose of the Ascension and Enthronement.
   F. The Results of the Ascension and Enthronement.

Chapter II

CHRISTOLOGY

Christology, fundamentally, is the doctrine of Christ. Blessed is he who knows Him as Lord and Saviour.

Sometimes we are warned that we can preach too much of Christ, in that we may not emphasize enough the doctrines of God and of the Holy Spirit. Let us say here, that one cannot preach too much of Jesus Christ. Furthermore, there is no such thing as jealousy in the Godhead. From Scripture we can see that God would have us emphasize Christ more than we do: "And he is the head of the body, the church: who is the beginning, the firstborn from the dead; that in all things he might have the *preeminence*" (Col. 1:18).

I. Names and Titles of Christ.

We believe in the verbal inspiration of the Holy Scripture. That is, we believe that every single word in the originals is the direct word chosen by God with which to convey His will to us. Believing thusly, we attach much importance to the titles and names of the Lord Jesus Christ. The most well-known name of our Saviour is:

A. *Jesus.*

The name *Jesus* is found in the Four Gospels 612 times, and it is found in the balance of the New Testament 71 times. The name *Christ* alone is found in the Four Gospels only 56 times, while in the remainder of the New Testament the name *Christ* is found 256 times.

Jesus is found *before* His death, burial and resurrection, while *Christ* is found *after*.

Jesus is the personal name of the Lord. It is His earthly name, the name under which He was born, lived, and died. It is the name of His humiliation; of suffering; of sorrow. It is the name of the One who humbled Himself. The name *Jesus*, at the time of our Lord, was not uncommon, there were many who were named Jesus. *Jesus* is the Greek form for the Hebrew word *Joshua,* and both mean "Jehovah our Saviour." This name, *Jesus,* was the one which was nailed over Him on the Cross.

Again we emphasize the fact that the name *Jesus* is prominent in the Gospels, while the name *Christ* is mentioned more in the Epistles. The name *Jesus* was more prominent *before* salvation was made and completed, while the name *Christ* is prominent *after* the work of salvation was finished. A Christian is not a person who believes in *Jesus* – the whole world believes there's a Jesus – but a Christian is one who believes in the LORD Jesus Christ. He is Lord! With this knowledge, that a person is saved by declaring Jesus as Lord (Rom. 10:9, R.V.), and believing that God hath raised Him from the dead (and we know by I Corinthians 15:1-3 that the Gospel is the death, burial and resurrection of the Lord Jesus Christ as the sinner's Substitute), we state that there is very little "gospel" in the Four Gospels. The Four Gospels give very little of the doctrine of salvation for sinners; only in the last few chapters of each Gospel is the death, burial and resurrection of Christ recorded. Hence, the name *Jesus* is predominant.

The Epistles are the writings which bring out so clearly the doctrine of salvation by grace through faith in the substitutionary sacrifice of Christ. The Epistles are full of the doctrine of salvation; hence the emphasis upon the name *Christ* and *Lord!* Before Calvary it is *Jesus* which is emphasized; after Calvary it is *Christ* which is emphasized: "Therefore let all the house of Israel know assuredly, that God hath made that same *Jesus,* whom ye have crucified, both Lord and Christ" (Acts 2:36); "Being found in fashion as a man, he humbled himself, and became obedient unto death, even the death of the cross. Wherefore God also hath highly exalted him, and given him a name which is above every name: that at the name of Jesus every knee should bow, of things in heaven, and things in earth, and things under the earth; and that every tongue should confess that Jesus Christ is Lord, to the glory of God the Father" (Phil. 2:8-11).

This is interesting to point out: when He was upon this earth (before He was crucified), He was never called Jesus to His face. It was always Lord, Master, or Rabbi by His followers: "Ye call me Master and Lord: and ye say well; for so I am" (John 13:13); "Why call ye me, Lord, Lord, and do not the things which I say?" (Luke 6:46).

The reason why the name *Jesus* is mentioned most in the Gospels (612 times) is that the Gospels emphasize His humility; the reason why the name *Christ* is mentioned most in the Acts and Epistles is that these writings emphasize His exaltation! There is a reason why the name *Jesus* is mentioned in the Epistle to the Hebrews eight times: the Holy Spirit would have us know that this Person was a *man.* The institution of the Lord's Supper is a perfect illustration of the emphasis on the name *Jesus* in the Gospels, and on the title *Christ* in the Epistles: "As they were eating, *Jesus* took bread, and blessed it, and brake it, and gave it to the disciples, and said, Take, eat; this is my body" (Matt. 26:26); "I have received of the *Lord* that which also I delivered unto you, That the *Lord Jesus* the same night in which he was betrayed took bread" (I Cor. 11:23).

Men of the world, the demons of Satan, all addressed Him as Jesus, but never as Lord. Christian Science, Universalism and Unitarianism believe in a Jesus, but they claim that He cannot save, for they state that there is no sin to be saved from. Every false system of religion has the Lord Jesus Christ as the Object of its attack. Every false system reasons away sin; and in doing so, the need of a Saviour is ruled out. It says that Jesus died a needless death; and in doing that, He did not know what He was doing; in doing that, He must not have been the Son of God, for God knows all things. Do you not see that every attack upon the Son of God, Jesus our Lord, whether it be in regard to His blood, His resurrection, His substitutionary sacrifice or His second coming, is nothing but a subtle assault upon the *deity* of Christ.

We do not get our name from Jesus, but from Christ: we are *Christians.* Yes, we know that this name *Christian* was first given to the believers by those who hated God and His Christ; nevertheless, we are proud to take His dear name and to bear His reproach.

Never, remember, did unbelievers call the Saviour Lord, they called Him Jesus; and never did believers call Him Jesus, with one exception (and the exception makes the rule): "He said unto them, What things? And they said unto him, Concerning *Jesus* of Nazareth, which was a prophet mighty in deed and word before God and all the people: and how the chief priests and our rulers delivered him to be condemned to death, and have crucified him. But we trusted that it had been he which should have redeemed Israel: and beside all this, to day is the third day since these things were done" (Luke 24:19-21). These were the words of the disappointed disciples – "we trusted that it had been he" – all their hopes were shattered when Jesus was crucified. They did not know the Scriptures, nor had they remembered the Lord's words that He would rise again from the dead, and thus they spoke of Him as a Lost Cause; and they, here, called Him *Jesus.* If Christ had not risen from the dead, their hopes, and not only theirs, but ours as well, would have been destroyed; He would have been just plain *Jesus.* "But now is *Christ* risen from the dead, and become the firstfruits of them that slept" (I Cor. 15:20). He is Christ and Lord! Not mere man, but the God-man.

To believers He is Lord. We should never use adjectives with Him. He is not the Blessed Jesus, the Sweet Jesus, although He is all that; He is the Lord Jesus Christ! When we pray, we should pray in Christ's name, not in Jesus' name.

B. Christ.

We have dealt at length with the name *Christ* as it is used, but let us add these details:

The name *Christ* means the Anointed One. This is the *official* title of the Son of God. Whenever we hear the word "anointed," remember how, and under what circumstances, men were anointed. We know that men were anointed as kings, and prophets, and priests: "Samuel also said unto Saul, The LORD sent me to anoint thee to be king over his people, over Israel: now therefore hearken thou unto the voice of the words of the LORD" (I Sam. 15:1); "Jehu the Son of Nimshi shalt thou anoint to be *king* over Israel: and Elisha the son of Shaphat of Abel-meholah shalt thou anoint to be *prophet* in thy room" (I Kings 19:16); "The LORD spake unto Moses, saying, Take Aaron and his sons with him, and the garments, and the *anointing oil,* and a bullock for the sin offering, and two rams, and a basket of unleavened bread. . . . And he poured of the *anointing oil* upon Aaron's head, and anointed him, to sanctify him" (Lev. 8:1, 2, 12).

1. *Christ Has Been Anointed Prophet.* "Moses truly said unto the fathers, A *prophet* shall the Lord your God raise up

unto you of your brethen, like unto me; him shall ye hear in all things whatsoever he shall say unto you. And it shall come to pass, that every soul, which will not hear that *prophet,* shall be destroyed from among the people" (Acts 3:22, 23).

2. *Christ Has Been Anointed Priest.* "Seeing then that we have a great *high priest,* that is passed into the heavens, Jesus the Son of God, let us hold fast our profession. For we have not an *high priest* which cannot be touched with the feeling of our infirmities; but was in all points tempted like as we are, yet without sin" (Heb. 4:14, 15).

3. *Christ Has Been Anointed King.* "Behold, thou shalt conceive in thy womb, and bring forth a son, and shalt call his name Jesus. He shall be great, and shall be called the Son of the Highest: and the Lord God shall give unto him the *throne* of his father David: and he shall reign over the house of Jacob for ever; and of his *kingdom* there shall be no end" (Luke 1:31-33).

In the Gospels *Christ* is pictured as *King* of Israel: in the Epistles *Christ* is pictured as *Head* of the Church.

C. *Messiah.*

"He first findeth his own brother Simon, and saith unto him, We have found the *Messias* [Messiah], which is, being interpreted, the Christ" (John 1:41); "The woman saith unto him, I know that *Messias* cometh, which is called Christ: when he is come, he will tell us all things" (John 4:25).

Messiah is the Hebrew word with the same meaning as *Christ,* which is the "Anointed One." The Old Testament is full of the *Messiah* prediction, while the New Testament is full of *Christ* fulfillment; the Old Testament is written in the Hebrew language, while the New Testament is written in the Greek language.

D. Lord.

This is Christ's title of deity, that of authority. All three names of God, as found in the Old Testament, are compounded into that one name, *Lord.* In the study of the names of God, we saw that the word "God" in the Authorized Version comes from the Hebrew word *Elohim,* which is the office of God; and that the word "LORD," or "GOD," comes from the Hebrew word *Jehovah,* which is the personal name of God; and that the word "lord," or "Lord" (small letters), comes from the Hebrew word *Adonai,* meaning Master.

In the New Testament the word "Lord" comes from the

Greek word *kurios,* which is translated in the Authorized Version as Lord, God, Master, and Sir. This rendering is equivalent to the Old Testament *Adonai* – Master. And Christ, the Lord, is our Master: "And, ye masters, do the same things unto them, forbearing threatening: knowing that your Master also is in heaven; neither is there respect of persons with him" (Eph. 6:9); "Masters, give unto your servants that which is just and equal; knowing that ye also have a Master in heaven" (Col. 4:1).

As stated above, the title "Lord" also includes another name for God, and that is LORD or Jehovah, and we know this by the way it is used in the New Testament. The New Testament quotes from the Old Testament Scriptures, using the word "Lord," while the Old Testament word is "LORD," or "Jehovah": "Jesus said unto him, It is written again, Thou shalt not tempt the Lord [Old Testament: Jehovah] thy God" (Matt. 4:7). In this verse it is also seen that *Elohim* (God) is ascribed to the Lord, who is the Lord Jesus Christ.

In salvation we must acknowledge that Jesus Christ is Jehovah, God, and Master: "If thou shalt confess with thy mouth Jesus as *Lord* [Jehovah, God, Master – all three], and shalt believe in thy heart that God raised him from the dead, thou shalt be saved" (Rom. 10:9, A.R.V.).

If we have declared Him as Lord (Jehovah, God, Master), then we recognize Him as the One who owns us, the One who determines our walk and life, the One who only has the right to us and everything we possess. We have a great responsibility to Him; His will is to be the will of our lives: "Be ye not unwise, but understanding what the will of the Lord [Jesus Christ: Jehovah, God, Master] is" (Eph. 5:17). Even in marriage one should abide by the will of the Lord Jesus Christ: "The wife is bound by the law as long as her husband liveth; but if her husband be dead, she is at liberty to be married to whom she will; only in the Lord" (I Cor. 7:39). These words take on a deeper meaning as you realize that a Christian should not only marry another Christian, but that he should do so only if it is according to the will of the Lord. And *after* marriage the will of the Lord should be desired: "Wives, submit yourselves unto your own husbands, as it is fit in the Lord" (Col. 3:18).

No man can call Jesus *Lord,* except by the Holy Spirit, for the flesh (sin, carnal nature) does not recognize Christ as Lord: "I give you to understand, that no man speaking by the Spirit of God calleth Jesus accursed: and that no man can say that Jesus is the Lord, but by the Holy Ghost" (I Cor. 12:3).

E. Jesus Christ.

This is another title of the Lord, which is the combination of His personal name (Jesus) with His official title (Christ). The emphasis is on the first word – Jesus, what He *was* to what He *is*. That is, Jesus, who once humbled Himself, is now exalted.

F. Christ Jesus.

The emphasis is on the first word here also – Christ, which means He who was exalted, was once humbled; "Let this mind be in you, which was also in Christ Jesus: who, being in the form of God, thought it not robbery to be equal with God: but made himself of no reputation, and took upon him the form of a servant, and was made in the likeness of men: and being found in fashion as a man, he humbled himself, and became obedient unto death, even the death of the cross" (Phil. 2:5-8).

G. The Lord Jesus Christ.

This is the Lord's fullest title: "Blessed be the God and Father of our Lord Jesus Christ, who hath blessed us with all spiritual blessings in heavenly places in Christ" (Eph. 1:3).

H. I Am.

This is an Old Testament title brought forth into the New Testament. Jehovah appeared unto Moses in the burning bush and commanded that he should tell Pharaoh to let the children of Israel go from the land of bondage. "Moses said unto God, Behold, when I come unto the children of Israel, and shall say unto them, The God of your fathers hath sent me unto you; and they shall say to me, What is his name? what shall I say unto them? And God said unto Moses, I AM THAT I AM: and he said, Thus shalt thou say unto the children of Israel, *I AM* hath sent me unto you" (Ex. 3:13, 14).

The Lord Jesus called Himself the great I AM when He was in Gethsemane. As the crowd came with lanterns, torches and weapons, the Lord went forth to meet them, asking, "Whom seek ye? They answered him, Jesus of Nazareth. Jesus saith unto them, I am . . ." (John 18:4, 5). But, you may add, the Scriptures say, "I am he," not merely, "I am." To this we reply, Look at the word "he"; it is in italics, and all italicized words have been supplied by the translators and can therefore be left out. The Lord Jesus actually said, "I am." When the Lord announced that He was the great I am, what did they do? "As soon then as he had said unto them, I am, they went backward, and fell to the ground" (John 18:6). Still another portion of the Word bears out the fact that Christ Jesus was the great I Am. "Jesus saith unto them, Verily, verily, I say unto you, Before Abraham was, I am" (John 8:58). "In him dwelleth all the fulness of the Godhead bodily" (Col. 2:9).

I. *The Son of God.*

This is the Lord's title of personal glory and deity. "The angel answered and said unto her, The Holy Ghost shall come upon thee, and the power of the Highest shall overshadow thee: therefore also that holy thing which shall be born of thee shall be called the Son of God" (Luke 1:35). "The Jews answered him, We have a law, and by our law he ought to die, because he made himself the Son of God" (John 19:7). See also John 5:18.

The Lord Jesus is *the* Son of God. A Christian is *a* Son of God. The Lord Jesus is *the* Son of God by relation and nature; the Christian is *a* Son of God by regeneration and adoption. The Lord Jesus has been *the Son* of God from all time and eternity; the Christian becomes *a child* of God when he trusts in Christ, the Lord.

J. *The Son of Man.*

This seems to be the favorite title of the Lord, the one by which He called Himself time and again: "Jesus said unto him, Foxes have holes, and birds of the air have nests; but the Son of man hath not where to lay his head" (Luke 9:58).

This is the Millennial title of Christ. Wherever it is recorded, it is used in connection with the coming kingdom reign of the Lord Jesus Christ. Even in the Old Testament the same thing holds true. Some may take issue with this, stating that Ezekiel takes upon himself that same title, the son of man. However, we refer the reader to the passages where it is used; there the coming Millennial Kingdom is in view. For example, in Ezekiel 37 is the prophecy of the Valley of Dry Bones, the whole house of Israel, which shall come to life again when the Lord prophecies unto them to return to the Land of Palestine; that will be the Millennium.

This is the Lord's title and not man's. You are *a* son of man, but He is *the* Son of man.

The title, the Son of man, is found eighty-eight times in the New Testament: once in Acts; once in Hebrews; twice in Revelation; and eighty-four times in the Gospels; not once in the Epistles. The Epistles concern the Church, not the coming kingdom of the Millennium. Christ is *King* of the Kingdom, but *Head* of the Church. And as the Church is not the Kingdom, therefore, the Millennial Title (the Son of man) of Christ is not found in the Epistles to the Churches.

K. The Son of Abraham.

The Gospel of Matthew is described as "the book of the generation of Jesus Christ, the son of David, the son of Abraham" (Matt. 1:1). "Now to Abraham and his seed were the promises made. He saith not, And to seeds, as of many; but as of one, And to thy seed, which is Christ" (Gal. 3:16).

The Messiah (Christ) was to be a Jew. Christ was a Jew, for He was a Son of Abraham, and thus the Messiah!

L. The Son of David.

This is the *royal title* of the Lord Jesus: "When he heard that it was Jesus of Nazareth, he began to cry out, and say, Jesus, thou son of David, have mercy on me" (Mark 10:47).

M. *The Son of the Highest.*

The title of pre-eminence: "He shall be great, and shall be called the Son of the Highest: and the Lord God shall give unto him the throne of his father David" (Luke 1:32).

N. Second Man.

"Second Man" indicates that there was one man before Him – only one – and that man was Adam: "The first man is of the earth, earthy: the *second man* is the Lord from heaven" (I Cor. 15:47).

O. Last Adam.

"Last Adam" indicates that there is no man to follow Him. There are only two men in the records of God: Adam and Christ. Thus, the world is divided under these two headships: Adam and Christ. All are of Adam by the natural birth; only those are of Christ who have experienced the new birth.

"It is written, The first man Adam was made a living soul; the last *Adam* was made a quickening spirit" (I Cor. 15:45).

P. The Word.

"In the beginning was the Word, and the Word was with God, and the Word was God. The same was in the beginning with God" (John 1:1, 2).

As spoken words reveal the invisible thoughts of man, so the visible (living) Word reveals to us the invisible God.

Q. Emmanuel.

"Behold, a virgin shall be with child, and shall bring forth a son, and they shall call his name Emmanuel, which being interpreted is, God with us" (Matt. 1:23). As the Scripture tells us, it means "God with us." Remember, the Lord Jesus is Emmanuel – God with us; He will never leave nor forsake us (Heb. 13:5, 6).

R. Saviour.

"Unto you is born this day in the city of David a Saviour, which is Christ the Lord" (Luke 2:11). Not a helper, but a Saviour!

S. Rabbi.

This comes from the Hebrew word meaning teacher. "Then Jesus turned, and saw them following, and saith unto them, What seek ye? They said unto him, Rabbi (which is to say, being interpreted, Master,) where dwellest thou?" (John 1:38).

T. Rabboni.

This is the same as the word "rabbi," meaning Teacher, but comes from the Chaldean. "Jesus saith unto her, Mary. She turned herself, and saith unto him, Rabboni; which is to say, Master" (John 20:16).

U. Master.

"When the Pharisees saw it, they said unto his disciples, Why eateth your Master with publicans and sinners?" (Matt. 9:11). The meaning here is "Instructor." The idea of Owner is not here implied, as in the word "Lord" (Adonai). The world today recognizes that Jesus is a great Master (Instructor), but will not own Him as Lord. The Lord Jesus is not merely our Instructor: He is our God, our Jehovah, our Lord!

II. The Incarnation of Christ

This is a cardinal truth of Christianity. It is the fundamental foundation upon which our faith rests. Without the incarnation, Christianity could not stand. There is no way of getting rid of the incarnation without getting rid of Christianity. Mere man did not reveal this to us but God Himself did, through the revelation of His Word: "I would that ye knew what great conflict [fear or care] I have for you, and for them at Laodicea . . . that their hearts, might be comforted, being knit together in love, and unto all riches of the full assurance of understanding, to the acknowledgment of the mystery of God, and of the Father, and of Christ, in whom are hid all the treasures of wisdom and knowledge" (Col. 2:1-3).

The word "incarnation" comes from the Latin word meaning enfleshment; thus, when we speak of the incarnation of Christ Jesus, the Son of God, we mean the "enfleshment" of God – God manifest in the flesh.

A. The Fact of the Incarnation.

Two of the Gospels, Matthew and Luke, record the full account of it. Both accounts are different, but both agree in the true facts. Matthew, which portrays Christ as the King throughout the whole Book, describes His birth as: "He who is born King of the Jews," tracing His line through Solomon to David. Luke, which reveals Christ as the perfect Man, emphasizes the humanity (human nature) of Jesus, showing that His lineage went back through Mary, to Nathan (another son of David), then to David, and on to Abraham, and finally to the first man, Adam.

1. *As To the Virginity of Mary.* Both Matthew and Luke state she was a virgin. "Now the birth of Jesus Christ was on this wise: When as his mother Mary was espoused to Joseph, before they came together, she was found with child of the Holy Ghost" (Matt. 1:18). "In the sixth month the angel Gabriel was sent from God unto a city of Galilee, named Nazareth, to a virgin espoused to a man whose name was Joseph, of the house of David; and the virgin's name was Mary. . . . Then said Mary unto the angel, How shall this be, seeing I know not a man?" (Luke 1:26, 27, 34).

2. *As To Her Discovered Motherhood Before Her Marriage to Joseph.* "Joseph also went up from Galilee . . . to be taxed with Mary his espoused wife, being great with child" (Luke 2:5). See also Matthew 1:18-20.

3. *As To the Divine Paternity.* If Joseph was not Jesus Christ's father, then who was? *God*, of course: "Behold, thou shalt conceive in thy womb, and bring forth a son, and shalt call his name JESUS. He shall be great, and shall be called the

Son of the Highest: and the Lord God shall give unto him the throne of his father David. . . . And the angel answered and said unto her, The Holy Ghost shall come upon thee, and the power of the Highest shall overshadow thee: therefore also that holy thing which shall be born of thee shall be called the Son of God" (Luke 1:31, 32, 34). See also Matthew 1:18-20.

B. The Manner of the Incarnation.

The reason why so many do not believe in the virgin birth of Jesus Christ is that they think His birth was the birth of a mere baby, and not the birth of God, the Son. Remember, this is the incarnation – the enfleshment of God, God manifest in the flesh!

1. *As Testified By Matthew.*

a. *In the Genealogy of Christ.* Tracing the Lord's descent from Abraham in chapter one, verses one through seventeen, we notice that the word "begat" is mentioned thirty-nine times, but is omitted after the name Joseph, the husband of the Virgin, Mary. Joseph did *not* beget Jesus Christ: "Jacob begat Joseph the husband of Mary, of whom was born Jesus, who is called Christ" (Matt. 1:16).

Then, one may ask, why is this genealogy mentioned in the first place? The reason is this: the future King of Israel *had* to come through this line (David, Solomon, etc.); and, in order to prove that Jesus was the rightful heir to the throne of David, it had to be shown that He came from this line. When Joseph married the Virgin Mary, her virgin-born Son became the *legal* heir of Joseph and first in line for the throne.

Was Christ an actual son of David? Certainly He was, but not through Joseph to Solomon and David. He was a son of David by His mother; she, herself, was a princess in Israel, tracing her lineage through Nathan (another son of David) on to David. By blood Christ Jesus was a son of David through Mary; legally He was a son of David through Joseph.

b. *In the Attitude of Joseph.* For this let us turn to Matthew 1:18-25: "Now the birth of Jesus Christ was on this wise: When as his mother Mary was espoused to Joseph, before they came together, she was found with child of the Holy Ghost. Then Joseph her husband, being a just man, and not willing to make her a publick example, was minded to put her away privily. But while he thought on these things, behold, the angel of the Lord appeared unto him in a dream, saying, Joseph, thou son of David, fear not to take unto thee Mary thy wife: for that which is conceived in her is of the Holy Ghost. And she shall bring forth a son, and thou shalt call his name JESUS: for he shall save his people from their sins. Now all this was done, that it might be fulfilled which was spoken of the Lord by the prophet, saying, Behold, a virgin shall be with child, and shall bring forth a son, and they shall call his name Emmanuel, which being interpreted is, God with us. Then Joseph being raised from sleep did as the angel of the Lord had bidden him, and took unto him his wife: and knew her not till she had brought forth her firstborn son: and he called his name JESUS."

Now if this does not speak of the virgin birth, how would you state it? In his own mind, Joseph was convinced of the impurity of Mary, his espoused wife. He reasoned that if he had not known her some other man must have. Living under the law, a just man, he thought of two things to do: divorce her; or have her exposed and stoned to death. He never once conceived of the idea of taking her and making her his wife; inneed, not until the angel appeared unto him and commanded him to do so; and this he did.

Men today, even some preachers, think it is smart to deny that Jesus was of a virgin birth. They say that Joseph was the father, but Joseph said he was not.

c. *In the Worship of the Wise Men.* "There came wise men . . . saying, Where is he that is born King of the Jews? for we have seen his star in the east, and are come to worship him. . . . And when they were come into the house, they saw the young child with Mary his mother, and fell down, and worshipped him" (Matt. 2:2, 11a).

These wise men were indeed wise men. They worshiped the Baby, and not the mother Mary. These men were men of God, taught and led by God; they would not have worshiped the Baby if Joseph had been the father.

d. *In the Expressions of "the Young Child and His Mother."* Four times is this statement made (Matt. 2:11, 13, 14, 20); never does it say, "your wife and your child." In connection with this we note another statement: "When they were departed, behold, the angel of the Lord appeareth to Joseph in a dream, saying, Arise, and take the young child and his mother, and flee into Egypt; and be thou there until I bring thee word: for Herod will seek the young child to destroy him. When he arose, he took the young child and his mother by night, and departed into Egypt: and was there until the death of Herod: that it might be fulfilled which was spoken of the Lord by the prophet, saying, Out of Egypt have I called my son." (Matt. 2:13-15). *My* Son. Not Joseph's, but God's!

2. *As Testified by Luke.*

a. *In the Enunciation to Zacharias.* "The angel said unto him, Fear not, Zacharias: for thy prayer is heard; and thy wife Elisabeth shall bear thee a son, and thou shalt call his name John. And thou shalt have joy and gladness; and many shall rejoice at his birth. For he shall be great in the sight of the Lord, and shall drink neither wine nor strong drink; and he shall be filled with the Holy Ghost, even from his mother's womb. And many of the children of Israel shall he turn to the Lord their God. And he shall go before him in the spirit and power of Elias, to turn the hearts of the fathers to the children, and the disobedient to the wisdom of the just; to make ready a people prepared for the Lord" (Luke 1:13-17).

Herein Zacharias was told that he was to have a son who would be the forerunner of the Christ, the Son of God.

b. *In the Enunciation to Mary.* "The angel said unto her, Fear not, Mary: for thou hast found favour with God. And, behold, thou shalt conceive in thy womb, and bring forth a son, and shalt call his name Jesus" (Luke 1:30, 31).

Mary became a woman with child out of wedlock, which was evil unto God; but Mary found favor in God's sight. Thus, if Mary had become with child by man, and God still blessed her while in that condition, then God would be a God of evil. But we know He found favor with her, and she with Him, for she was with child, but by the Holy Ghost.

c. *In the Praise of Elizabeth.* "She [Elizabeth] spake out with a loud voice, and said, Blessed art thou among women, and blessed is the fruit of thy womb. And whence is this to me, that the mother of my Lord should come to me? For, lo, as soon as the voice of thy salutation sounded in mine ears, the babe leaped in my womb for joy. And blessed is she that believed: for there shall be a performance of those things which were told her from the Lord" (Luke 1:42-45).

Was this the praise to Mary? No!

d. *In the Song of Mary.* "Mary said, My soul doth magnify the Lord, and my spirit hath rejoiced in God my *Saviour* . . ." (Luke 1:46-55). This was not a song of a woman that had conceived and was to bear in shame; it was a song filled with joy and praise to God, who had selected her to bring forth the Messiah.

e. *In the Prophecy of Zacharias.* "Thou, child, shalt be called the prophet of the Highest: for thou shalt go before the face of the Lord to prepare his ways" (Luke 1:76). This is only a portion of the prophecy of the father of John the Baptist concerning the work of John, then just born. He declares that the One whom John shall go before is the Son of God, and not the son of a man.

f. *In the Experience of Shepherds.* "There were in the same country shepherds abiding in the field, keeping watch over their flock by night. And, lo, the angel of the Lord came upon them, and the glory of the Lord shone round about them: and they were sore afraid. And the angel said unto them, Fear not: for, behold, I bring you good tidings of great joy, which shall be to all people. For unto you is born this day in the city of David a Saviour, which is Christ the Lord. And this shall be a sign unto you; Ye shall find the babe wrapped in swaddling clothes, lying in a manger. And suddenly there was with the angel a multitude of the heavenly host praising God, and saying, Glory to God in the highest, and on earth peace, good will toward men" (Luke 2:8-14).

When Christ was born, Heaven shouted a message of praise. Would all this have happened over a bastard child? Of course not! But Jesus was what the Word says He is – Christ the Lord! – the virgin son of Mary.

C. The Objections to the Incarnation.

Many of the enemies of God are within the body of professed believers – those who claim to be Christians, but deny the virgin birth of Christ. Someone may ask: "When a person is to be saved, does he have to believe in the virgin birth of Christ to be saved? Is this one doctrine which one must believe and understand to be saved?" Let us answer by asking this: "Do you believe that it is possible for a saved person not to believe in the virgin birth of Christ?" Of course not! All saved, born-again saints of God will believe that our Saviour was virgin born. The only thing that a lost person has to do to be saved is to repent of his sins and trust Christ as his Saviour, believing that He died for his sins and that He rose again from the dead. Saved people will believe in the virgin birth of our Lord.

Those who say they are Christians, and deny the virgin birth, are mere "professors" and not "possessors." These enemies within, and those without the professing Church, object to the virgin birth by the following arguments:

1. *The Scholarship of the Day is Against It.* This statement is not true, but it would not matter much if it were, for we know that "the carnal mind is enmity against God: for it is not subject to the law of God, neither indeed can be" (Rom. 8:7). The unconverted heart knows not God nor of the things of God; and, of course, it would not believe in the virgin birth of Jesus Christ. Unregenerated scholars may not accept this divine truth, but there are great minds of this world sitting upon the chairs of learning in our leading colleges and universities – saved men – who believe and testify to the virgin birth of Jesus. Really, a person is not indeed educated until he believes God and His Word: "The fear of the LORD is the beginning of knowledge" (Prov. 1:7).

2. *The New Testament is Silent Concerning It.* Certainly Matthew is not silent concerning it; surely Luke is not silent concerning it. God has provided *two witnesses,* for "in the mouth of two or three witnesses shall every word be established" (II Cor. 13:1). God fulfills the Law, thus establishing the truth concerning the virgin birth of our Redeemer. What if there were only *one* witness? It still would be true, for it is God who speaketh.

a. *But There is the Testimony of Mark.* By this we present indirect evidence which proves the virgin birth of Christ. There is nothing said against the virgin birth. Mark does not record the birth of the Lord; does he mean to state that Christ never existed? Of course not. The Gospel of Mark presents Jesus as the Perfect Servant; and when considering a servant, no one cares to know his genealogy; thus the birth of Christ is omitted. The first verse of Mark's Gospel states: "The beginning of the gospel of Jesus Christ, the Son of God." Any Hebrew knows that this means that Jesus Christ was on an equal with God, and we know that the record tells us of things Jesus Christ did which no other man could ever do.

b. *But There is the Testimony of John.* "In the beginning was the Word, and the Word was with God, and the Word was God. . . . And the Word was made flesh, and dwelt among us, (and we beheld his glory, the glory as of the only begotten of the Father,) full of grace and truth" (John 1:1, 14). Indeed this is not the record of a mere man, but the Son of Man, the Son of God, God Himself!

c. *But There is the Testimony of Paul.* While stating that these arguments are of Mark, John, Paul, and others, let us bear in mind that, while these men penned these words, the words are the words of God, and they express His mind upon the virgin birth of His Son.

Paul was separated "unto the gospel of God . . . concerning his Son Jesus Christ our Lord, which was made of the seed of David according to the flesh; and declared to be the Son of God with power, according to the spirit of holiness, by the resurrection from the dead. . . . what the law could not do, in that it was weak through the flesh, God sending his own Son in the likeness of sinful flesh, and for sin, condemned sin in the flesh" (Rom. 1:3, 4; 8:3). "Ye know the grace of our Lord Jesus Christ, that, though he was rich, yet for your sakes he became poor, that ye through his poverty might be rich" (II Cor. 8:9). See also Philippians 2:5-7; Galatians 4:4; I John 4:2; Colossians 2:8.

3. *The Early Church Didn't Believe It.* This is another false argument against the virgin birth which can be refuted easily. The early creeds of the Church plainly declared the virgin birth.

a. *The Apostles' Creed.* This dates back to the second century. The word "creed" comes from the Latin, *credo,* which means, "I believe." These creeds came first orally, then written.

b. *The Nicene Creed.* This goes back to the fourth century. When Arius stated that Jesus was a created being, and not the Son from all eternity, a council was called to settle the fact that Christ, though born of the virgin, has existed co-eternally with the Father. The Council at Constantinople (381) was called. This council also refers to the fact of the virgin birth of Christ.

c. *The Te Deum Laudamus.* This was an ancient hymn preserved by the Church, which proved that the Early Church believed in the virgin birth of Christ.

4. *It Is Against the Laws of Nature.* To this argument against the virgin birth, we reply, "It most certainly *is* against the laws of nature." For this was not the birth of a mere baby, but the birth of the Son of God in the flesh. Did you ever

take time to consider that this might have been the only way by which God could have come in the flesh – by the virgin birth?

There are three ways by which God made human beings not according to the laws of nature: (1) When He made Adam without the aid of a man and woman; (2) when He made Eve without the aid of a woman; (3) when He made Christ without the aid of a man.

5. *It Is Too Much Like Mythology.* It is true that many idolatrous religions have taught that their gods were the offsprings of women, but not wholly of virginity; rather, that these women had carnal relations with other gods which produced the people's gods. Can there be any comparison between the birth of Jesus Christ and the reported stories of those myths? Of course not! The virgin births of the men of mythology are not virgin, but the result of carnal intercourse.

6. *In Calling Himself the Son of Man Christ Denied the Virgin Birth.* Remember, the Lord Jesus Christ never said, "I am *a* Son of *a* man"; but, "I am *the* Son of Man."

7. *The Need of a Purification Proved That This Was a Natural Birth.* Under the law of Israel all women were unclean. The purpose of this law was hygenic, to save the woman's health, protecting her from the pleasure of her husband while she was still in a weakened condition, caused by childbirth.

D. The Objects of the Incarnation.

What were the purposes of the virgin birth?

1. *To Reveal the Invisible God.* "No man hath seen God at any time; the only begotten Son, which is in the bosom of the Father, he hath declared him" (John 1:18). Jesus Christ is the Exposition of God, the Revealer of God. If you want to know what God is like, look upon Jesus.

2. *To Fulfill Prophecy.*

a. *The Seed as an Example.* "I will put enmity between thee and the woman, and between thy seed and her seed; it shall bruise thy head, and thou shalt bruise his heel" (Gen. 3:15). A woman does not have seed; seed belongs to the man. But this Scripture mentions the "seed of the woman." This is contrary to nature and refers, of course, to the virgin birth – fulfilled when Mary gave birth to Jesus Christ.

b. *The Virgin as an Example.* "The Lord himself shall

give you a sign; Behold, a virgin shall conceive, and bear a son, and shall call his name Immanuel." (Is. 7:14). This Scripture means exactly what we mean.

3. *To Fulfill the Davidic Covenant.* "There shall come forth a rod out of the stem of Jesse, and a Branch shall grow out of his roots. . . . And in that day there shall be a root of Jesse, which shall stand for an ensign of the people; to it shall the Gentiles seek: and his rest shall be glorious" (Is. 11:1, 10). "Behold, the days come, saith the LORD, that I will raise unto David a righteous Branch, and a King shall reign and prosper, and shall execute judgment and justice in the earth. In his days Judah shall be saved, and Israel shall dwell safely: and this is his name whereby he shall be called, THE LORD OUR RIGHTEOUSNESS" (Jer. 23:5, 6). "Men and brethren, let me freely speak unto you of the patriarch David, that he is both dead and buried, and his sepulchre is with us unto this day. Therefore being a prophet, and knowing that God had sworn with an oath to him, that of the fruit of his loins, according to the flesh, he would raise up Christ to sit on his throne; he seeing this before spake of the resurrection of Christ, that his soul was not left in hell, neither his flesh did see corruption" (Acts 2:29-31). See also I Samuel 7:4-17; Luke 1:32, 33.

4. *To Sacrifice For Our Sins.* "Ye know that he was manifested to take away our sins; and in him is no sin" (I John 3:5). "It is not possible that the blood of bulls and of goats should take away sins. Wherefore when he cometh into the world, he saith, Sacrifice and offering thou wouldest not, but a body hast thou prepared me. . . . Above when he said, Sacrifice and offering and burnt offerings and offering for sin thou wouldest not, neither hadst pleasure therein; which are offered by the law; then said he, Lo, I come to do thy will, O God. He taketh away the first, that he may establish the second. By the which will we are sanctified through the offering of the body of Jesus Christ once for all" (Heb. 10:4, 5, 8-10). "Moreover, brethren, I declare unto you the gospel which I preached unto you, which also ye have received, and wherein ye stand; by which also ye are saved, if ye keep in memory what I preached unto you, unless ye have believed in vain. For I delivered unto you first of all that which I also received, how that Christ died for our sins according to the scriptures;

and that he was buried, and that he rose again the third day according to the scriptures" (I Cor. 15:1-4).

a. *A Sacrifice of Beast Never Took Away Sin.* It is God who instituted animal sacrifice. Yet all the blood for centuries shed upon Jewish altars never took one sin away. Why, then, was it commanded? It was commanded in order to provide a "covering" for sins until the blood of Christ would come and "wash" them away. No, animal sacrifices could never take away sin, for the sacrifice must come up to the level of man, for whom it is sacrificed.

b. *The Sacrifice Must Be Sinless.* We agree that a "man must be sacrificed for a man"; animals do not come up to the level of man. Yet one sinful man cannot be offered up as a sacrifice for another sinful man, for if the first sinful man must die, he must die for his *own* sin.

c. *The Sacrifice Must Be an Infinite Sacrifice.* Not only must the sacrifice come up to the level of man, for whom it is offered, but it must come up to the level of *God,* whom it must satisfy! Jesus, our Lord, fulfilled all! "His own self bare our sins in his own body on the tree, that we, being dead to sin, should live unto righteousness: by whose stripes ye were healed" (I Peter 2:24).

5. *To Provide the Redeemed With a High Priest.* "In all things it behoved him to be made like unto his brethren, that he might be a merciful and faithful high priest in things pertaining to God, to make reconcilation for the sins of the people. . . . Wherefore, holy brethren, partakers of the heavenly calling, consider the Apostle and High Priest of our profession, Christ Jesus" (Heb. 2:17; 3:1).

Today we have One, even Jesus Christ, who stands for us before God. We have an accuser (Rev. 12:10), who accuses us daily before God, but we also have an advocate with the Father, who maketh intercession for us.

6. *To Show Believers How To Live.* "He that saith he abideth in him ought himself also so to walk, even as he walked" (I John 2:6). "For even hereunto were ye called: because Christ also suffered for us, leaving us an example, that ye should follow his steps" (I Peter 2:21).

7. *To Become the Head of a New Creation.* "He that sat upon the throne said, Behold, I make all things new. And he said unto me, Write: for these words are true and faithful"

(Rev. 21:5). See also II Corinthians 5:17; I Corinthians 15: 45, 47.

E. *The Perpetuity of the Incarnation.*

By this we mean the "everlasting of the incarnation." God will always be manifested in the flesh in the person of His Son Jesus Christ.

1. *Is Essential To the Integrity of Our Lord's Manhood.* Our Lord, now in glory, has His manhood. He is man *today.*

2. *Is Essential To Our Lord's High Priesthood.* "Forasmuch then as the children are partakers of flesh and blood, he also himself likewise took part of the same; that through death he might destroy him that had the power of death, that is, the devil; and deliver them who through fear of death were all their lifetime subject to bondage. For verily he took not on him the nature of angels; but he took on him the seed of Abraham. Wherefore in all things it behoved him to be made like unto his brethren, that he might be a merciful and faithful high priest in things pertaining to God, to make reconciliation for the sins of the people. For in that he himself hath suffered being tempted, he is able to succour them that are tempted" (Heb. 2:14-18). "And they truly were many priests, because they were not suffered to continue by reason of death: but this man, because he continueth ever, hath an unchangeable priesthood. Wherefore he is able also to save them to the uttermost that come unto God by him, seeing he ever liveth to make intercession for them. For such an high priest became us, who is holy, harmless, undefiled, separate from sinners, and made higher than the heavens; who needeth not daily, as those high priests, to offer up sacrifice, first for his own sins, and then for the people's: for this he did once, when he offered up himself. For the law maketh men high priests which have infirmity; but the word of the oath, which was since the law, maketh the Son, who is consecrated for evermore" (Heb. 7:23-28). "For Christ is not entered into the holy places made with hands, which are the figures of the true; but into heaven itself, now to appear in the presence of God for us" (Heb. 9:24). "Looking unto Jesus the author and finisher of our faith; who for the joy that was set before him endured the cross, despising the shame, and is set down at the right hand of the throne of God" (Heb. 12:2).

3. *Is Essential To Our Lord's Return and Millennium Reign.* "While they looked stedfastly toward heaven as he went up, behold, two men stood by them in white apparel; which also said, Ye men of Galilee, why stand ye gazing up into heaven? *This same Jesus,* which is taken up from you into heaven, shall so come in like manner as ye have seen him go into heaven" (Acts 1:10, 11). "I have said, Mercy shall be built up for ever; thy faithfulness shalt thou establish in the very heavens. I have made a covenant with my chosen. I have sworn unto David my servant, Thy seed will I establish for ever, and build up thy throne to all generations" (Ps. 89:2-4). "In that day will I raise up the tabernacle of David that is fallen, and close up the breaches thereof; and I will raise up his ruins, and I will build it as in the days of old" (Amos 9:11). See also Isaiah 9:6, 7; 55:3, 4.

F. The Proofs of the Incarnation.

The proofs of the incarnation are centered in Christ Himself!

1. *Such As His Sinless Life.* "We have not an high priest which cannot be touched with the feeling of our infirmities; but was in all points tempted like as we are, yet without sin" (Heb. 4:15). "For he hath made him to be sin for us, who knew no sin; that we might be made the righteousness of God in him" (II Cor. 5:21). Only God, in human flesh, could live the sinless life.

2. *Such As His Resurrection.* "Now is Christ risen from the dead, and become the firstfruits of them that slept" (I Cor. 15:20). Would He have been raised from the dead had He not been the incarnate Son of God? Of course not.

III. The Two Natures of Christ

There can be no Christianity without Christ. Orthodoxy of any person, or any church, can be settled upon this question: What think ye of Christ?

We wonder why the modernists of today try to lay Christ low. There are those who try to prove that He never existed. In one great university, a certain professor went to lengths to prove that Christ was only a figment of the mind. After many lectures, he completed his tirade, and then asked for comments. One student humbly asked, "If Christ never existed, why are you attacking Him?"

Why do not the enemies leave Him alone if He never

existed? Why have anything to do with Him if He never rose from the dead? But He does exist; He has been resurrected; He ever lives!

Who is He? has been the question for two thousand years. We have the testimonies and confessions of men who saw Him: *John the Baptist* – "Behold the Lamb of God, which taketh away the sin of the world" (John 1:29); "I saw, and bare record that this is the Son of God" (John 1:34); *Andrew* – "We have found the Messias, which is, being interpreted, the Christ" (John 1:41); *Philip* – "We have found him, of whom Moses in the law, and the prophets, did write, Jesus of Nazareth, the son of Joseph" (John 1:45); *Peter* – "Thou art the Christ, the Son of the living God" (Matt. 16:16).

Among the people there was division caused by this question, Who is He? "Many of the people therefore, when they heard this saying, said, Of a truth, this is the Prophet. Others said, This is the Christ. But some said, Shall Christ come out of Galilee? Hath not the scripture said, That Christ cometh of the seed of David, and out of the town of Bethlehem, where David was? So there was a division among the people because of him" (John 7:40-43). See also John 9:17, 18; 10:9-20; Luke 5:21.

Men questioned the deity of Christ, but the demons never did. They acknowledged Him as being their Creator and coming Judge: "Behold, they cried out, saying, What have we to do with thee, Jesus thou Son of God? art thou come hither to torment us before the time?" (Matt. 8:29).

At the trial of the Lord Jesus, this same question predominated: "Jesus stood before the governor: and the governor asked him, saying, Art thou the King of the Jews? And Jesus said unto him, Thou sayest" (Matt. 27:11). See also Matthew 26:63; Luke 22:67, 70.

And as He hung upon the Cross, the question still agitated the minds of his enemies: "They that passed by reviled him . . . saying, Thou that destroyest the temple, and buildest it in three days, save thyself. If thou be the Son of God, come down from the cross" (Matt. 27:40).

As we have the testimonies and confessions of those who saw Him, we ourselves who trust Him, and love Him, have the Witness (Holy Spirit) within that He is the Christ, the Son of the living God: "For he dwelleth with you, and shall be in you" (John 14:17a); "No man can say that Jesus is the Lord, but by the Holy Ghost" (I Cor. 12:3b).

A. *The Humanity of Christ.*

In other days it was the humanity of Christ which was under attack, and not His deity. No matter what age we may live in, Satan is the common enemy, and it is he who keeps going the continued attack upon our Lord.

1. *He was Perfectly Human.* By this we mean that our Lord, though He has been from all time and eternity, yet when He became flesh, He possessed a perfect human body, soul and spirit. Man, we know, has a body, soul and spirit: "The very God of peace sanctify you wholly; and I pray God your whole spirit and soul and body be preserved blameless unto the coming of our Lord Jesus Christ" (I Thess. 5:23).

a. *His Human Physical Body.* Yes, the Lord Jesus, in His humanity, possessed a *body*: "For in that she hath poured this ointment on my body, she did it for my burial" (Matt. 26:12; see also Hebrews 10:5); a *soul*: "Now is my soul troubled; and what shall I say? Father, save me from this hour: but for this cause came I unto this hour" (John 12:27; see also Matthew 26:38); and a *spirit;* "Immediately when Jesus perceived in his spirit that they so reasoned within themselves, he said unto them, Why reason ye these things in your hearts" (Mark 2:8; see also Luke 23:46; Luke 10:21).

b. *His Human Appearance.* The woman at the well recognized Jesus as a human being: "How is it that thou, being a Jew, askest drink of me, which am a woman of Samaria? for the Jews have no dealings with the Samaritans" (John 4:9). And after Christ's resurrection He still maintained His human appearance; for Mary, supposing Jesus to be the gardener, recognized Him as a human being: "She, supposing him to be the gardener, saith unto him, Sir, if thou have borne him hence, tell me where thou hast laid him, and I will take him away" (John 20:15b).

c. *His Human Parent.* Though God was His Father, yet the Lord Jesus did have a human mother, thus proving that He was human: "When the fulness of the time was come, God sent forth his Son, made of a woman, made under the law" (Gal. 4:4); Paul was separated unto the gospel "concerning his Son Jesus Christ our Lord, which was made of the seed of David, according to the flesh" (Rom. 1:3); "The third day there was a marriage in Cana of Galilee; and the mother of Jesus was there" (John 2:1). See also Matthew 2:11; 13:55; John 1:14.

d. *His Human Development.* Being perfectly human, the Lord was born, and He grew as other boys and girls: "The child grew, and waxed strong in spirit, filled with wisdom: and the grace of God was upon him. . . . And Jesus increased in wisdom and stature, and in favour with God and man" (Luke 2:40, 52).

e. *His Human Limitation.* Being God, the Son of God became man, and when He did, He limited Himself to the realm of the human. Thus, He possessed human limitations, which were sinless infirmities. As we thus speak, let us not confuse infirmity with sin. He had human infirmities, but no sin. He *hungered* ("When he had fasted forty days and forty nights, he was afterward an hungred" – Matt. 4:2); He *thirsted* ("After this, Jesus knowing that all things were now accomplished, that the scripture might be fulfilled, saith, I thirst" – John 19:28); He became *weary* ("Now Jacob's well was there. Jesus therefore, being *wearied* with his journey, sat thus on the well: and it was about the sixth hour" – John 4:6); He *slept* ("Behold, there arose a great tempest in the sea, insomuch that the ship was covered with the waves: but he was asleep" – Matt. 8:24). See Matthew 26:36-40, for these verses describe in full the testing of Christ in the garden such as only a human being can endure.

f. *His Human Name.* His human name was a name common to all of that time: "And she shall bring forth a son, and thou shalt call his name JESUS: for he shall save his people from their sins" (Matt. 1:21). See also Luke 2:21.

g. *His Human Suffering and Death.* His suffering and death was common to that which is experienced by man. The Scriptures abound in the fact that He possessed a human body and suffered as a human (Matt. 26:26-35; John 19:20; Luke 22:44).

If Jesus was not man, He could not have died, for God, in His true essence, cannot die! And He *did* die "Neither by the blood of goats and calves, but by his own blood he entered in once into the holy place, having obtained eternal redemption for us" (Heb. 9:12). He rose from the dead! And He is *still* man!

2. *He Is the Perfect Human.*

a. *As He Transcends All Limitation of Character.* Everything is combined in Him. Look at all the attributes of man, and you will find that some men possess one kind while other men possess other attributes; but in Him we find completeness – all the attributes of men.

We believe that the character of Jesus is free from forgery. It takes a Plato to forge a Plato, and it would have taken a Jesus to have forged a Jesus.

Think of His *power* compared with His *humility*: He drives the money-changers out of the temple at one moment, and then washes the disciples feet at another.

(1) *He Has All Perfection.* He never ran for fear. No one ever frightened Him. He was never elated with success; we are. The Devil never baffled Him. He is the Man above all men. You cannot put anyone on the same level with the Lord Jesus. Take the leaders of the world – Caesar, Alexander the Great, yea, even godly men, such as Moody and Billy Sunday – they can never come up to Him. You cannot put the gods of men upon the same platform with the Lord Jesus. There is only *one* place for our Saviour, and that is the *throne!*

(2) *He Is Without Sin.* He is a perfect human being, the only One the world has ever seen. Turn to II Corinthians 5:21 and read the description of Him: "He hath made him to be sin for us, who knew no sin; that we might be made the righteousness of God in him." This verse of Scripture does not mean that Christ never sinned, although He never did, but rather that He was without a sinful nature.

If a man lived all his life without sin, he still would not be perfect. By living without sin, he would only be triumphing over a sinful nature. Christ never had a sinful nature. "that holy thing which shall be born of thee shall be called the Son of God" (Luke 1:35c). There has been only *one* Holy Baby ever to be born into this world, and they called Him *Jesus!* No drunkard can help a drunkard. A man does not have to become a thief to help a thief. The Lord Jesus did not take upon Himself a sinful nature in order to help us who do have a sinful nature.

When the Lord Jesus was in the wilderness for forty days, He knew what hunger was. He knows how it is with us when we go hungry. No man ever died at the stake, or went through a time of testing, as He did upon the Cross. He knows what it is to suffer. We have something in us that wants us to sin, but He never wanted to sin – that is what He suffered: the Devil trying to make Him want to sin.

That age-old question may now be raised: "Could the Lord Jesus have sinned had He wanted to?" The question is thrown aside by stating, "He could not have wanted to, being the Son of God." But, someone may add, if He could not have sinned, then why the temptation? If He could not have sinned, then the temptation was a mockery! That is exactly the answer! For He was not tested to see if He would sin, but He was tested to show (to prove) that He *would not* sin.

This is something to consider also: if the Lord Jesus could have sinned here upon earth, then it is still possible for Him to sin in Heaven as He maketh intercession for us. But He could not have sinned upon earth, and He cannot sin in heaven. He is our perfect High Priest.

b. *As He Transcends All Limitations of Time.* He is for all time. His teachings are not out-of-date. They are up-to-date! The books of our colleges and universities are not over ten years old; they are ever changing. But His words stand sure.

He is the One who has said, "Heaven and earth shall pass away, but my words shall never pass away." But there is no record of Him writing a book of His life – yet His words *are* true, for they have *not* passed away!

c. *As He Transcends All Limitations of All Nationalities.* The Jew was exclusive of all people, and the Lord Jesus came from the most exclusive race of people, yet He belongs to all kindreds and tribes! *He belongs to all.* The Chinaman thinks of Him as being Chinese; the Englishman thinks of Him as being English. When we are saved, we claim Him as our own, no matter to what race we belong.

Christ was liar, lunatic, or *Lord!* No modernist ever says He was a liar – He only *thought* He was God. Then He must have been a lunatic. Of course He was not a liar nor a lunatic; He was the Son of God! The God man!

B. The Deity of Christ.

1. *Divine Predictions.* "The Lord said unto my Lord, Sit thou at my right hand, until I make thine enemies thy foot-

stool" (Ps. 110:1); "Thou, Beth-lehem Ephratah, though thou be little among the thousands of Judah, yet out of thee shall he come forth unto me that is to be ruler in Israel; whose goings forth have been from of old, from everlasting" (Mic. 5:2). See also Isaiah 7:14; 9:8; Jeremiah 23:6; and Genesis 3:15.

2. *Divine Names.*

a. *He Is Called God.* "Thomas answered and said unto him, My Lord and my God" (John 20:28); "Christ came, who is over all, God blessed for ever. Amen" (Rom. 9:5); "We know that the Son of God is come, and hath given us an understanding, that we may know him that is true, and we are in him that is true, even in his Son Jesus Christ. This is the true God, and eternal life" (I John 5:20). See also Matthew 1:23; John 1:1; compare Psalm 45:6, 7 with Hebrews 1:8.

b. *He is Called the Son of God.* This implies sameness with God. "Devils also came out of many, crying out, and saying, Thou art Christ the Son of God. And he rebuking them suffered them not to speak: for they knew that he was Christ" (Luke 4:41); "Verily, verily, I say unto you, The hour is coming, and now is, when the dead shall hear the voice of the Son of God: and they that hear shall live" (John 5:25); "For what the law could not do, in that it was weak through the flesh, God sending his own Son in the likeness of sinful flesh, and for sin, condemned sin in the flesh" (Rom. 8:3). Look up these other Scriptures: Mark 1:1; Matthew 27:40, 43; John 19:7; 10:36; 11:4.

c. *He Is Called Lord.* "The Son of man is Lord even of the sabbath day" (Matt. 12:8); "Ye call me Master and Lord: and ye say well; for so I am" (John 13:13); "And they said, Believe on the Lord Jesus Christ, and thou shalt be saved, and thy house" (Acts 16:31); "He hath on his vesture and on his thigh a name written, KING OF KINGS, AND LORD OF LORDS" (Rev. 19:16).

d. *He Is Called Other Divine Names.* "When I saw him, I fell at his feet as dead. And he laid his right hand upon me, saying unto me, Fear not; I am the first and the last" (Rev. 1:17). See also Revelation 22:13.

3. *Divine Equality.* "Now, O Father, glorify thou me with thine own self with the glory which I had with thee before the world was" (John 17:5); "He that seeth me seeth him

that sent me" (John 12:45); "Being in the form of God, [Christ Jesus] thought it not robbery to be equal with God" (Phil. 2:6a); "In him dwelleth all the fulness of the Godhead bodily" (Col. 2:9).

4. *Divine Relationship.* His name is coupled with the Father's. "I and my Father are one" (John 10:30). "The grace of the Lord Jesus Christ, and the love of God, and the communion of the Holy Ghost, be with you all. Amen" (II Cor. 13:14); "Now our Lord Jesus Christ himself, and God, even our Father, which hath loved us, and hath given us everlasting consolation and good hope through grace, comfort your hearts, and stablish you in every good word and work" (II Thess. 2:16, 17).

5. *Divine Worship.* Worship belongs only to God. Christ received true worship. Therefore, Christ is God! "There came wise men . . . saying, Where is he that is born King of the Jews? for we have seen his star in the east, and are come to worship him. . . . And when they were come into the house, they saw the young child with Mary his mother, and fell down and worshipped him: and when they had opened their treasures, they presented unto him gifts; gold, and frankincense, and myrrh" (Matt. 2:2, 11). The wise men did not come to worship Mary, but Christ Jesus. In later years he accepted worship: "They that were in the ship came and worshipped him, saying, Of a truth thou art the Son of God" (Matt. 14:33). See also Matthew 9:18; Luke 24:52. If Christ had not been God, then this worship would have been idolatry. It is God's command that the Son should be worshiped. "And again, when he bringeth in the firstbegotten into the world, he saith, And let all the angels of God worship him" (Heb. 1:6). "That all men should honour the Son, even as they honour the Father. He that honoureth not the Son honoureth not the Father which hath sent him" (John 5:23). This is true of all ages, that Christians have worshiped Christ as God. Born-again men would not have been satisfied with the worshiping of the mere man.

6. *Divine Attributes.*

a. *Omnipotence.* "Jesus came and spake unto them, saying, All power is given unto me in heaven and in earth" (Matt. 28:18). He has power over *death*: "Jesus said unto her, I am the resurrection, and the life: he that believeth in me, though he were dead, yet shall he live: and whosoever liveth and believeth in me shall never die. Believest thou this?" (John 11:25, 26). He has power over *nature*: "By him were all things created, that are in heaven, and that are in earth, visible and invisible, whether they be thrones, or dominions, or principalities, or powers: all things were created by him, and for him: and he is before all things, and by him all things consist" (Col. 1:16, 17). He has power over *demons*: "They were all amazed, and spake among themselves, saying, What a word is this! for with authority and power he commandeth the unclean spirits, and they come out" (Luke 4:36).

b. *Omniscience.* "Now are we sure that thou knowest all things, and needest not that any man should ask thee: by this we believe that thou camest forth from God" (John 16:30). "He [Peter] said unto him, Lord, thou knowest all things; thou knowest that I love thee. Jesus saith unto him, Feed my sheep" (John 21:17c). See also Matthew 9:4; 12:25; Luke 6:8; 9:47; 10:22; John 1:48, 49; John 4:16-19; Mark 2:8.

This one question of the doctors of Jerusalem proves the omniscience of the Lord Jesus: "How knoweth this man letters, never having learned?" (John 7:15). This leads us to know that Christ was never taught by man. He needed no schooling, nor tutors. His disciples sat at His feet – at whose feet did He sit? At no one's! Paul was a student of Gamaliel – who taught Jesus? No one! Christ said, "Learn of me" – when did He ever say, "Teach me"? Never! We are sometimes advised to go to a higher authority, but to what authority did He go? To none other, for He had all authority. When did Jesus ever say, "I don't remember, I will have to look it up?" Never! He was never caught off guard. In Mark 12:13 we have these words: "And they send unto him certain of the Pharisees and of the Herodians to catch him in his words." They tried to trap Him in His words, but He was all wise and put His persecutors into confusion.

(1) *How He Taught.*

(a) *With Simplicity.* His illustrations were made on the spot. He drew them from life itself. He had no need of a filing system.

(b) *With Authority.* You never heard the Lord say, "We may as well suppose" (See Matthew 7:29; Mark 1:22).

(2) *What He Taught.*

(a) *Doctrine.* What He taught is not popular today. The modernists substitute ethics for doctrine; they believe in salvation by ethical living.

(b) *Ethics.* Christ certainly did teach ethics, but doctrine was first. Ethics must have doctrine for its foundation.

c. *Omni-sapience.* "In whom are hid all the treasures of wisdom and knowledge." (Col. 2:3).

d. *Omnipresence.* "Lo, I am with you alway, even unto the end of the world" (Matt. 28:20). "No man hath ascended up to heaven, but he that came down from heaven, even the Son of man which is in heaven" (John 3:13).

e. *Immutability.* "They shall perish; but thou remainest; and they all shall wax old as doth a garment; and as a vesture shalt thou fold them up, and they shall be changed: but thou art the same, and thy years shall not fail" (Heb. 1:11, 12). "This man, because he continueth ever, hath an unchangeable priesthood" (Heb. 7:24). "Jesus Christ the same yesterday, and to day, and for ever" (Heb. 13:8). Jesus may change His position, but His Person never changes.

f. *Everlastingness.* "In the beginning was the Word, and the Word was with God, and the Word was God. The same was in the beginning with God" (John 1:1, 2). "Thou, Beth-lehem Ephratah, though thou be little among the thousands of Judah, yet out of thee shall he come forth unto me that is to be ruler in Israel; whose goings forth have been from of old, from everlasting" (Mic. 5:2). "Jesus said unto them, Verily, verily, I say unto you, Before Abraham was, I am" (John 8:58). "Fear not; I am the first and the last" (Rev. 1:17c).

g. *Holiness.* "Who did no sin, neither was guile found in his mouth" (I Peter 2:22). "Ye know that he was manifested to take away our sins; and in him is no sin" (I John 3:5). See also Hebrews 7:26.

h. *Love.* Paul prays that the Ephesians may be able "to know the love of Christ, which passeth knowledge, that ye may be filled with all the fulness of God" (Eph. 3:19).

(1) *It is Spontaneous.*

(2) *It is Eternal.*

(3) *It is Infinite.*

(4) *It is Inexhaustible.*

(5) *It is Invincible.* See Ephesians 5:25; Revelation 1:5.

i. *Righteousness and Justice.* "Ye denied the Holy One and the Just, and desired a murderer, to be granted unto you" (Acts 3:14).

7. *Divine Offices.*

a. *Creation.* All creation is by the act of God; Christ created; therefore, Christ is God. "Thou, Lord, in the beginning hast laid the foundation of the earth; and the heavens are the works of thy hands" (Heb. 1:10). See John 1:3; Colossians 1:16; Ephesians 3:9; John 1:10.

b. *Preservation.* "Who being the brightness of his glory, and the express image of his person, and upholding all things by the word of his power, when he had by himself purged our sins, sat down on the right hand of the Majesty on high" (Heb. 1:3). "He is before all things, and by him all things consist"—all things hang together (Col. 1:17).

c. *Pardon.* "He said unto her, Thy sins are forgiven" (Luke 7:48). See also Mark 2:5-10.

d. *Resurrection.* "This is the Father's will which hath sent me, that of all which he hath given me I should lose nothing, but should raise it up again at the last day. And this is the will of him that sent me, that everyone which seeth the Son, and believeth on him, may have everlasting life: and I will raise him up at the last day" (John 6:39, 40).

e. *Transformation.* "Beloved, now are we the sons of God, and it doth not yet appear what we shall be: but we know that, when he shall appear, we shall be like him; for we shall see him as he is" (I John 3:2). See also Philippians 3:21 (R.V.).

f. *Judgment.* "The Father judgest no man, but hath committed all judgment unto the Son" (John 5:22). See also Acts 17:31; Matthew 16:27; Matthew 25:31; Romans 2:16; 14:10; II Corinthians 5:10; Revelation 22:12.

g. *Salvation.* "I give unto them eternal life; and they shall never perish, neither shall any man pluck them out of my hand" (John 10:28). See also John 5:25; 6:47; 10:10; 17:2.

C. *The Blending of the Two Natures in One Person.*

Man cannot understand it. This is one proof that the Bible is the Word of God, for if man had written the Bible he would have left the two natures of Christ out of it. These are infinite facts, and God does not seek to explain, but makes a simple declaration of fact; Christ possessed a human nature and a divine nature – both are complete. It is not Scriptural to say Christ is God and man; rather, He is the God-Man. A type of His dual nature can be found in the boards of the tabernacle. The boards were of wood and gold – one board, with two materials; not two boards. The wood never became gold, and the gold never became wood. Christ had but one personality, not two. Two natures, with one personality.

We try to make John 1:14 read, "The Word became a man"; but it says, "The Word was made flesh."

If we make Christ have two personalities, then we make the Godhead a Foursome instead of a Trinity.

D. Errors Concerning the Two Natures of Christ.

1. *Ebionitism.* This error was prevalent during the first century of the Christian Church. It denied the deity of Christ. It stated that Christ had a relationship with God after His baptism.

2. *Corinthianism.* This was most popular during the days of the Apostle John. According to this error, Christ possessed no deity until He was baptized.

3. *Docetism.* This error found its way into the Church during the latter part of the second century. It maintained that Christ did not possess a human body. He had a body, He had a celestial body. Thus Docetism denied Christ's humanity. Such error is the "spirit of anti-Christ" (I John 4:1-3).

4. *Arianism.* This error denied the divine nature of Christ. Arianism maintained that there was a time when the Son never existed, that God lived and then begat His Son after Him. Thus it denied Christ's pre-existence.

5. *Apollinarianism.* This error maintained that Christ possessed an incomplete human body. The Apollinarians reasoned: sin is sown in the soul of all men; God had no sin; therefore Christ had no soul; therefore He had an incomplete body.

6. *Nestorianism.* Nestorians took the two natures of Christ and made two persons out of them. That is, God came and dwelt in a perfect man; therefore God was in Christ, instead of Christ being God.

7. *Eutychianism.* The Eutychians took the two natures of Christ and ran them together and made one new nature.

8. *Monothelitism.* This error consisted of the belief that Christ had two natures, but only one will.

9. *Unitarianism.* The Unitarians deny the Trinity. Thus they deny the deity of Christ altogether.

10. *Christian Science.* This belief is a denial of the humanity of Christ.

11. *Millennial Dawnism.* This belief denies the personal existence of our Lord Jesus Christ.

IV. The Death of Christ

The Cross is the fundamental truth of the revealed Word of God. By the Cross we do not mean the tree, but the Sacrifice upon that tree.

We see the emblems of Christ and Him crucified in Genesis, and so on through the Old Testament. The only reason for Bethlehem is Calvary. Our salvation depends upon Christ dying upon the Cross.

A. *The Fact of the Death.*

1. *Old Testament Anticipation.*

a. *In Type.*

(1) Coats of Skin (Gen. 3:21).
(2) Abel's Lamb (Gen. 4:4).
(3) Offering of Isaac (Gen. 22).
(4) Passover Lamb (Ex. 12).
(5) The Levitical Sacrificial System (Lev. 1:1–7:16).
(6) The Brazen Serpent (Num. 21; John 3:14, 15).
(7) The Slain Lamb (Is. 53:6, 7; John 1:29).

b. *In Prediction.*

(1) Seed of the Woman (Gen. 3:15).
(2) The Sin Offering of Psalm 22.
(3) The Vicarious Sufferings of Isaiah 53.
(4) The Cut-off Messiah of Daniel 9:26.
(5) The Smitten Shepherd of Zachariah 13:6, 7.

2. *New Testament Revelation.*

a. *In General.* One third of the Book of Matthew, more than one third of Mark, one fourth of Luke, and one half of John deals with the last week of Christ before His crucifixion.

b. *In Particular.*

(1) *The Heart of Christ Must Be Noted.*

(a) *His death.* "If when we were enemies, we

were reconciled to God by the death of his Son, much more, being reconciled, we shall be saved by his life" (Rom. 5:10). See also Philippians 2:8; Hebrews 2:9, 14; Revelation 5:6-12.

(b) *His Cross.* "We preach Christ crucified, unto the Jews a stumbling block, and unto the Greeks foolishness" (I Cor. 1:23). See also Galatians 3:1; 6:14; Ephesians 2:16; Colossians 1:20.

(c) *His Blood.* "This is my blood of the new testament, which is shed for many for the remission of sins" (Matt. 26:28). See also Mark 14:24; Ephesians 1:7; Colossians 1:14; I John 1:7; Hebrews 9:12, 25; Revelation 1:5; 5:9.

(2) *The Three Statements Concerning His Death Must Be Studied.*

(a) *Made Sin for Us.* "He hath made him to be sin for us, who knew no sin; that we might be made the righteousness of God in him" (II Cor. 5:21).

(b) *Died the Just for the Unjust.* "Christ also hath once suffered for sins, the just for the unjust, that he might bring us to God, being put to death in the flesh, but quickened by the Spirit" (I Peter 3:18).

(c) *Made a Curse For Us.* "Christ hath redeemed us from the curse of the law, being made a curse for us: for it is written, Cursed is every one that hangeth on a tree" (Gal. 3:13).

B. The Form of the Death.

1. *A Natural Death.* His death was a death such as experienced by man. It had to be a natural death, for He was The Man dying for all men.

2. *An Abnormal Death.* God cannot die, but God had to die if He was to become man's substitute. Therefore He became a creature who could die. However, He contracted no sin while He lived.

Man dies today because of sin; but He had no sin. Apart from our sins, He would never have tasted death.

3. *A Preternatural Death.* Christ's death was marked out and determined beforehand. Before the fall of Adam God anticipated it. Before man sinned, God made provision for Calvary, for Christ is the Lamb slain "before the foundation of the world" (I Peter 1:20). Were the sins that man committed before Calvary taken away by the blood of bulls and goats? No!

For all sins, whether committed before or after the Cross, were put on Him at Calvary (Rom. 3:25).

4. *A Supernatural Death.* While we have stated that His death was a natural death, yet it was different from the death of other men. "Therefore doth my Father love me, because I lay down my life, that I might take it again. No man taketh it from me, but I lay it down of myself. I have power to lay it down, and I have power to take it again. This commandment have I received of my Father" (John 10:17, 18).

His death was of His own volition. He lay down His life Himself; no one took it from Him. Usually it took two days for a man to die by crucifixion, but He died in six hours. Matthew 27:46 and 50 state that He cried out with a loud voice. His strength had not left Him. He died in His strength. He *gave* His life; no one took it from Him. He bowed His head in death; He was majestic, even upon the cross.

Thus we see Christ suffering two deaths for us: the first death, the separation of the soul and spirit from the body; the second death, the separation of the individual from God. Christ suffered the second death first, and the first death last. He suffered the second death when He was separated from the Father, for He cried, "My God, my God, why hast thou forsaken me?" (Matt. 27:46). Christ, the very son of God, was able to suffer in six hours what the sinner will endure throughout eternity.

C. Unscriptural Theories Concerning the Death.

"Christ died for our sins according to the *scriptures*" (I Cor. 15:3b). Anything that is not of the Scripture is false.

1. *The Death of Christ Was a Martyr's Death.* "In this He died to show us that truth is worth dying for." How does the child of God meet this argument? Simply by the following: Why didn't Christ say so? Why didn't Paul say so? Why didn't Peter say so? And why didn't John and Luke say so? If Christ had died a martyr's death, why didn't the apostles say, "Believe on Stephen's death and be saved, for Stephen was a martyr?" If Christ died as a martyr, why didn't the Father comfort Him at His death as He has done others down through the centuries? But He cried out, "My God, my God, why hast thou forsaken me?'

2. *The Death of Christ Was Accidental.* By the above statement critics mean that He was the victim of a mob. This

we know is not true, for He was conscious of His future death. Seven times in the Gospel of John He speaks of "mine hour," which was in the future, and which was Calvary. *He need not have died.* Nails did not hold Christ upon the cross, but His will. "Come down from the cross, if thou be the Son of God," cried the mob; but Christ did not come from heaven to come down from the cross.

3. *The Death of Christ Was a Moral Example.* This theory holds that a drunkard has only to think on Christ and he will improve. To refute this we ask, "Why didn't it improve the ones who crucified Him?" If Christ's example is for the improvement of the world, then Christianity is a failure. Why not look upon the cross of Peter, as he was crucified downward? Man needs more than improvement.

4. *The Death of Christ Was an Exhibit of God's Displeasure with Sin.* In other words some people think that God's displeasure with sin is pictured on the cross rather than in hell. If the preceding statement is true, why the incarnation? Why not crucify a plain sinner, instead of the best Man who ever lived?

5. *The Death of Christ Was to Show Man That God Loves Him.* God does love man, and the Cross does show that God loves him, but the death of Christ was not only to show God's love.

6. *The Death of Christ Was the Death of a Criminal.* Can it be possible that one could hold to this theory? The answer is "yes." And we refute this theory by stating that Pilate found no fault in Him. A study of the trial, as found in the Gospels, will disprove this theory.

D. Scriptural Names of Christ's Death.

1. *Atonement.* This is an Old Testament idea which means "to cover." The only place that the word "atonement" can be found in the New Testament is in Romans 5:11, but this is a mistranslation; it should be translated "reconciliation." However, the word "atonement" is a New Testament idea meaning "at-one-ment" – at one with God through the sacrifice of His Son.

2. *Sacrifice.* "Purge out therefore the old leaven, that ye may be a new lump, as ye are unleavened. For even Christ our Passover is sacrificed for us" (I Cor. 5:7). See also Ephesians 5:2; Hebrews 9:26; 10:12.

3. *Offering.* "By the which will we are sanctified through the offering of the body of Jesus Christ once for all. . . . for by one offering He hath perfected forever them that are sanctified" (Heb. 10:10, 14).

4. *Ransom.* "The Son of man came not to be ministered unto, but to minister, and to give His life a ransom for many" (Matt. 20:28). Also I Peter 1:18, 19; I Timothy 2:5, 6. We have been redeemed (bought back) by the Price, which is the blood of Jesus Christ.

5. *Propitiation.* "He is the propitiation for our sins: and not for ours only, but also for the sins of the whole world" (I John 2:2). See also I John 4:10; Romans 3:25. In Hebrews 9:5 the word "propitiation" is translated "mercy seat," which is correct, for in the above Scriptures also the word "propitiation" means "mercy seat." The law demanded death for sin; therefore, the blood of the sacrifice was placed on the mercy seat (Ex. 25:22; Lev. 16:13, 14), showing that death had taken place. God looked upon the mercy seat and saw blood – life – and was satisfied. Since Calvary, God looks upon our Mercy Seat, which is Christ, and is satisfied. Therefore, the underlying thought of propitiation is "satisfaction."

6. *Reconciliation.* "To wit, that God was in Christ, reconciling the world unto himself, not imputing their trespasses unto them; and hath committed unto us the word of reconciliation" (II Cor. 5:19). See also Colossians 1:20. The word "reconciliation" means to cause, or affect a thorough change. Never in Scripture does it say that God is reconciled. It is man who has to be reconciled; it is man who needs a thorough change.

7. *Substitution.* Substitution is not a Scriptural word, but it surely is a Scriptural idea. "He was wounded for our transgressions, he was bruised for our iniquities: the chastisement of our peace was upon him; and with his stripes we are healed. All we like sheep have gone astray; we have turned every one to his own way; and the LORD hath laid on him the iniquity of us all" (Is. 53:5, 6). See also I Peter 3:18; II Corinthians 5:1.

8. *Testator.* A testament is a will that goes into effect at the death of the testator. Thus, our inheritance is that which we shall receive, which is made possible by the death of the Lord Jesus. "He is the mediator of the new testament, that by

means of death, for the redemption of the transgressions that were under the first testament, they which are called might receive the promise of eternal inheritance. For where a testament is there must also of necessity be the death of the testator. For a testament is of force after men are dead: otherwise, it is of no strength at all while the testator liveth" (Heb. 9:15-17). See also Colossians 1:12-14; Ephesians 1:1-7.

E. The Objectives of the Death.

1. *The Manifestation of Divine Character.* "Now the righteousness of God without the law is manifested, being witnessed by the law and the prophets. . . . To declare, I say, at this time his righteousness: that he might be just, and the justifier of him which believeth in Jesus" (Rom. 3:21, 26).

2. *The Vindication of Divine Law.* The law is unto death. There is no mercy in law, only justice. The law condemns the sinner to death; Christ took the sinner's place; therefore, Christ paid the law's demand.

3. *The Foundation of Divine Pardon.* This statement will go unchallenged in the New Testament. There is one essential feature of forgiveness, and that is: the one who forgives must take upon himself all wrong (or loss) that has been committed. For example, if a person is robbed of ten dollars, and the culprit is found, but is forgiven, who then stands the loss? It is he who forgave.

F. The Extent of the Death.

1. *General Statements.*

a. *Its Universality.* His death was for all men – for those who believe, and those who believe not. "We see Jesus, who was made a little lower than the angels for the suffering of death, crowned with glory and honour; that he by the grace of God should taste death for every man" (Heb. 2:9). See also I Timothy 2:6; 4:10; Titus 2:11; I John 2:2; II Peter 3:9.

b. *Its Limitation.* Christ's work upon the cross was conditional, as the efficiency of it depended upon the repentance and acceptation of Christ by the sinner. "We labor and suffer reproach, because we trust in the living God, who is the Saviour of all men, especially of those that believe" (I Tim. 4:10).

2. *Particular Statement.*

a. *Christ Died for the Believer.* "Who gave himself for us, that he might redeem us from all iniquity, and purify unto himself a peculiar people, zealous of good works" (Titus 2:14). See also Ephesians 5:2; Galatians 2:20; I Timothy 4:10.

b. *Christ Died for the Church.* "Husbands, love your wives, even as Christ loved the church, and gave himself for it; that he might sanctify and cleanse it with the washing of water by the word, that he might present it to himself a glorious church, not having spot, or wrinkle, or any such thing; but that it should be holy and without blemish" (Eph. 5:25-27).

c. *Christ Died for Sinners.* "Christ also hath once suffered for sins, the just for the unjust, that he might bring us to God, being put to death in the flesh, but quickened by the Spirit" (I Peter 3:18). See also I Timothy 1:15; Romans 5:10.

d. *Christ Died for the World.* "They sing a new song, saying, Worthy art thou to take the book, and to open the seals thereof: for thou wast slain, and didst purchase unto God with thy blood men of every tribe, and tongue, and people, and nation" (Rev. 5:9, R.V.). See also John 3:16; 1:9; I John 2:2.

G. *The Results of the Death.*

1. *In Relation to the Sinner.*

a. *Provides a Substitute.* "We see Jesus, who was made a little lower than the angels for the suffering of death . . . that he by the grace of God should taste death for every man" (Heb. 2:9).

b. *Provides a Ransom.* "Who gave himself a ransom for all, to be testified in due time" (I Tim. 2:6).

c. *Provides a Propitiation.* Because of the death of Christ, God is "mercy seated" – satisfied. "He is the propitiation for our sins: and not for ours only, but also for the sins of the whole world" (I John 2:2).

d. *Provides for Non-imputation of Sin.* "God was in Christ, reconciling the world unto himself, not imputing their trespasses unto them: and hath committed unto us the word of reconciliation" (II Cor. 5:19).

e. *Provides an Attraction.* "I, if I be lifted up from the earth, will draw all men unto me" (John 12:32).

f. *Provides a Salvation.* "The grace of God that bringeth salvation hath appeared to all men" (Titus 2:11).

g. *Provides a Gracious Invitation.* "God so loved the world, that he gave his only begotten Son, that whosoever believeth in him should not perish, but have everlasting life" (John 3:16).

2. *In Relation to the Believer.*

a. *Reconciliation.* "All things are of God, who hath reconciled us to himself by Jesus Christ, and hath given to us the ministry of reconciliation" (II Cor. 5:18).

b. *Redemption.* "We have redemption through his blood, the forgiveness of sins, according to the riches of his grace" (Eph. 1:7). See also Galatians 3:13.

c. *Justification.* "Being justified by faith, we have peace with God through our Lord Jesus Christ" (Rom. 5:1).

d. *Exoneration.* "There is therefore now no condemnation to them which are in Christ Jesus" (Rom. 8:1, R.V.).

e. *Possession.* "What? Know ye not that your body is the temple of the Holy Ghost which is in you, which ye have received of God, and ye are not your own? For ye are bought with a price: therefore glorify God in your body, and in your spirit, which are God's" (I Cor. 6:19, 20).

f. *Sanctification.* "We are sanctified through the offering of the body of Jesus Christ once for all" (Heb. 10:10).

g. *Perfection.* "By one offering he hath perfected forever them that are sanctified" (Heb. 10:14).

h. *Admission.* "Having therefore, brethren, boldness to enter into the holiest by the blood of Jesus, by a new and a living way, which he hath consecrated for us, through the veil, that is to say, his flesh; and having a high priest over the house of God; let us draw near with a true heart in full assurance of faith, having our hearts sprinkled from an evil conscience, and our bodies washed with pure water" (Heb. 10:19-22).

i. *Identification.* "The love of Christ constraineth us; because we thus judge, that one died for all, therefore all died" (II Cor. 5:14, R.V.).

j. *Liberation.* "Since then the children are sharers in flesh and blood, he also himself in like manner partook of the same; that through death he might bring to nought him that had the power of death, that is, the devil; and might deliver all them who through fear of death were all their lifetime subject to bondage" (Heb. 2:14, 15, R.V.).

k. *Donation.* "He that spared not his own Son, but delivered him up for us all, how shall he not with him also freely give us all things?" (Rom. 8:32).

3. *In Relation to Satan.*

a. *Dethronement.* "Now is the judgment of this world: now shall the prince of this world be cast out" (John 12:31).

b. *Nullification.* "Since then the children are sharers in flesh and blood, he also himself in like manner partook of the same; that through death he might bring to nought him that had the power of death, that is, the devil" (Heb. 2:14, R.V.).

c. *Defeat.* "Who hath delivered us from the power of darkness, and hath translated us into the kingdom of his dear Son" (Col. 1:13). See also Ephesians 6:12.

4. *In Relation to the Material Universe.* "It pleased the Father that in him should all fulness dwell; and, having made peace through the blood of his cross, by him to reconcile all things unto himself; by him, I say, whether they be things in earth, or things in heaven" (Col. 1:19, 20).

Some teach that Philippians 2:9-11 reveals the fact of universal salvation, but this is not so. This passage declares the truth of universal adoration.

V. The Resurrection of Christ

A. The Importance of the Resurrection.

In the Bible there are several accounts of people having been brought back to life. These people, however, were not resurrected, but restored, for they died again. But our Lord was resurrected, having died once and for all and having been raised from the dead. He now liveth and abideth forever.

His death was necessary, because He was made sin for us.

1. *Its Place in Scripture.* There are thirteen or fourteen references in the New Testament concerning the ordinance of baptism, and even fewer Scriptures referring to the Lord's Supper. However, the fact of His resurrection is mentioned over one hundred times.

2. *Its Part in Apostolic Testimony.* "With great power gave the apostles witness of the resurrection of the Lord Jesus: and great grace was upon them all" (Acts 4:33). See also Acts 2:32; 17:18; 23:6.

3. *Its Prominence in the Gospel.* If Christ be not risen there is no Gospel. "Moreover, brethren, I declare unto you the gospel which I have preached unto you, which also ye have received, and wherein ye stand; by which also ye are saved if ye keep in memory what I preached unto you, unless ye be-

lieved in vain. For I delivered unto you first of all that which I also received, how that Christ died for our sins according to the scriptures; and that he was buried, and that he rose again the third day according to the scriptures" (I Cor. 15:1-4).

4. *Its Preeminence in Salvation* (I Cor. 15:12-20).

a. *First Proposition.* "Now if Christ be preached that he rose from the dead, how say some among you that there is no resurrection of the dead?" (verse 12).

b. *Second Proposition.* "But if there be no resurrection of the dead, then is Christ not risen" (verse 13). If we are not to be raised from the dead, then Christ is not risen.

c. *Third Proposition.* "And if Christ be not risen, then is our preaching vain, and your faith is also vain" (verse 14). If Christ is not risen, Christianity is a sham.

d. *Fourth Proposition.* "Yea, and we are found false witnesses of God; because we have testified of God that he raised up Christ: whom he raised not up, if so be that the dead rise not" (verse 15). If Christ be not raised, every evangelical preacher is a fraud.

e. *Fifth Proposition.* "For if the dead rise not, then is not Christ raised: and if Christ be not raised, your faith is vain; ye are yet in your sins" (verses 16 and 17). If He be not risen, He is still dead, and therefore cannot redeem us. The penalty paid for any crime is not fully paid until the one for whom it was paid is free. As long as Christ was in the tomb, the penalty for our sins was not paid; but His resurrection shows that the penalty *has* been paid. And, remember, this Scripture was written to those who were not in their sins.

f. *Sixth Proposition.* "Then they also which are fallen asleep in Christ are perished" (verse 18). In other words, they have all gone like the beasts of the field, if Christ did not rise from the dead.

g. *Seventh Proposition.* "If in this life only we have hope in Christ, we are of all men most miserable" (verse 19). If all of our hope is staked upon the resurrection of Christ, and if He has not risen, then we are of all men most to be pitied. We have done nothing else to secure salvation, and if our Saviour be not risen, we have no Saviour. We had better look into some other religion.

h. *Eighth Proposition.* "But now is Christ risen from the dead, and become the firstfruits of them that slept" (verse 20). Praise the Lord, *He is risen! He is alive!* We are saved by a living Redeemer. We, of all men, are the only sinners who are saved.

B. The Meaning of the Resurrection.

By the resurrection we mean the *bodily* resurrection, not the spiritual resurrection.

1. *Provision of the Tomb.* Guards were placed there to guarantee against the removal of His body, not His Spirit. "So they went, and made the sepulchre sure, sealing the stone, and setting a watch" (Matt. 27:66).

2. *Recognition of the Disciples.* "Then saith he to Thomas, Reach hither thy finger, and behold my hands; and reach hither thy hand, and thrust it into my side: and be not faithless, but believing. And Thomas answered and said unto him, My Lord and my God" (John 20:27, 28).

3. *Testimony of the Apostles.* "This Jesus hath God raised up, whereof we are all witnesses" (Acts 2:32).

4. *A Testimony of the Lord Himself.* "He began to teach them, that the Son of man must suffer many things, and be rejected of the elders, and of the chief priests, and scribes, and be killed, and after three days rise again" (Mark 8:31).

5. *The Announcement of Our Transformation.* "Our conversation is in heaven; from whence also we look for the Saviour, the Lord Jesus Christ: who shall change our vile body, that it may be fashioned like unto his glorious body, according to the working whereby he is able even to subdue all things unto himself" (Phil. 3:20, 21).

C. The Unscriptural Theories Concerning the Resurrection.

1. *The Unburied Body Theory.* By this statement unbelievers maintain that the tomb was never filled, that the two thieves, and Christ, were thrust out upon the trash heap. However, this is refuted by the Jew's own law: "If a man have committed a sin worthy of death, and he be put to death, and thou hang him on a tree; his body shall not remain all night upon the tree, but thou shalt surely bury him the same day; for he that is hanged is accursed of God; that thou defile not thy land which Jehovah thy God giveth thee for an inheritance" (Deut. 21:22, 23).

2. *The Unemptied Grave Theory.* Those that hold to this say that He is still there. Surely common sense would refute this argument, for if Christ had not arisen, the Devil would

have caused His body to have been found sometime during the last two thousand years.

3. *The Removal Theory.* This is that theory which proposes that Joseph moved the body out of the tomb. Of this argument we ask, "If he removed the body, why didn't he also remove the clothing?" All will have to admit that if Joseph *did* remove the body, it would have had to be done in secret. If done in secret, why wasn't the stone rolled back against the door?

4. *The Mistaken Woman Theory.* This theory contends that the woman misunderstood what the man in the sepulchre had said. We refute this contention by saying that the Word does not so declare it, and the Word is the only authority and witness we have.

5. *The Deliberate Deception Theory.* This supposition clings to the idea that Christ did not die at all, but rather that He fainted on the cross and was revived by the cool air of the tomb. If this be the case, where did He go? Surely, as He was an object of interest to the entire populace, He would have been recognized and openly accepted or rejected.

6. *The Fraud Theory.* This states that the apostles plainly lied and deceived those that heard them. However, all of the apostles, except John, met a martyr's death. Why? Because of their devotion to Christ and His resurrection. Would they have sacrified their lives for a lie? Of course not!

7. *The Self-Deception Theory.* In other words, this speculation declares that the apostles had an illusion; that is, they thought that He arose from the dead, and kept on thinking it, until after a while they believed it. We know, from human experience, that delusions soon fade away, and we awaken to reality. The apostles could not have deceived themselves very long.

8. *The Hallucination Theory.* This idea supposes that they thought they had actually seen the resurrected Saviour, when it was merely an hallucination caused by nerves and excitement. Can you imagine Peter becoming delirious, and Thomas hysterical?

9. *The Recollection Theory.* This view sees the hysterical apostles fleeing to Samaria, and while alone in this place, they began to think that Jesus is still with them. That is where we get the idea that He arose from the dead. The Scriptures,

nevertheless, declare that they remained in Jerusalem behind closed doors until He revealed Himself to them.

10. *The Misunderstood Theory.* This reasoning admits that the Saviour died, but states that the apostles preached the resurrection of His Spirit, and not His body. However, people took it wrong. The word "resurrection" is never connected with the spirit, but rather with the body, for the spirit never dies.

11. *The Spiritual Vision Theory.* This supposition maintains that the apostles actually saw something. What they saw was a lying vision, not the Lord. The Devil had fooled them. But, if there was anything the Devil did not want them to believe, it was the resurrection of Christ, whether, a lying vision or the actual thing. Christ Himself dispels this argument by declaring, after His resurrection, that "a spirit does not have flesh and bones."

12. *The Twins Theory.* Those who offer this suggestion say that Christ had a twin, and that three days after He had been crucified and buried, His twin showed himself, declaring that he was Christ risen from the dead. We ask, "Where was this twin hidden for thirty-three years?"

D. The Proofs of the Resurrection.

1. *The Empty Tomb.* The Gospels declare that the people held two views concerning His resurrection. One group, consisting of unbelievers, said that someone stole His body; the other group contended that He was raised by Divine Power. The empty tomb proves the latter. A Roman watch, composed of sixty men, with four groups of fifteen each, were stationed to watch the tomb. Each group guarded the tomb for a six-hour period. The watch was ordered to guard the tomb against the theft of the body of Christ. Now the enemy did not wish to steal the body; they wanted it buried. We know that the apostles did not steal it, as they were afraid. Even at His crucifixion they fled. The soldiers were paid by the unbelievers to bear false testimony. Is it not peculiar that the Jewish priests did not prosecute the soldiers, if the body had actually been stolen? Had the disciples stolen the body, would not the priests have hounded them until they admitted such a deed? Why did they not do *something?* Simply because they did not believe the story.

A *new tomb*: there was but one body in it, and there is no question as to who rose from the dead when the tomb became empty. It was carved out of the rock – solid rock behind, above, below, and on the side. There were no other entrances.

2. *The Undisturbed Grave Clothes.* In the Orient the bodies of the dead are wound with grave clothes, from the neck down to the feet, in a manner similar to that used on Egyptian mummies. The head is wrapped with a napkin. When this wrapping was duly done, the body was stretched out on a ledge. When Peter came in to examine the grave clothes, he saw that they were undisturbed – the body of Christ had shot through the grave clothes without bursting a single thread. Peter discovered that the grave clothes were unmolested; the clothes appeared as though they were still wrapped around the body – but there was no body.

As for the tomb, the door was not opened to let Christ out – He was *already* out! He came out of the tomb just as He had come out of the grave clothes. Yes, He was out of the tomb long before the stone was rolled away. The soldiers had been guarding a sealed, empty tomb for nearly twelve hours.

3. *The Appearances of Christ.* In I Corinthians 15:1-11 we have recorded the number of witnesses who actually saw the Lord, the risen Saviour. This number does not include the women. The highest number of witnesses required to establish the truth in America is seven: one for murder; two for treason; three for a will; and seven for an oral will. The number of witnesses recorded in the Word is over five hundred. Certainly, according to the accepted jurisprudence, there is sufficient evidence that He arose from the dead.

4. *The Character of Christ.* No greater proof is needed in contending for His resurrection than His character. To think that such a shameful end would come to Him who was the Perfect One! Surely, God in His justice would not have allowed the only man without sin to remain in the tomb.

5. *The New Testament.* The twenty-seven books composing the New Testament are the *effect;* the *cause* is a risen Christ. Without Christ's resurrection, there would not have been any New Testament. The death of Christ had sorely depressed the disciples. Their faith was shattered. If Christ had not appeared unto them, they would never have written about Him. The story of His life grew out of His resurrection.

6. *The Apostles' Church.* The apostles began preaching at Jerusalem only seven weeks after the crucifixion. Right there

in Jerusalem, where Jesus had been crucified and buried, the apostles declared Christ to have risen from the dead. If Christ had not risen, the enemies could have produced the body, for they had crucified Him. The silence of the Jews was as much proof of His resurrection as the writings of the disciples.

7. *The Transformed Disciples.* The resurrection brought about a transformation of the disciples. Before, they had seen Christ die, and thus their faith was shattered. Two of them said, "We hoped that it was he who should redeem Israel" (Luke 24:21, R.V.) Sad words – no hope. All faith was now dead. They were meeting together behind closed doors, frightened, afraid for their lives, when the Lord appeared. It was hard to convince them of His resurrection, even though He actually appeared before them. But when they were convinced, *nothing* could ever change them.

How about doubting Thomas? He was not present at Christ's first appearance before the disciples, and, therefore, he doubted. I am glad that Thomas doubted, for now I am relieved of doubt. His unbelief was removed at the second appearance of the Saviour; consequently, all of our doubts concerning the resurrection should be removed.

8. *The Conversion of Saul.* The Church never had a greater enemy than Saul of Tarsus. He was a well-known individual in Judaism, belonging to the sect known as the Pharisees, who believed in the future resurrection of the dead, but certainly not in the resurrection of Jesus. What changed this terrible persecutor of the Church into the mighty preacher of Christ? *The resurrection of Christ!* From the day on the road to Damascus, he never doubted the resurrection. He suffered at the hands of his own countrymen and in the courts of the foreigner because of his belief in Christ's resurrection.

9. *Christian Experience.* Since we have been born again hope has been placed in our hearts: that our sins have been taken away and that our own resurrection is assured. This hope could only be guaranteed by a risen Saviour. We are not saved from our sins by a living mother, nor by a dead Jew, but by a Living Lord.

10. *The Gospel Record.* The Gospels were written or dictated by witnesses, "chosen before of God, even to us, who did eat and drink with him after he rose from the dead"

(Acts 10:41b). In reading the Gospels, we notice the little details, words and phrases, which prove to us how natural and how true to life the accounts are.

E. *The Result of the Resurrection.*

1. *In Relation to Christ Himself.*

a. *It Was the Seal of His Father's Acceptance.* In other words, Christ's sacrifice was sufficient and accepted by God. "It is God's 'amen' to His Son's 'it is finished.'"

b. *It Was the Mark of His Divine Sonship.* Christ was "declared to be the Son of God with power, according to the spirit of holiness, by the resurrection from the dead" (Rom. 1:4). On being nailed to the cross, He was accursed of God. God would not let His Son remain accursed; therefore God raised Him from the dead.

c. *It Was the Demonstration of His Victory.*

(1) *Over the Devil.* If only the Devil could have kept Him in the grave, complete victory would have been Satan's. However, Christ arose from the dead, guaranteeing salvation for every believing soul. The believer is commanded to put on the whole armour of God in order to withstand the wiles of the Devil. One piece of that armour is the helmet of Salvation.

(2) *Over Death.* "Yet a little while, and the world seeth me no more; but ye see me: because I live, ye shall live also. At that day ye shall know that I am in my Father, and ye in me, and I in you" (John 14:19, 20). See also II Timothy 1:10.

d. *It Was the Illustration of Incorruptibility.* God's purpose and grace "is now made manifest by the appearing of our Saviour Jesus Christ, who hath abolished death, and hath brought life and immortality [incorruptibility] to light through the gospel" (II Tim. 1:10).

2. *In Relation to the Believer.*

a. *Proves His Justification.* "Jesus our Lord . . . was delivered for our offences, and was raised again for our justification" (Rom. 4:24, 25).

b. *Illustrates His Power.* Paul prayed that God might give the Ephesians "the spirit of wisdom and revelation in the knowledge of him . . . that ye may know . . . what is the exceeding greatness of his power to usward who believe, according to the working of his mighty power, which he wrought in Christ, when he raised him from the dead, and set him at his own right hand in the heavenly places" (Eph. 1:17, 18,19, 20).

c. *Provides a High Priest.* "He is able to save them to the uttermost that come unto God by him, seeing he ever liveth to make intercession for them" (Heb. 7:25). See also Romans 8:34; Hebrews 3:1; 7:22.

d. *Begets a Living Hope.* "Blessed be the God and Father of our Lord Jesus Christ, which according to his abundant mercy hath begotten us again unto a lively hope by the resurrection of Jesus Christ from the dead, to an inheritance incorruptible, and undefiled, and that fadeth not away, reserved in heaven for you" (I Peter 1:3, 4).

e. *Guarantees Our Resurrection.* "He which raised up the Lord Jesus shall raise up us also by Jesus, and shall present us with you" (II Cor. 4:14). See also I Corinthians 15:22; I Thessalonians 4:14.

3. *In Relation to the World.*

a. *Gives Evidence of His Truth.* All that he spake is substantiated by His resurrection, for God would not have raised a liar from the dead and declare Him to be His Son. His act proved His favor.

b. *Gives Evidence of Universal Resurrection.* "As in Adam all die, even so in Christ shall all be made alive" (I Cor. 15:22).

c. *Gives Evidence of World Judgment.* "He hath appointed a day, in the which he will judge the world in righteousness by that man whom he hath ordained; whereof he hath given assurance unto all men, in that he hath raised him from the dead" (Acts 17:31).

VI. The Ascension and Enthronement of Jesus Christ

His ascension is a historical fact. If His resurrection is denied, then His ascension must also be denied. It is hard for some people to grasp the thought that a glorified, living Body is in glory; but He *is* up there, nevertheless.

A. *The Meaning of the Ascension and Enthronement.*

1. *Of the Ascension.* It is that event, after His resurrection, in which He departed visibly from the earth to heaven. "When he had spoken these things, while they beheld, he was taken up; and a cloud received him out of their sight. And while they looked stedfastly toward heaven as he went

up, behold, two men stood by them in white apparel; which also said, Ye men of Galilee, why stand ye gazing up into heaven? this same Jesus, which is taken up from you into heaven, shall so come in like manner as ye have seen him go into heaven" (Acts 1:9-11).

2. *Of the Enthronement* (Exaltation). This is that act of God by which he gave to the risen and ascended Lord full power and glory, allowing Him to sit down on the right hand of God's throne. "This Jesus hath God raised up, whereof we are all witnesses. Therefore, being by the right hand of God exalted, and having received of the Father the promise of the Holy Ghost, he hath shed forth this, which ye now see and hear" (Acts 2:32, 33). "To him that overcometh will I grant to sit with me in my throne, even as I also overcame, and am set down with my Father in His throne" (Rev. 3:21). Christ is not now sitting on His own throne, but upon His Father's throne.

B. The Message of the Ascension and Enthronement.

1. *In Prophecy.*

a. *Testimony of a Psalmist.* "Thou wilt not leave my soul in hell; neither wilt thou suffer thy Holy One to see corruption. Thou wilt show me the path of life: in thy presence is fulness of joy; at thy right hand there are pleasures for evermore" (Ps. 16:10, 11). See also Psalm 68:18; 110:4, 5.

b. *Testimony of the Saviour.* "What and if ye shall see the Son of man ascend up where he was before?" (John 6:62). See also John 16:28.

c. *Testimony of Luke.* "It came to pass, when the time was come that he should be received up, he stedfastly set his face to go to Jerusalem" (Luke 9:51).

2. *In History.*

a. *Testimony of Mark.* "So then after the Lord had spoken unto them, he was received up into heaven, and set on the right hand of God" (Mark 16:19).

b. *Testimony of Luke.* "It came to pass, while he blessed them, he was parted from them, and carried up into heaven" (Luke 24:51). See also Acts 1:9-11.

c. *Testimony of Stephen.* "He, being full of the Holy Ghost, looked stedfastly into heaven, and saw the glory of God, and Jesus standing on the right hand of God, and said,

Behold, I see the heavens opened and the Son of man standing on the right hand of God" (Acts 7:55, 56).

d. *Testimony of Peter.* "Who is gone into heaven, and is on the right hand of God; angels and authorities and powers being made subject unto him" (I Peter 3:22). See also Acts 3:15, 20, 21; 5:30, 31.

e. *Testimony of Paul.* "Who is he that condemneth? It is Christ that died, yea rather, that is risen again, who is even at the right hand of God, who also maketh intercession for us" (Rom. 8:34). See also Ephesians 1:20, 21; 4:8-10; Colossians 3:1; I Timothy 3:16.

f. *Testimony of John.* The entire first chapter of the Book of Revelation declares John's testimony of the ascended and enthroned Christ.

C. *The Nature of the Ascension and Enthronement.*

1. *He Bodily and Visibly Ascended.* Luke wrote "of all that Jesus began both to do and teach, until the day in which he was taken up, after that he through the Holy Ghost had given commandments unto the apostles whom he had chosen" (Acts 1:1, 2). See also Acts 1:9-11.

2. *He Passed Through the Heavens.* "Having then a great high priest, who hath passed through the heavens, Jesus the Son of God, let us hold fast our confession" (Heb. 4:14).

3. *He Was Made Higher Than the Heavens.* This means that He was made higher than all the created beings in heaven. "Such an high priest became us, who is holy, harmless, undefiled, separate from sinners, and made higher than the heavens" (Heb. 7:26).

4. *He Sat Down on the Right Hand of God.* "Now in the things which we are saying the chief point is this: We have such a high priest, who sat down on the right hand of the throne of the Majesty in the heavens" (Heb. 8:1, R. V.). See also Ephesians 1:20; Colossians 3:1.

D. *The Necessity of the Ascension and Enthronement.*

1. *For the Demonstration of His Complete Achievement.* "Him hath God exalted with his right hand to be a Prince and a Saviour, for to give repentance to Israel, and forgiveness of sins" (Acts 5:31). He said, "Lo, I come to do thy will, O God. . . . By the which will we are sanctified through the offering of the body of Jesus Christ once for all" (Heb. 10: 9, 10). In the tabernacle here upon earth there were no chairs,

and this fact signified that the showing work was never complete. He entered heaven and sat down on the throne, and thus declared that the work of our redemption was a finished act.

2. *For the Facilitation of Human Worship.* "The hour cometh and now is, when the true worshippers shall worship the Father in spirit and in truth: for the Father seeketh such to worship him. God is a Spirit: and they that worship him must worship him in spirit and in truth" (John 4:23, 24).

3. *For the Bestowment of the Holy Ghost.* "I tell you the truth; It is expedient for you that I go away: for if I go not away, the Comforter will not come unto you; but if I depart, I will send him unto you" (John 16:7).

4. *For the Constitution of His Headship Over the Church.* "[God] hath put all things under his feet, and gave him to be the head over all things to the church, which is his body, the fulness of him that filleth all and in all" (Eph. 1:22, 23).

E. The Purpose of the Ascension and Enthronement.

1. *He Entered Heaven as a Forerunner.* "The forerunner is for us entered, even Jesus, made a high priest forever after the order of Melchisedec" (Heb. 6:20). Another word for "forerunner" is "captain," "prince leader," "one who has others to follow him." The Lord Jesus precedes us; if death comes while He tarries, we will go on to be with Him.

2. *He Entered Heaven as a Gift-Bestower.* "He saith, When he ascended up on high, he led captivity captive, and gave gifts unto men. . . . and he gave some, apostles; and some, prophets; and some, evangelists; and some, pastors and teachers" (Eph. 4:8, 11).

3. *He Entered Heaven as a Place-Preparer.* "I go to prepare a place for you. And if I go and prepare a place for you, I will come again, and receive you unto myself; that where I am, there ye may be also" (John 14:2, 3).

F. The Results of the Ascension and Enthronement.

1. *Gives Us an Intercessor with God.* "Christ is not entered into the holy places made with hands, which are the figures of the true; but into heaven itself, now to appear in the presence of God for us" (Heb. 9:24). See also Hebrews 7:25.

2. *Gives Us Access to God.* "Seeing then that we have a great high priest, that is passed into the heavens, Jesus the Son of God, let us hold fast our profession. For we have not an

high priest which cannot be touched with the feelings of our infirmities; but was in all points tempted like as we are, yet without sin. Let us therefore come boldly unto the throne of grace, that we may obtain mercy, and find grace to help in time of need" (Heb. 4:14-16).

3. *Gives Us Ableness for Service.* "Verily, verily, I say unto you, He that believeth on me, the works that I do shall he do also; and greater works than these shall he do; because I go unto my Father" (John 14:12). "Greater works" does not mean healing or speaking in tongues, but the spreading of the Gospel of salvation. For example, Peter spoke, and three thousand believed; he spoke again, and five thousand others believed.

4. *Gives Us Confidence in God's Providences.* "We know that all things work together for good to them that love God, to them who are the called according to his purpose" (Rom. 8:28).

5. *Gives Us Our Heavenly Position.* "[God] hath raised us up together, and made us sit together in heavenly places in Christ Jesus" (Eph. 2:6).

PNEUMATOLOGY
(The Doctrine of the Holy Spirit)

Outline for Chapter III

PNEUMATOLOGY

I. The Personality of the Holy Spirit.
  A. Personal Property.
  B. Personal Pronouns.
  C. Personal Acts.
  D. Personal Reactions.
  E. Personal Relationships.
  F. Personal Designations.

II. The Deity of the Holy Spirit.
  A. He Is Identified as the Old Testament Deity.
  B. He Is Called God.
  C. He Possesses Divine Attributes.
  D. He Performs the Works of God.
  E. He Exercises the Sovereignty of God.
  F. He Is to Be Recognized as God.
  G. He Is to Be Depended Upon as God.
  H. He, God, Can Be Sinned Against.

III. The Work of the Holy Spirit.
  A. As Set Forth in the Old Testament.
  B. As Set Forth in the New Testament.

Chapter III

PNEUMATOLOGY

Pneumatology is derived from the Greek word *pneuma,* meaning spirit, wind, or breath. Thus, pneumatology is the doctrine of the Spirit, or breath of God: the doctrine of the Holy Spirit.

The doctrine of the Holy Spirit is indeed a Bible doctrine. The Bible is the only source from whence we can secure any information concerning Him. The Christian religion alone has the Holy Spirit.

As we study the doctrine of the Holy Spirit, let us keep in mind that *Christ* is the center of the Book, the theme of the entire secret writings. If we put someone in His place, confusion will result. The Holy Spirit cannot displace the Son of God. The Holy Spirit did not come to speak of (or from) Himself, but of Christ. One who speaks continually about the Spirit and omits the Son shows evidence that he really does not have the Spirit.

I. Personality of the Holy Spirit

Here is one word of caution: Do not call the Holy Spirit "It." We sometimes confuse personality with visibility. Personality is not an attribute of a body; it is the attribute of a spirit. You yourself have never been seen; you are not a body, but a spirit having a body.

A. *Personal Property.*

1. *He Possesses Intelligence.* "To one is given by the Spirit the word of wisdom; to another the word of knowledge by the same Spirit" (I Cor. 12:8). See also Isaiah 11:2, 3; Nehemiah 9:20; I Peter 1:11; II Peter 1:21; I Corinthians 2:10, 11.

2. *He Possesses a Will.* "All these worketh that one and the selfsame Spirit, dividing to every man severally as he will" (I Cor. 12:11).

3. *He Possesses Power.* "Now the God of hope fill you

with all joy and peace in believing, that ye may abound in hope, through the power of the Holy Ghost. . . . through mighty signs and wonders, by the power of the Spirit of God; so that from Jerusalem, and round about Illyricum, I have fully preached the gospel of Christ" (Rom. 15:13, 19). See also Zechariah 4:6; Isaiah 11:2; Ephesians 3:16.

4. *He Possesses Knowledge.* "God hath revealed them unto us by his Spirit: for the Spirit searcheth all things, yea, the deep things of God. For what man knoweth the things of a man, save the spirit of man which is in him? Even so the things of God knoweth no man, but the Spirit of God. Now we have received not the spirit of the world, but the spirit which is of God; that we might know the things that are freely given to us of God" (I Cor. 2:10-12).

5. *He Possesses Love.* "Now I beseech you, brethren, for the Lord Jesus Christ's sake, and for the love of the Spirit, that ye strive together with me in your prayers to God for me" (Rom. 15:30).

B. Personal Pronouns.

The personal name of the Holy Spirit is unknown. The title "Holy Spirit" is a designation – what He is; it is not His name. The silence of the Scriptures concerning His personal name is very significant. He withholds His own name, that the name of the Lord Jesus Christ may be exalted. The title "Holy Spirit" is a neuter noun in the Greek, but whenever a pronoun is in its place, the pronoun used is always masculine. "I will pray the Father, and he shall give you another Comforter, that *he* may abide with you forever; even the Spirit of truth; whom the world cannot receive, because it seeth *him* not, neither knoweth *him*: but ye know *him;* for *he* dwelleth with you, and shall be in you. . . . But the Comforter, which is the Holy Ghost, *whom* the Father will send in my name, *he* shall teach you all things, and bring all things to your remembrance, whatsoever I have said unto you" (John 14:16, 17, 26). See also John 16:7, 8, 13-15; Romans 8:16, 26, R.V.

C. Personal Acts.

Why do we act like human beings? Because we are human. Why does the Holy Spirit act like a person? Because He is a person.

1. *He Speaks.* "As they ministered to the Lord, and fasted,

the Holy Ghost said, Separate me Barnabas and Saul for the work whereunto I have called them" (Acts 13:2).

2. *He Intercedes.* "Likewise the Spirit also helpeth our infirmities: for we know not what we should pray for as we ought: but the Spirit himself maketh intercession for us with groanings which cannot be uttered" (Rom. 8:26).

3. *He Testifies.* "When the Comforter is come, whom I will send unto you from the Father, even the Spirit of truth, which proceedeth from the Father, he shall testify of me" (John 15:26).

4. *He Commands.* "Now when they had gone through Phrygia and the region of Galatia, and were forbidden of the Holy Ghost to preach the word in Asia, after they were come to Mysia, they assayed to go into Bithynia: but the Spirit suffered them not" (Acts 16:6, 7).

5. *He Oversees.* "Take heed therefore unto yourselves, and to all the flock, over which the Holy Ghost hath made you overseers, to feed the church of God, which he hath purchased with his own blood" (Acts 20:28).

6. *He Guides.* "Howbeit when he, the Spirit of truth, is come, he will guide you into all truth: for he shall not speak of himself, but whatsoever he shall hear, that shall he speak: and he will show you things to come" (John 16:13).

7. *He Teaches.* "The Comforter, which is the Holy Ghost, whom the Father will send in my name, he shall teach you all things, and bring all things to your remembrance, whatsoever I have said unto you" (John 14:26).

D. Personal Reactions.

Acts can be committed against the Spirit that can only be committed against a person. The Holy Spirit has feelings.

1. *He May Be Grieved.* "Grieve not the holy Spirit of God, whereby ye are sealed unto the day of redemption" (Eph. 4:30).

2. *He May Be Vexed.* "They rebelled, and vexed his holy Spirit: therefore he was turned to be their enemy, and he fought against them" (Is. 63:10).

3. *He May Be Tested.* "Then Peter said unto her, How is it that ye have agreed together to tempt the Spirit of the Lord? behold the feet of them which have buried thy husband are at the door, and shall carry thee out" (Acts 5:9).

4. *He May Be Resisted.* "Ye stiffnecked and uncircum-

cized in heart and ears, ye do always resist the Holy Ghost: as your fathers did, so do ye" (Acts 7:51).

5. *He May Be Blasphemed.* "He that shall blaspheme against the Holy Ghost hath never forgiveness, but is in danger of eternal damnation: because they said, He hath an unclean spirit" (Mark 3:29, 30).

E. *Personal Relationships.*

1. *With the Father.* "Go ye therefore, and teach all nations, baptising them in the name of the Father, and of the Son, and of the Holy Ghost" (Matt. 28:19).

2. *With Christ.* "He shall glorify me: for he shall receive of mine, and shall shew it unto you" (John 16:14).

3. *With the Christians.* "It seemed good to the Holy Ghost, and to us, to lay upon you no greater burden than these necessary things" (Acts 15:28).

F. *Personal Designations.*

1. *The Name Paraclete.* This is the Greek word meaning Comforter: one who is called to help. "When the Comforter is come, whom I will send unto you from the Father, even the spirit of truth, which proceedeth from the Father, he shall testify of me" (John 15:26).

2. *Other Specifications.*

a. *Spirit of Promise.* "After that ye believed [in Christ], ye were sealed with that holy Spirit of promise" (Eph. 1:13).

b. *Spirit of Might.* "The spirit of the LORD shall rest upon him, and the spirit of wisdom and understanding, the spirit of counsel and might, the spirit of knowledge and of the fear of the LORD" (Is. 11:2).

c. *Spirit of Truth.* "He shall give you another Comforter . . . even the Spirit of truth; whom the world cannot receive, because it seeth him not, neither knoweth him: but ye know him; for he dwelleth with you, and shall be in you" (John 14:16, 17).

II. THE DEITY OF THE HOLY SPIRIT.

He is a divine person. He is God! He is co-equal, co-eternal, co-existent with the Father and the Son. However, He is designated as the third person of the Trinity. In our own lives, there may be persons who are equal in station, but in position they are subordinate to others. It is the same with the Holy Spirit. As a Being, He is equal with the Father and the Son, but in position He is subordinate to the Father and gives precedence to the Son. Take note: there is no jealousy in the Godhead!

A. He Is Identified as the Old Testament Deity.

Jesus of the New Testament is Jehovah of the Old Testament; the Holy Spirit of the New Testament is the Jehovah of the Old Testament. "This shall be the covenant that I shall make with the house of Israel; After those days, saith the LORD, I will put my law in their inward parts, and write it in their hearts; and will be their God, and they shall be my people" (Jer. 31:33). "By one offering he hath perfected for ever them that are sanctified. Whereof the Holy Ghost is a witness to us: for after that he had said before, This is the covenant that I will make with them after those days saith the Lord, I will put my laws into their hearts and in their minds will I write them" (Heb. 10:14, 15, 16).

B. He Is Called God.

1. *In Acts* 5:3, 4. "Peter said, Ananias, why hath Satan filled thine heart to lie to the Holy Ghost, and to keep back part of the price of the land? While it remained, was it not thine own? and after it was sold, was it not in thine own power? why hast thou conceived this thing in thine heart? thou hast not lied unto men, but unto God." Ananias and Sapphira died instantly for lying unto the Holy Spirit. They lied in the time of consecration. They were not struck dead because of withholding their money, but because they claimed to have given it all. They lied unto the Church, thus to the Holy Ghost.

2. *In I Corinthians* 3:16. "Know ye not that ye are the temple of God, and that the Spirit of God dwelleth in you." We are the temple of God because the Spirit dwells within.

3. *In II Corinthians* 3:17, R.V. "Now the Lord is the Spirit: and where the Spirit of the Lord is, there is liberty."

C. He Possesses Divine Attributes.

1. *Omnipotence.* "The angel answered and said unto her, The Holy Ghost shall come upon thee, and the power of the Highest shall overshadow thee: therefore also that holy thing which shall be born of thee shall be called the Son of God" (Luke 1:35).

2. *Omniscience.* "The Spirit searcheth all things, yea, the deep things of God" (I Cor. 2:10). See also Luke 2:25-32.

3. *Omnipresence.* "Whither shall I go from thy spirit?

or whither shall I flee from thy presence? If I ascend up into heaven, thou art there: if I make my bed in hell, behold, thou art there. If I take the wings of the morning, and dwell in the uttermost parts of the sea; even there shall thy hand lead me, and thy right hand shall hold me" (Ps. 139:7-10).

4. *Everlastingness.* "How much more shall the blood of Christ, who through the eternal Spirit offered himself without spot to God, purge your conscience from dead works to serve the living God?" (Heb. 9:14).

5. *Love.* "Now I beseech you, brethren, for the Lord Jesus Christ's sake, and for the love of the Spirit, that ye strive together with me in your prayers to God for me" (Rom. 15:30).

6. *Holiness.* "Grieve not the holy Spirit of God, whereby ye are sealed unto the day of redemption" (Eph. 4:30).

D. He Performs the Works of God.

1. *Creation.* "In the beginning God created the heavens and the earth. And the earth was without form, and void; and darkness was upon the face of the deep. And the Spirit of God moved upon the face of the waters" (Gen. 1:1, 2). "Thou sendest forth thy spirit, they are created: and thou renewest the face of the earth" (Ps. 104:30). "The Spirit of God hath made me, and the breath of the Almighty hath given me life" (Job 33:4).

2. *Regeneration.* "Jesus answered and said unto him, Verily, verily, I say unto thee, Except a man be born again, he cannot see the kingdom of God . . . Jesus answered, Verily, verily, I say unto thee, Except a man be born of water and of the Spirit, he cannot enter into the kingdom of God. That which is born of the flesh is flesh; and that which is born of the Spirit is spirit. Marvel not that I say unto thee, ye must be born again. The wind bloweth where it listeth, and thou hearest the sound thereof, but canst not tell whence it cometh, and whither it goeth: so is every one that is born of the Spirit" (John 3:3, 5-8).

3. *Resurrection.* "If the Spirit of him that raised up Jesus from the dead dwell in you, he that raised up Christ from the dead shall also quicken your mortal bodies by his Spirit that dwelleth in you" (Rom. 8:11).

4. *Transformation.* "If Christ be in you, the body is dead because of sin; but the Spirit is life because of righteousness" (Rom. 8:10).

5. *Salvation.* "Ye are washed . . . ye are sanctified . . . ye are justified in the name of the Lord Jesus, and by the Spirit of our God" (I Cor. 6:11).

E. He Exercises the Sovereignty of God.

"All these worketh that one and the selfsame Spirit, dividing to every man severally as he will" (I Cor. 12:11). See also Zechariah 4:6.

F. He Is to Be Recognized as God.

1. *As Set Forth in the Great Commission.* "Jesus came and spake unto them saying, All power is given unto me in heaven and in earth. Go ye therefore, and teach all nations, baptizing them in the name of the Father, and of the Son, and of the Holy Ghost: teaching them to observe all things whatsoever I have commanded you: and, lo, I am with you alway, even unto the end of the world. Amen" (Matt. 28:18-20).

2. *As Set Forth in the Apostolic Benediction.* "The grace of the Lord Jesus Christ, and the love of God, and the communion of the Holy Ghost, be with you all. Amen" (II Cor. 13:14).

3. *As Set Forth by Scriptural Designation.* "He that hath an ear, let him hear what the Spirit saith unto the churches" (Rev. 3:22).

4. *As Set Forth in the Church's Administration.* "Now there are diversities of gifts but the same Spirit. And there are differences of administrations, but the same Lord. And there are diversities of operations, but it is the same God which worketh all in all" (I Cor. 12:4-6).

G. He Is to Be Depended Upon as God.

"When they shall lead you, and deliver you up, take no thought beforehand what ye shall speak, neither do ye premeditate: but whatsoever shall be given you in that hour, that speak ye: for it is not ye that speak, but the Holy Ghost" (Mark 13:11). See also Romans 8:26.

H. He, God, Can Be Sinned Against.

"Peter said, Ananias, why hast Satan filled thine heart to lie to the Holy Ghost, and to keep back part of the price of the land? While it remained was it not thine own? and after it was sold, was it not in thine own power? why hast thou conceived this thing in thine heart? thou hast not lied unto men, but unto God" (Acts 5:3, 4).

III. The Work of the Holy Spirit

A. As Set Forth in the Old Testament.

Someone has said that the Holy Spirit is mentioned eighty-eight times in the Old Testament. However, the teaching of the Holy Spirit is not as clear in the Old Testament as it is in the New.

1. *His Manifestations.*

a. *As Coming Upon Men.* "Balaam lifted up his eyes, and he saw Israel abiding in his tents according to their tribes; and the spirit of God came upon him" (Num. 24:2). "Then the Spirit of the Lord came upon Jephthah, and he passed over Gilead, and Manasseh, and passed over Mizpeh of Gilead, and from Mizpeh of Gilead he passed over unto the children of Ammon" (Judg. 11:29). See also Judges 3:10; 14:6.

b. *As Clothing Men.* "The Spirit of Jehovah came upon [Hebrew – *clothed itself with*] Gideon; and he blew a trumpet; and Abiezer was gathered together after him" (Judg. 6:34). See also II Chronicles 24:20.

c. *As Poured Out Upon Men.* "Upon the land of my people shall come up thorns and briers . . . until the spirit be poured upon us from on high, and the wilderness be a fruitful field, and the fruitful field be counted for a forest" (Is. 32:13, 15).

d. *As Filling Men.* "I have filled him with the spirit of God, in wisdom, and in understanding, and in knowledge, and in all manner of workmanship" (Ex. 31:3). See also Micah 3:8.

e. *As Resting Upon Men.* "The Lord came down in a cloud, and spake unto him, and took of the spirit that was upon him, and gave it unto the seventy elders: and it came to pass, that when the spirit rested upon them they prophesied, and did not cease" (Num. 11:25). See also Numbers 11:26; Isaiah 11:2.

The Holy Spirit is never represented as indwelling the believer. The Holy Spirit filled them, but never took his abode within them.

No Old Testament saint was ever baptized with the Holy Ghost. That initial baptism came at Pentecost, fifty days after Christ arose from the dead.

2. *His Ministration.*

a. *In Relation to Creation.*

(1) *Generation.*

(a) *Of Heavens and Earth.* "By the word of the LORD were the heavens made; and all the host of them by the breath of his mouth. He gathered the waters of the sea together as an heap: he layeth up the deep in storehouses. Let all the earth fear the LORD: let all the inhabitants of the world stand in awe of him. For he spake, and it was done; he commanded, and it stood fast" (Ps. 33:6-9). See also Job 26:13.

(b) *Of Animals.* "O LORD, how manifold are thy works! in wisdom hast thou made them all: the earth is full of thy riches. . . . Thou sendest forth thy spirit, they are created: and thou renewest the face of the earth" (Ps. 104: 24, 30).

(c) *Of Man.* "The Spirit of God hath made me, and the breath of the almighty hath given me life" (Job 33:4). See also Genesis 1:26, 27; 2:7.

(2) *Regeneration.*

(a) *Of the Fallen Earth.* "The Spirit of God moved upon the face of the waters" (Gen. 1:2b).

(b) *Of Fallen Man.* "Then said he unto me, Prophesy unto the wind, prophesy, son of man, and say to the wind, Thus saith the Lord God; Come from the four winds, O breath, and breathe upon these slain, that they may live. So I prophesied as he commanded me, and the breath came into them, and they lived and stood upon their feet, an exceeding great army" (Ezek. 37:9, 10). See also Isaiah 55:3.

(3) *Preservation.* "Thou sendest forth thy spirit, they are created: and thou renewest the face of the earth" (Ps. 104:30).

b. *In Relation to Satan.* From the beginning the Holy Spirit has been the antagonizer of Satan. "The LORD said, My spirit shall not always strive with man, for that he also is flesh: yet his days shall be an hundred and twenty years" (Gen. 6:3).

c. *In Relation to Israel.*

(1) *Her Fathers* (Abraham, Isaac, and Jacob etc.). "Pharaoh said unto his servants, Can we find such a one as this is, a man in whom the Spirit of God is?" (Gen. 41:38).

(2) *Her Founders* (Moses and his helpers). "The

LORD said unto Moses, Gather unto me seventy men of the elders of the people, and officers over them; and bring them unto the tabernacle of the congregation, that they may stand there with thee. And I will come down and talk with thee there: and I will take of the spirit which is upon thee, and will put it upon them; and they shall bear the burden of the people with thee, that thou bear it not thyself alone" (Num. 11: 16, 17). See also Numbers 27:18, 19; Deuteronomy 34:9; Nehemiah 9:20.

(3) *Her Judges.* "The Spirit of the LORD came upon him, and he judged Israel, and went out to war" (Judg. 3:10a).

(4) *Her Kings.* Saul: "The Spirit of God came upon Saul when he heard those tidings, and his anger was kindled greatly" (I Sam. 11:6). See also I Samuel 6:14 – an evil spirit was sent by God as judgment upon Saul.

David: "Then Samuel took the horn of oil and anointed him in the midst of his brethren: and the Spirit of the LORD came upon David from that day forward. So Samuel rose up, and went to Ramah" (I Sam. 16:13). See also Psalms 51:11, 12; 143:10.

(5) *Her Priests.* "The Spirit of God came upon Zechariah the son of Jehoiada the priest, which stood above the people" (II Chron. 24:20a).

(6) *Her Prophets.* "Yea, they made their heart as an adamant stone, lest they should hear the law, and the words which the LORD of hosts hath sent in his spirit by the former prophets: therefore came a great wrath from the Lord of hosts" (Zech. 7:12). See also Nehemiah 9:30; Ezekiel 2:2; Daniel 5:1-14; Micah 3:8.

(7) *Her Sanctuary.*

(a) *The Tabernacle.* Nothing was left to human wisdom; it was not made by the natural ability of man. "He hath filled him with the spirit of God, in wisdom, in understanding, and in knowledge, and in all manner of workmanship" (Ex. 35:31). See also Exodus 28:3; 31:1-5.

(b) *The Temple.* "Then David gave to Solomon his son the pattern of the porch and of the houses thereof, and of the treasuries thereof, and of the upper chambers thereof, and of the inner parlours thereof, and of the place of the mercy seat, and the pattern of all that he had by the spirit, of the courts of the house of the LORD, and of all the chambers round about, of the treasuries of the house of God, and of the treasuries of the dedicated things" (I Chron. 28:11, 12).

d. *In Relation to Messiah.* "The Spirit of the Lord GOD is upon me; because the LORD hath anointed me to preach good tidings unto the meek; he hath sent me to bind up the brokenhearted, to proclaim liberty to the captives, and the opening of the prison to them that are bound; to proclaim the acceptable year of the LORD and the day of vengeance of our God; to comfort all that mourn" (Is. 61:1, 2). See also Isaiah 11:2.

e. *In Relation to the Millennium.* "It shall come to pass afterward that I will pour out my spirit upon all flesh, and your sons and your daughters shall prophesy, your old men shall dream dreams, your young men shall see visions: and also upon the servants, and upon the handmaids in those days will I pour out my spirit" (Joel 2:28, 29). "Afterward" means after Israel's restoration. See also Ezekiel 36:25-28; 37:14.

f. *In Relation to Inspiration.* "Now these be the last words of David. David the son of Jesse said, and the man who was raised up on high, the anointed of the God of Jacob, and the sweet psalmist of Israel, said, The Spirit of the LORD spake by me, and his word was in my tongue" (II Sam. 23:1, 2). See also Numbers 24:2; Acts 1:16; 4:25; I Peter 1:10-12; II Peter 1:21; II Timothy 3:16, 17.

B. *As Set Forth in the New Testament.*

1. *The Holy Spirit and Christ.*

a. *Reference to His Work in the Old Dispensation.*

(1) *In Preaching.* "Christ also hath once suffered for sins, the just for the unjust, that he might bring us to God, being put to death in the flesh, but quickened by the Spirit: by which also he went and preached unto the spirits in prison; which sometime were disobedient, when once the longsuffering of God waited in the days of Noah, while the ark was preparing, wherein few, that is, eight souls were saved by water" (I Peter 3:18-20). This passage of Scripture has been used by several cults, which teach that God gives man a second chance beyond death. They interpret this portion of the Word as follows: Christ, between His crucifixion and resurrection, went to Hades and offered salvation to the wicked dead. If they believed in Him then, they were saved.

We know that the above theory is not true, for, "It is appointed unto men once to die, but after this the judgment" (Heb. 9:27). No second chance here. The correct interpretation is that Christ, by the Holy Spirit in Noah, preached the Gospel to the people, warning them of world judgment. They refused the message; they died in the flood; thus, their spirits are now in prison, waiting for the last resurrection.

(2) *In Prophecy.* "The prophets have searched diligently . . . what, or what manner of time the Spirit of Christ which was in them did signify, when it testified beforehand the sufferings of Christ, and the glory that should follow" (I Peter 1:10, 11).

(3) *In Type.* The Tabernacle is a type of Christ. Everything about it reveals the Saviour. And it was the Holy Spirit who endowed men to build the Tabernacle. "See, I have called by name Bezaleel the son of Uri, the son of Hur, of the tribe of Judah: and I have filled him with the spirit of God, in wisdom, and in understanding, and in knowledge, and in all manner of workmanship, to devise cunning works, to work in gold, and in silver, and in brass, and in cutting of stones, to set them, and in carving of timber, to work in all manner of workmanship. And I, behold, I have given with him Aholiab, the son of Ahisamach, of the tribe of Dan: and in the hearts of all that are wisehearted I have put wisdom, that they may make all that I have commanded thee" (Ex. 31:2-6).

b. *Reference to His Work in His Earthly Manifestation.*

(1) *The Birth of Christ.* "The angel answered and said unto her, The Holy Ghost shall come upon thee, and the power of the Highest shall overshadow thee: therefore also that holy thing which shall be born of thee shall be called the Son of God" (Luke 1:35). *Never* in Scripture do we find that Jesus is declared to be the Son of the Spirit. The Holy Spirit produced the body, sinless; "a body hast thou prepared me" (Heb. 10:5c), not the Person.

(2) *The Baptism of Christ.* "Now when all the people were baptized, it came to pass, that Jesus also being baptized, and praying, the heaven was opened, and the Holy Ghost descended in a bodily shape like a dove upon him, and a voice came from heaven, which said, Thou art my beloved Son; in thee I am well pleased" (Luke 3:21, 22). See also Mark 1:10, 11; John 1:32, 34.

(3) *The Testing of Christ.* "Jesus being full of the

Holy Ghost returned from Jordan, and was led by the Spirit into the wilderness, being forty days tempted of the devil" (Luke 4:1, 2a). See also Matthew 4:1; Mark 1:12.

(4) *The Anointing of Christ.* "God anointed Jesus of Nazareth with the Holy Ghost and with power: who went about doing good, and healing all that were oppressed of the devil; for God was with him" (Acts 10:38). See also Luke 4:16-21.

(5) *The Teaching of Christ.* "He whom God hath sent speaketh the words of God: for he giveth not the Spirit by measure" (John 3:34, R.V.).

(6) *The Miracles of Christ.* "If I cast out devils by the Spirit of God, then the kingdom of God is come unto you" (Matt. 12:28).

(7) *The Life of Christ.* "Jesus being full of the Holy Ghost returned from Jordan and was led by the Spirit into the wilderness" (Luke 4:1). See also Luke 10:21, R.V.; Hebrews 9:14.

(8) *The Death of Christ.* "How much more shall the blood of Christ, who through the eternal Spirit offered himself without spot to God, purge your conscience from dead works to serve the living God?" (Heb. 9:14).

(9) *The Resurrection of Christ.* "If the Spirit of him that raised up Jesus from the dead dwell in you, he that raised up Christ from the dead shall also quicken your mortal bodies by his Spirit that dwelleth in you" (Rom. 8:11).

(10) *The Pre-ascension Commands of Christ.* Luke tells us that in his Gospel he wrote "of all that Jesus began both to do and teach, until the day in which he was taken up, after that he through the Holy Ghost had given commandments unto the apostles whom he had chosen" (Acts 1:1, 2). See also Acts 1:8.

c. *Reference to His Work During This Dispensation.*

(1) *He Glorifies Christ.* "He shall glorify me: for he shall receive of mine, and shall shew it unto you" (John 16:14).

(2) *He Witnesses to Christ.* "The God of our fathers raised up Jesus, whom ye slew and hanged on a tree. Him hath God exalted with his right hand to be a Prince and a Saviour, for to give repentance to Israel, and forgiveness of sins. And we are his witnesses of these things; and so is also the

Holy Ghost, whom God hath given to them that obey him" (Acts 5:30-32).

(3) *He Enthrones Christ.* "I give you to understand, that no man speaking by the Spirit of God calleth Jesus accursed: and that no man can say that Jesus is the Lord but by the Holy Ghost" (I Cor. 12:3).

2. *The Holy Spirit and the World.*

a. *Conviction.* "When he is come, he will reprove [convict] the world of sin, and of righteousness, and of judgment. Of sin, because they believe not on me; of righteousness, because I go to my Father, and ye see me no more: of judgment, because the prince of this world is judged" (John 16:8-11).

(1) *Of Sin.* It is not the business of the Holy Spirit to convict the world of murder, adultery, etc; the law of the land does this. The Holy Spirit convicts the world of *unbelief*: "because they believe not on me" (John 16:9). Many times we get the word "convict" confused by thinking that it means to feel guilty; but that is not the meaning at all. "Convict" means to be found guilty as charged. The sinner has already been found guilty of sin – unbelief – whether he feels it or not. Yes, the sinner is already convicted, condemned, and waiting to be sentenced. "He that believeth on him is not condemned; but he that believeth not is condemned *already*, because he hath not believed in the name of the only begotten Son of God. . . . the wrath of God abideth upon him" (John 3:18, 36c). The Great White Throne is not the place to determine the guilt of the sinner (to convict him as a sinner), but the place to sentence him to the degree of punishment which his works merit.

(2) *Of Righteousness.* In what manner does the Spirit convict the world of righteousness? The Holy Spirit does not convict the world of the righteousness it has, but convicts the world where righteousness is – in Christ: "because I go to my Father" (John 16:10).

(3) *Of Judgment.* If the world rejects Christ, there is nothing left but judgment. "Neither is there salvation in any other: for there is none other name under heaven given among men, whereby we must be saved" (Acts 4:12). The world's conception of future judgment is confusing. Man has one false idea after another. Yet these universal beliefs, however wrong they may be, are proof positive that there is a time

when man must give an account of himself unto God. The Bible is the only true source of the Great White Throne judgment.

b. *Regeneration.* "If any man be in Christ, he is a new creature: old things are passed away; behold, all things are become new" (II Cor. 5:17). See also John 3:5. Man may lower the bars, thinking he can become a child of God another way, but God does not. He still requires that you must be born again.

c. *Hindrances of Evil.* "The mystery of iniquity does already work: only he who now letteth will let, until he be taken out of the way" (II Thess. 2:7). Lawlessness will one of these days be headed up in one man, the Antichrist. There is a Person in the world who keeps sin from taking full sway even today; and that person is the Holy Spirit. During the Great Tribulation, when the Antichrist is revealed, the Holy Spirit shall step aside, taking His constraining hand off of sinful man, allowing him to plunge unto the depths of degradation.

3. *The Holy Spirit and the Church.* See Ephesians 1:22, 23; 2:12-16; 3:4-16.

a. *The Holy Spirit Constitutes the Church.* The Spirit's baptism is the operation by which the Church is constituted. "By one Spirit are we all baptized into one body, whether we be Jews or Gentiles, whether we be bond or free, and have been all made to drink into one spirit" (I Cor. 12:13).

There are seven references to the baptism of the Holy Spirit. Five are prophetic (Matt. 3:11; Mark 1:8; Luke 3:16; John 1:33; Acts 1:5); one historic (Acts 11:16); and one didactic (I Cor. 12:13). In the five prophetic Scriptures, we find that two speak of the baptism of the Spirit, and of fire. The baptism of the Spirit, and of fire, are not the same. The baptism of the Spirit speaks of the formation of the Church, while baptism of fire speaks of judgment. Matthew 3:11 and Luke 3:16 are those passages which speak of the baptism of fire. It was in these Scriptures that Christ was addressing His messages to saved people and to "vipers" (unbelievers). Mark's and John's accounts include no "baptism of fire," for they are not addressed to "vipers."

All five prophetic portions point to the future; the one historic passage looks back; therefore, the baptism of the Spirit comes in between the two. This is Pentecost.

The baptism of the Holy Spirit was not that enduement of power which enabled the apostles to do miracles, for they performed miracles before they were baptized with the Spirit. The Church is an organism, not an organization, and the baptism of the Spirit is that act of God which unites believers into that organism. Whenever the words "baptism of the Spirit" are used, they are always applied collectively, to a group, never to an individual. When were "we" and the Corinthians (I Cor. 12:13) baptized with the Spirit? At Pentecost, once and for all. When one receives Christ, he is sealed in Christ with the Spirit. "In whom ye also trusted, after that ye heard the word of truth, the gospel of your salvation; in whom also after that ye believed, ye were sealed with that holy Spirit of promise" (Eph. 1:13). He receives the baptism of the Spirit at the same time also.

As far as *God* is concerned, there is only *one* Calvary, and there is only *one* Pentecost. The sinner, however, must appropriate Calvary by faith, and he must acknowledge Pentecost by faith, to make both a reality to his own soul. This takes place immediately upon his acceptance of Christ as his Lord and Saviour.

We would like to give an explanation of the following verse, inasmuch as many use it for the above argument: "One Lord, one faith, one baptism" (Eph. 4:5). This does not speak of the Spirit's baptism, but of water baptism. The preceding verse explains the Spirit's baptism: "There is one body, and one Spirit, even as ye are called in one hope of your calling" (Eph. 4:4). That one body is constituted by the baptism of the Spirit.

Pentecost always came fifty days after the Feast of Firstfruits. The Feast of Firstfruits was a type of the resurrection of Christ. The second chapter of Acts records the account of the hundred and twenty disciples in the upper room waiting for the fifty days to expire. The Holy Spirit did not come in answer to their prayer, for all of their prayers and fasting would not have hastened His coming. He came on time. It is inconceivable to think of the Spirit coming forty-nine, or even fifty-one days after His resurrection. He came on time – *fifty* days after the resurrection.

The Holy Spirit would have come had they not prayed. They would have been baptized and indwelt by the Spirit had they not prayed, but they would not have received power; they would not have been filled with the Spirit had they not prayed. More will be said about the filling of the Spirit later.

The Feast of Passover was fulfilled at Calvary. Christ will never die again. The Feast of Pentecost was fulfilled by the baptism of the Spirit, and there will be no more Pentecost. There will never be a re-fulfillment of the Passover Lamb, and there will never be a re-fulfillment of Pentecost.

The original Feast of Pentecost was also known as the Feast of Weeks, when the *harvest* was gathered. In Leviticus 23:22 we read: "When ye reap the harvest of your land, thou shalt not make clean riddance of the corners of thy fields when thou reapest, neither shalt thou gather any gleaning of thy harvest: thou shalt leave them unto the poor, and to the stranger: I am the LORD your God." Thus, we see that the harvest was for three classes:

1. Israel in General.
2. The Poor.
3. Strangers.

All three received blessings of the harvest. The baptism of the Spirit, which was the fulfillment of the Feast of Harvest (Weeks), was for three classes of people:

1. Israel. At Jerusalem (Acts 2:37, 39).
2. Samaritans (the Poor). At Samaria (Acts 8:9-17).
3. Gentiles (Strangers). At Caesarea (Acts 10:34-44).

The following is the process by which the above three classes received the Holy Spirit:

1. The Jews at Jerusalem.
   (a) By faith in Christ.
   (b) Then by water baptism.
   (c) And then by receiving the Holy Spirit.
2. The Samaritans at Samaria.
   (a) By faith in Christ.
   (b) Then by water baptism.
   (c) Then by laying on of hands.
   (d) Then by receiving the Holy Spirit.
3. The Gentiles at Caesarea.
   (a) By faith in Christ.
   (b) Then by receiving the Holy Spirit.
   (c) Then by water baptism.

There were two operations of the Spirit on the day of Pentecost. They must not be confused. The two operations were the "baptism" and the "filling." The believers were baptized with the Spirit at Pentecost, although the word "baptism" cannot be found in Acts 2. We know that the baptism occurred then, because of the words spoken by the Lord Jesus only a short time before His ascension. "John truly baptized with water; but ye shall be baptized with the Holy Ghost not many days hence" (Acts 1:5).

There are some who believe that speaking in tongues was a sign of the baptism of the Spirit, but if you look closely, you will notice that they spoke in tongues because they were *filled* with the Spirit. No one was converted while tongues were spoken on the day of Pentecost, but three thousand were saved when Peter preached. Peter declared, "*This is that* which was spoken by the prophet Joel: And it shall come to pass in the last days, saith God, I will pour out of my Spirit upon all flesh; and your sons and your daughters shall prophesy, and your young men shall see visions, and your old men shall dream dreams; and on my servants and on my handmaidens I will pour out in those days of my Spirit; and they shall prophesy" (Acts 2:16-18). "This is that." What? The event? The speaking in tongues? No. "This" is a quotation from Joel, and I am quoting him. Peter was giving Joel as an example, for He, God, who will bring to pass those things which Joel has prophesied, has caused these things to happen which you have witnessed.

b. *The Spirit Abides in the Church.* "Know ye not that ye are the temple of God, and that the Spirit of God dwelleth in you?" (I Cor. 3:16).

c. *The Spirit Builds the Church.* "Ye also are builded together for an habitation of God through the Spirit" (Eph. 2:22).

d. *The Spirit Administers the Church.*

(1) *He Appoints the Officers.* "Take heed therefore unto yourselves, and to all the flock, over the which the Holy Ghost hath made you overseers, to feed the Church of God, which he hath purchased with his own blood" (Acts 20:28). See also Acts 6:3, 5, 10.

(2) *He Directs the Work.* "As they ministered to the Lord, and fasted, the Holy Ghost said, Separate me Barnabas and Saul for the work whereunto I have called them" (Acts 13:2). See also Acts 29; 10:19; 16:7.

4. *The Holy Spirit and the Christian.*

a. *Beginning in the Spirit.* "O foolish Galatians, who hath bewitched you, that ye should not obey the truth, before whose eyes Jesus Christ hath been evidently set forth, crucified among you? This only would I learn of you, Received ye the Spirit by the works of the law, or by the hearing of faith? Are ye so foolish? having begun in the Spirit, are ye now made perfect by the flesh?" (Gal. 3:1-3).

We become Christians by the operation of God alone. A new life is imparted by the Holy Spirit. It is a new birth: "Ye must be born again. . . . That which is born of the flesh is flesh; and that which is born of the Spirit is spirit" (John 3:7, 6). God has never fellowshiped with unregenerated men in any dispensation until man received a new nature from Him.

b. *Indwelling of the Spirit.* "What? know ye not that your body is the temple of the Holy Ghost which is in you, which ye have of God, and ye are not your own" (I Cor. 6:19). What assurance does the Christian have of the Spirit's indwelling? By feeling? By some great ecstasy? No – by the Word of God! The Spirit indwells the believer when he acts upon what Christ has done, when he accepts Christ Jesus by faith. The proof of His indwelling is not based upon feeling, for one's feelings may change from one day to another. Christ's work upon Calvary never changes.

"In the last day, that great day of the feast, Jesus stood and cried, saying, If any man thirst, let him come unto me, and drink. He that believeth on me as the scripture hath said, out of his belly shall flow rivers of living water. (But this spake he of the Spirit, which they that believe on him should receive: for the Holy Ghost was not yet given; because that Jesus was not glorified.)" (John 7:37-39). This portion of God's Word plainly states that the disciples had not as yet received the Holy Spirit, but would in the future – and they did so at Pentecost. Another passage reveals that they were not as yet indwelt by the Spirit until Pentecost: "For he dwelleth *with* you, and shall be *in* you" (John 14:17c). Before Pentecost, the Spirit was *with* them; after Pentecost, the Spirit was *in* them. No believer is to pray as David did, "Cast me not away from thy presence; and take not thy holy spirit from me" (Ps. 51:11), for David was not indwelt by the Holy Spirit. The Christian is! "Ye are not in the flesh, but in the Spirit, if so be that the Spirit of God dwell in you. Now if any man have not the Spirit of Christ, he is none of his" (Rom. 8:9).

Still another Scripture which has confused the child of God is Luke 11:13: "If ye then, being evil, know how to give good gifts unto your children; how much more shall your heavenly Father give the Holy Spirit to them that ask Him?" Some propose that we must ask for the Spirit in order to have Him; but remember, this was spoken *before* Pentecost. We have no place in Scripture which says that one should ask for the Spirit *after* Pentecost. Would the Father have given the Spirit to the disciples *before* Pentecost if they had asked for Him? The Lord Jesus said He would, but the truth is, they did not ask for Him.

The last Scripture we shall deal with concerning the indwelling of the Spirit is John 20:22: "And when he had said this, he breathed on them, and saith unto them, Receive ye the Holy Ghost." Many say that at this time the disciples were indwelt by the Holy Spirit, instead of at Pentecost. We know, however, that they did not receive the Holy Spirit at that time, for they were commanded that "they should not depart from Jerusalem, but wait for the promise of the Father which, saith he, ye have heard of me. For John truly baptized with water; but ye shall be baptized with the Holy Ghost not many days hence" (Acts 1:4, 5). Now, if they had already received the Holy Ghost, why were they to wait to receive Him?

c. *Sealing of the Holy Spirit.* "In whom ye also trusted, after that ye heard the word of truth, the gospel of your salvation: in whom also after that ye believed, ye were sealed with that holy Spirit of promise" (Eph. 1:13).

"Sealing" is used many times in Scripture.

(1) *The Sealer.* The Sealer is God the Father. "Now he which stablisheth us with you in Christ, and hath anointed us, is God; who hath also sealed us, and given the earnest of the Spirit in our hearts" (II Cor. 1:21, 22).

(2) *The Sealed.* There are two who are sealed by the Father — the Son and believers. "Labour not for the meat which perisheth, but for that meat which endureth unto everlasting life, which the Son of man shall give you: for him hath God the Father sealed" (John 6:27). "Grieve not the holy Spirit, whereby ye are sealed unto the day of redemption" (Eph. 4:30). The Son was sealed because of who He is. We are sealed because of Jesus and our position in Him. The time of the believer's sealing is when he accepts Christ as his Saviour: "In

whom, having also believed ye were sealed with the Holy Spirit of promise" (Eph. 1:13, R.V.).

(3) *The Seal.* The Holy Spirit Himself is the seal. The seal is not secured through some emotional experience, but through belief in Christ: "In whom, *having also believed,* ye were sealed with the holy Spirit of promise" (Eph. 1:13, R.V.).

(4) *Signification.*

(a) *The Seal Signifies Ownership.* If we are sealed we have the ownership seal of God upon us. "Nevertheless the foundation of God standeth sure, having this seal, The Lord knoweth them that are his. And, Let everyone that nameth the name of Christ depart from iniquity" (II Tim. 2:19).

(b) *The Seal Signifies Identification.* It is our identification for the future. "In whom [Christ] ye also trusted, after that ye heard the word of truth, the gospel of your salvation: in whom also after that ye believed, ye were sealed with that holy Spirit of promise, which is the earnest of our inheritance until the redemption of the purchased possession, unto the praise of his glory" (Eph. 1:13, 14).

(c) *The Seal Signifies Security.* In Revelation 7:4-8 there are 144,000 sealed. Satan is sealed in the bottomless pit during the Millennium, (Rev. 20:3). The Book of Revelation has seven seals that no man can open (Rev. 6-8). We, the believers, are sealed unto the time of our redemption (Eph. 1:13, 14).

(d) *The Seal Signifies a Finished Transaction.* "I subscribed the evidence, and sealed it, and took witnesses, and weighed him the money in the balances" (Jer. 32:10). The seal of the Holy Spirit is that legal evidence which testifies to the fact that we have entered into the finished work of Christ.

(e) *The Seal Signifies Genuineness.* "He received the sign of circumcision, a seal of the righteousness of the faith which he had yet being uncircumcised: that he might be the father of all them that believe, though they be not circumcised; that righteousness might be imputed unto them also" (Rom. 4:11). See also Esther 3:12.

(f) *The Seal Signifies Unchangeableness.* "Write ye also for the Jews, as it liketh you, in the king's name, and seal it with the king's ring: for the writing which is written in the king's name, and sealed with the king's ring, may no man reverse" (Esth. 8:8).

(g) *The Seal Signifies Value.* "Is not this laid up in store with me, and sealed up among my treasures?" (Deut. 32:34).

(h) *The Seal Signifies Impression.* The seal always left its impression in the wax. If we are sealed with the Spirit, His impression should be on us. "It is turned as clay to the seal; and they stand as a garment" (Job 38:14). "Ye are manifestly declared to be the epistles of Christ ministered by us, written not with ink, but with the Spirit of the living God; not in tables of stone, but in fleshly tables of the heart" (II Cor. 3:3).

d. *The Earnest of the Spirit.* "[God] hath also sealed us, and given the earnest of the Spirit in our hearts" (II Cor. 1:22). See also II Corinthians 5:5; Ephesians 1:13, 14.

"Earnest" is an emblem which speaks of the future. It is a part payment of that which will be paid in full at a future date. When earnest money is paid on a piece of property, both parties are bound. When God bestows His Earnest on us, He is bound for all time and eternity. The Holy Spirit is God's Earnest, God's down payment of our salvation. The believer has not all things as yet which he is to receive. There is more to follow. Indeed, this does stagger the imagination. If the Holy Spirit is only part of what we are to receive, and He is God, and God is *everything*, what will the *rest* be?

If earnest money has been placed upon a piece of property, and the purchaser should fail to complete the transaction, he will have lost his earnest money. God has given us His Earnest, the Holy Spirit. Should He fail to complete our salvation, He will have lost His Earnest; but we know this is impossible. Thus, it is a guarantee of our eternal salvation.

(1) *Illustrations of Earnest.*

(a) *The Presents to Rebecca* (Gen. 24). These presents were the earnest of what was to follow.

(b) *The Fruit of Canaan* (Num. 13). The fruit was the earnest of that which was promised, a foretaste of their inheritance which was to come.

(c) *The Gifts of Boaz* (Ruth 2). The handfuls of grain left for Ruth, and only for Ruth, were just an earnest of what Boaz had to offer in marriage.

(d) *The Firstfruit* (Lev. 23). This wave offering to God was man's earnest that one tenth of his harvest was yet to go to God.

(2) *Giver of the Earnest.* God is the Giver! "Now he which stablisheth us with you in Christ, and hath anointed us, is *God;* who hath also sealed us, and given the earnest of the Spirit in our hearts" (II Cor. 1:21, 22).

(3) *Description of the Earnest.* The Holy Spirit is the earnest: "The earnest of the *Spirit*" (II Cor. 1:22b).

(4) *The Place of the Earnest.* That place is our hearts: "The earnest of the Spirit in our *hearts*" (II Cor. 1:22b).

(5) *Guarantee of the Earnest.*

(a) *Guarantees Our Resurrection.* "Not only they, but ourselves also, which have the first fruits of the Spirit, even we ourselves groan within ourselves, waiting for the adoption, to wit, the redemption of our body" (Rom. 8:23).

(b) *Guarantees Our Inheritance.* "If children, then heirs; heirs of God, and joint heirs with Christ; if so be that we suffer with him, that we may be also glorified together" (Rom. 8:17).

(c) *Guarantees Our Glory.* "We are bound to give thanks alway to God for you, brethren beloved of the Lord, because God hath from the beginning chosen you to salvation through sanctification of the Spirit and belief of the truth: Whereunto he called you by our gospel, to the obtaining of the glory of our Lord Jesus Christ" (II Thess. 2:13, 14).

e. *Filling With the Spirit.* "They were all filled with the Holy Ghost, and began to speak with other tongues, as the Spirit gave them utterance" (Acts 2:4). "When they had prayed, the place was shaken where they were assembled together; and they were all filled with the Holy Ghost, and they spake the word of God with boldness" (Acts 4:31). "Be not drunk with wine, wherein is excess, but be filled with the Spirit" (Eph. 5:18).

The filling of the Spirit has to do with the life and work of the Christian, by which he is empowered to do that which is commanded by the Lord.

(1) *What?* There are many opinions as to the meaning of the "filling" of the Spirit. Some say it happens when a person is born again. The believer does receive the Holy Spirit at conversion but this is not the *filling* of the Spirit; it is the *regeneration* of the Spirit (Titus 3:5). Others propose that the "filling of the Spirit is that experience by which [the believer]

receives the Holy Spirit sometimes later after he is saved." However, the Word declares that *all* believers have received the Holy Spirit: "Now if any man have not the Spirit of Christ he is none of his" (Rom. 8:9).

The "filling" of the Spirit may be confusing to many because of that word "filling." They think of a material filling, as a vessel being filled with water. The Spirit, however, is not a material thing, but a Person. It is true that a half-empty vessel can be filled with more water, but it is impossible for the believer, who has the Spirit, to get more of Him. One cannot get more of God, but God can get more of him.

Now the believer already has the Spirit, yet he is told to be "filled" with Him. The believer is indwelt by the Spirit; he is sealed with the Spirit; he is baptized with (in) the Spirit, and he is regenerated by the Spirit; and still he is commanded to be "filled" with the Spirit. What is the "filling" of the Spirit? A better word or thought for "filling" is "controlled by" the Spirit. Thus, the Christian is admonished to be controlled by, to be possessed by, to be dominated by the Spirit. We know the full meaning now of the expression, "It is not how much of the Holy Spirit one has, but how much of one the Holy Spirit has."

(2) *How*? Is this experience secured through seeking, and through prayer? There is no passage in the Word where a person ever prayed for the "filling" of the Spirit and received it. It is all brought about by *yieldedness* to the Lord. When we are yielded to Him, our wills die, and His will is the will for our lives; our ambitions fall as ashes at our feet. Some may ask, "What is 'yieldedness' "? It is that act of the believer which places himself upon God's altar: "Walk in love, as Christ also hath loved us, and hath given himself for us an offering and a sacrifice to God for a sweet-smelling savour" (Eph. 5:2). The sweet-smelling savour offering spoken of here is the continual burnt offering: that offering which never lacked a sacrificial lamb, for when one was consumed, another was put in its place immediately – one in the morning and one at night. This was the only way it could be a continuous offering. This burnt offering was never instituted as a sin offering, but rather as a praise offering. The Christian is beseeched to give himself as a living sacrifice, a continual burnt

offering, showing forth the praises of Him who hath called him out of darkness into His marvelous light (I Peter 2:9).

(3) *When?* When does the Spirit take over? When does He control the believer? Just as *soon* as the believer yields – completely yields!

Are there a certain number of steps one must take in order to become yielded? No. What are the requirements, then, for yieldedness? *A complete subjection to the will of God!* For some it may take death to self; others, obedience to God's call; still others, the forsaking of known sin, etc. Whatever it may take to become yielded to the will of God – that is the requirement!

(4) *Why?* Should the believer ever ask this question? Is there a need for the "filling" of the Spirit? We answer "yes" to both of these questions. Some Christians do not understand that there is such a thing as the "filling" of the Spirit, and therefore they are powerless. In addition to God's command to be "filled" with the Spirit, we realize that this "filling" is mandatory for power in service and in life – not for selfish gain, but for the glory of the Lord Jesus Christ and the winning of the lost to Him.

(5) *What Then?* A survey of those who have been truly "filled" with the Spirit reveals these results:

(a) They Will Reproduce Christ.
(b) They Will Convict the World.
(c) They Will Love the Word.
(d) They Will Be Filled With Power.
(e) They Will Be Full of Life.

Contrast of Baptism With Filling

Baptism of the Spirit	*Filling of the Spirit*
1. Has to do with the body.	1. Has to do with the individual.
2. Baptism is external.	2. Filling is internal.
3. *Every* believer is baptized with the Spirit.	3. A believer may or may not be filled with the Spirit.
4. *No believer* is ever exhorted to be baptized with the Spirit.	4. *All believers* are exhorted to be filled with the Spirit.
5. An initial work at the time of salvation.	5. One may be filled years after the time of salvation.

6. The believer is baptized but once.	6. The believer may be filled many times.
7. No believer was ever baptized before Pentecost. Baptism puts the believers into the *Body*.	7. Some believers were filled before Pentecost. Filling is essential for *service*.

f. *The Fruits of the Spirit.* "The fruit of the Spirit is love, joy, peace, longsuffering, gentleness, goodness, faith, meekness, temperance: against such there is no law" (Gal. 5:22, 23). The fruit of the Spirit is true Christian character. You will notice that the word "fruit" is singular. One has presented this portion of Scripture in this manner: "The fruit of the Spirit is love: joy, peace, longsuffering, gentleness, goodness, faith, meekness, temperance: against such there is no law."

The life of our Lord is the greatest example of the fruit of the Spirit. Fruit always comes from the life within. When at Christmastime we see apples and oranges on Christmas trees, we know they have been tied on. You do not have to tie apples on apple trees; they grow there naturally. There are many social religions that are figuratively tying apples and oranges on Christmas trees. They pretend to bear fruit, but there is no life within, for they have not the Spirit; therefore, they have only the form of godliness and deny the power thereof. An apple tree does not *work* to produce apples; it simply *yields*. The same with the Christian. He does not bear the fruit of the Spirit by his own *labor*, but simply by *yieldedness*.

(1) *Fruit in Relation to the Individual.* Love; joy; peace.

(2) *Fruit in Relation to Men.* Longsuffering; gentleness; goodness.

(3) *Fruit in Relation to God.* Faith; meekness; temperance.

g. *Walking in the Spirit.* "This I say then, Walk in the Spirit, and ye shall not fulfill the lust of the flesh" (Gal. 5:16). Another way of saying it is: "By the Spirit be walking." The Spirit will do the walking. An old example is the suit of clothes: the person inside the suit does the walking. The responsibility of the suit is just to hang on. We should not have a will of our own, but like the suit, just hang on. Wherever the Spirit goes, we go. The will of the Spirit is our will.

h. *Renewing of the Spirit.* "Not by works of righteousness which we have done, but according to his mercy he saved us, by the washing of regeneration, and renewing of the Holy Ghost" (Titus 3:5).

This refers to a daily enduement of the Spirit to live a victorious Christian life. We never come to the time of self-sufficiency.

i. *Strengthening of the Spirit.* Paul prays that God might grant the Ephesians, "according to the riches of his glory, to be strengthened with might by his Spirit in the inner man" (Eph. 3:16). The saints have attested to the truth of this Scripture.

j. *Sowing to the Spirit.* "Be not deceived; God is not mocked: for whatsoever a man soweth, that shall he also reap. For he that soweth to his flesh shall of the flesh reap corruption, but he that soweth to the Spirit shall of the Spirit reap life everlasting" (Gal. 6:7, 8). This passage is not written to the unsaved, but to Christians. The Christian can sow to the flesh, that is, live in sin; however, reaping time will come.

k. *Leading of the Spirit.* "As many as are led by the Spirit of God, they are the sons of God" (Rom. 8:14). Some interpret this to mean that "those who ask the Spirit for advice in their decisions of life are thus assured they are the sons of God." Now it is a blessing to ask and receive of the Holy Spirit His will in our decisions, but this is not what this Scripture refers to. The leading of the Spirit has reference to His guidance of Christians on the way to glory.

> Though sorrow befall us and Satan oppose,
> God leads His dear children along.
> Through grace we can conquer, defeat all our foes,
> God leads His dear children along.
>
> Some through the waters, some through the flood,
> Some through the fire, but all through the blood.
> Some through great sorrow, but God gives a song,
> In the night season, and all the day long.

l. *Sanctification of the Spirit.* "Elect according to the foreknowledge of God the Father, through sanctification of the Spirit, unto obedience and sprinkling of the blood of Jesus Christ: Grace unto you, and peace, be multiplied" (I Peter 1:2).

m. *The Supply of the Spirit.* "I know that this shall turn

to my salvation through your prayer, and the supply of the Spirit of Jesus Christ" (Phil. 1:19).

n. *The Gifts of the Spirit.*

(1) *As to the Enumeration of the Gifts.* "Now concerning spiritual gifts, brethren, I would not have you ignorant . . . . For to one is given by the Spirit the word of wisdom; to another the word of knowledge by the same Spirit; to another faith by the same Spirit; to another the working of miracles; to another prophecy; to another discerning of spirits; to another divers kinds of tongues; to another the interpretation of tongues: but all these worketh that one and the selfsame Spirit, dividing to every man severally as he will" (I Cor. 12:1, 8-11).

(2) *As to the Bestowing of the Gifts.* The first thing we would like to point out is that the gifts are not given to man because of his desires and prayers, but according to the will of the Spirit: "dividing to every man severally as he will." The next thing we would call attention to is that gifts were given in order to substantiate the claims of Christ and His disciples, that Jesus Christ was truly the Son of God, and that the old dispensation of Law was at an end, and that the dispensation of Grace had begun. "How shall we escape, if we neglect so great salvation; which at the first began to be spoken by the Lord, and was confirmed unto us by them that heard him; God also bearing them witness, both with signs and wonders, and with divers miracles, and gifts of the Holy Ghost, according to his own will?" (Heb. 2:3, 4). Certainly there was a need for God to verify this new teaching which was begun by the Lord Himself inasmuch as the people had been under the traditions of the law for over fourteen hundred years, and thus it was hard for them to realize that God had done away with the Old Covenant and had established the New. Also, there were no New Testament Books yet written. Lastly, we emphasize the fact that no *one* believer receives every one of the gifts. "God hath set some in the Church, first apostles, secondarily prophets, thirdly teachers, after that miracles, then gifts of healings, helps, governments, diversities of tongues. Are all apostles? are all prophets? are all teachers? are all workers of miracles? Have all the gifts of healing? do all speak with tongues? do all interpret?" (I Cor. 12:28-30) The answer is *no.*

(3) *As to Utilization of the Gifts.* How were these

gifts to be used? The thirteenth chapter of I Corinthians plainly declares they should be motivated by love. Paul, by inspiration of the Holy Spirit, states that if he had *all* the gifts, and had not love, he would be nothing; his life would be fruitless, and his rewards nil.

Some may ask, "Is the gift of tongues for today?" "Doesn't the Bible say, 'Forbid not to speak with tongues'?" This subject will be dealt with more fully in the next section; however, something may be said about it here.

First Corinthians 14:39 does clearly state: "Wherefore, brethren, covet to prophesy, and forbid not to speak with tongues." But if chapter 14 is to be used as permission to speak with tongues, then they who speak in tongues must be governed by this same chapter as to their use of this gift. Should a person, then, be allowed to speak in tongues in a church service? Certainly, *if* it is done according to I Corinthians 14. "If any man speak in an unknown tongue, let it be by two, or at the most by three, and that by course; and let one interpret. But if there is no interpreter, let him keep silence in the church; and let him speak to himself, and to God" (I Cor. 14:27, 28). Whenever the gift of tongues is employed, only two or at the most, three, can speak at one service. This rule would eliminate much of the so-called tongue movement of today. Next in order is that the speaking shall be "by course" – one at a time. This would eliminate even more tongue movement, for sometimes scores, and even hundreds are upon the floor at the same time. Then the Scriptures say that if there is no interpreter, let there be no talking in tongues whatsoever. More would be eliminated if this were followed. Finally, "Let your women keep silence in the church" (I Cor. 14:34). This practically puts to an end all tongue movement, for the majority of those participating are women.

Many will rebel at the quoted passage, saying that it does not mean "tongues." If this does not mean "tongues," it refers to everything, including tongues, when it says for the women to keep silent in the churches. This, however, has reference only to tongues, for other portions of this same book of I Corinthians allow a woman to speak or pray in church. "But every woman that prayeth or prophesieth with her head uncovered dishonoureth her head: for that is even all one as if she were shaven" (I Cor. 11:5). "Prophesieth" means to "forth-tell";

thus, a woman is alowed to "forth-tell" the Word of God at Sunday school, upon the mission field, and in like places.

(4) *As to the Withholding of the Gifts.* Can it be possible that God withholds many of the gifts from the believers of today, which He gave at the first? Not only possible, but a certainty. In chapter 13 of I Corinthians, the Holy Spirit states, "Charity [love] never faileth: but whether there be prophecies, they shall fail; whether there be tongues, they shall cease; whether there be knowledge, it shall vanish away. For we know in part, and we prophesy in part. But when that which is perfect is come, then that which is in part shall be done away" (verses 8-10). Remember, I Corinthians 13 is speaking about "gifts" of the Spirit, and when it says prophecies shall fail, it does not mean that some of the prophecies foretold by men of God, as recorded in the Bible, will fail to be fulfilled. It means that the *gift* of prophecy will one day be withheld. When it says that "tongues shall cease," it does not mean that some time in the future all tongues will be silenced, but that the *gift* of the tongues will be withheld. And when it says that "knowledge shall vanish away," it does not mean that there will be a time when knowledge will not be in existence, but that the *gift* of knowledge will be withheld. When will the gifts of prophecy, tongues and knowledge be withheld? When "that which is perfect is come." This is not speaking of Christ's second coming, but rather of when the full revelation of God's Word is given. Have we the full revelation of God today? *Yes,* when the apostle John wrote, "The grace of our Lord Jesus Christ be with you all, Amen" (Rev. 22:21), God's full revelation was completed – that which was perfect had come. Therefore, since we have the full revelation, the gifts of prophecy, tongues, and knowledge have vanished away; they have been withheld. They are not for today.

Turning to Ephesians 4:11 we read, "He gave some, apostles; and some, prophets; and some evangelists; and some pastors and teachers." We note by this later revelation that no miraculous gifts are listed, as were listed in I Corinthians 12, 13 and 14. There is no need for the gifts of miracles anymore, because we have the full revelation of God. The child of God is blessed more by having the complete revelation of God than if he had all the miraculous gifts.

The claim is made by some that we need these gifts for signs of the "filling" of the Spirit. It is true that God gave these miraculous gifts for signs; not however, for the "filling" of the Spirit, but for the confirmation of Paul's apostleship (II Cor. 12:12); of Paul's confirmation to the Gentiles (Rom. 15:18, 19); of the confirmation of salvation through Christ (Heb. 2:3, 4); of the confirmation of the Word (Mark 16:20). Do we need these gifts today to confirm the Word, the Gospel, and the Apostle Paul? Two thousand years of Church history has confirmed them.

(5) *As to the Remainder of the Gifts.* "Now abideth faith, hope, love, these three; and the greatest of these is love" (I Cor. 13:13). These three gifts are possessed by every Christian. He, being controlled by the Holy Spirit, is to utilize them.

o. *Witness of the Spirit.* "The Spirit himself beareth witness with our spirit, that we are the children of God" (Rom. 8:16, R. V.).

The law states that in the mouth of two witnesses shall the truth be declared. Thus, we have the two witnesses who declare that we are the children of God. They are the Holy Spirit, and our spirit. How does the Holy Spirit bear witness to our salvation? Through the Word. How does our spirit bear witness? By feeling, or conscience? No. Feelings are deceiving. Our spirit bears witness by *faith* in God's Word. God's Word declares our salvation when we trust Christ; we believe it. Therefore, the Spirit bears witness "together with" our spirit.

p. *As to the Unction of the Spirit.* "Ye have an *unction* from the Holy One, and ye know all things. . . . But the *anointing* which ye received of him abideth in you, and ye need not that any man teach you: but as the same *anointing* teacheth you of all things, and in truth, and is no lie, and even as it hath taught you, ye shall abide in him" (I John 2:20, 27).

The words "unction" and "anointing" are the same in the Greek. "Anointing" in the Scriptures, whether in the Old or New Testament, was for some service. Kings and priests were anointed for their special service. Christ was anointed (Acts 10:38). The very name "Christ" means "anointed one." He was anointed Prophet (for the past); Priest (for the present); King (for the future). The believer in Christ receives his anointing for service when he is born again: "Ye *have* received." The anointing of the Spirit is not for a favored few. All believers are anointed: "*Ye* have received." The Spirit's anointing is once and for all: "abideth in you." There is no place in the Scriptures where one receives a fresh anointing. False religions may try to turn you away from Christ, to induce you away from your faith; but you, upon hearing their inducements, do not yield, because you have the unction of the Spirit. "And ye need not that any man teach you."

q. *As to Worship by the Spirit.* "We are the circumcision, who worship by the Spirit of God, and glory in Christ Jesus, and have no confidence in the flesh" (Phil. 3:3, R.V.). The only worship accepted by God has to be inspired by the Spirit. One does not worship Him with hands, feet and lips, but by the Spirit through the hands, feet and lips.

r. *As to Communion of the Spirit.* "The grace of the Lord Jesus Christ, and the love of God, and the communion of the Holy Ghost, be with you all. Amen" (II Cor. 13:14). The word "communion" is better translated "fellowship; partnership." Thus, "communion" means "participating, partaking, and sharing." The Holy Spirit and Christians have one thing in common – Jesus Christ!

s. *As to Praying in the Spirit.* "The Spirit also helpeth our infirmities: for we know not what we should pray for as we ought: but the Spirit himself maketh intercession for us with groanings which cannot be uttered. And he that searcheth the hearts knoweth what is the mind of the Spirit, because he maketh intercession for the saints according to the will of God" (Rom. 8:26, 27).

Is it wrong to pray to the Holy Spirit? There is no place in Scripture commanding us to do so, yet He is a member of the Godhead; when we pray to God, we pray to Him.

t. *As to the Warfare of the Spirit.* The flesh lusteth against the Spirit, and the Spirit against the flesh: and these are contrary one to the other: so that ye cannot do the things that ye would" (Gal. 5:17).

u. *As to the Teaching of the Spirit.* "God hath revealed them unto us by his Spirit: for the Spirit searcheth all things, yea, the deep things of God" (I Cor. 2:10). The Holy Spirit reveals His Word to only born-again Christians, and not to those outside of the Body of Christ. Man without the Spirit of God cannot learn the truths of God.

5. *The Holy Spirit and the Scriptures.*

a. *Inspiration.* "All scripture is given by *inspiration* of God" (II Tim. 3:16a). The literal meaning of "inspiration" is "God-breathed." No prophecy is of man's own ingenuity. We believe in the verbal inspiration of the Word of God. The words, not merely the thoughts, are inspired, as given by God in the original. Some may ask, "Did not God use human instruments?" Yes, but the use of human instruments did not lessen it as the Word of God. When you read the Pentateuch, you do not read the words of Moses, but you read the words of God. See I Corinthians 2:12, 13; 10:11; Romans 4:20-25; 15:4.

b. *Enlightenment.* The best way to study the Book is to know its author. The best interpreter of the Book is the writer, the Holy Spirit. Just as the Lord Jesus made known the Scriptures unto the disciples, so the Holy Spirit will do for us today (I Cor. 2:9-14).

6. *The Holy Spirit and Sins.*

a. *Grieving the Spirit.* "Grieve not the holy Spirit of God whereby ye are sealed unto the day of redemption" (Eph. 4:30). Grieve is a word that has to do with love. People who do not love you will never grieve over you. The Holy Spirit grieves over us; therefore, He must love us.

b. *Lying to the Spirit.* "Peter said, Ananias, why hast Satan filled thine heart to lie to the Holy Ghost?" (Acts 5:3). Ananias lied to the Church, the temple of the Holy Ghost. We, too, can lie to the Holy Spirit. We can sing a lie. Sometimes in an emotional meeting people dedicate their lives to definite Christian service, but shortly after they neglect this decision. This is lying to the Holy Ghost.

c. *Quenching the Spirit.* "Quench not the Spirit" (I Thess. 5:19). To "quench" means to "extinguish." One can quench the gifts of the Spirit, and can quench the Spirit in others by forbidding them to use the gifts of the Holy Spirit (Num. 11:28, 29).

d. *Resisting the Spirit.* "Ye do always resist the Holy Ghost" (Acts 7:51b).

e. *Insulting the Spirit.* "Of how much sorer punishment . . . shall he be thought worthy, who hath trodden under foot the Son of God . . . and hath done despite unto the Spirit of grace" (Heb. 10:29).

f. *Blaspheming Against the Spirit.* This is the so-called unpardonable sin found in Matthew 12:31, 32 and Mark 3:29, 30. If the grace of God, which will pardon *all* the sins of mankind, will not pardon *this* one, it must be an unusual sin. Murder is not the unpardonable sin. Unbelief is not the unpardonable sin. Where would we be if this were true? Rejection of Jesus Christ is not the unpardonable sin; however, the man who rejects Christ and dies, is indeed lost. The Spirit will not strive with man after death. His final rejection is not unpardonable, but unpardoned.

Man should distinguish between the following:

Unpardoned – Unpardonable
Unforgiven – Unforgivable
Unsaved – Unsavable

I believe the blasphemy against the Holy Ghost, which some term "unpardonable," was a dispensational sin, limited for thirty-three years, during Christ's stay on earth. There are no sinners on God's blacklist today. God has never commissioned any man to go cut and preach the message that there are some men He will not save.

Has anyone who has committed this blasphemy been saved? Yes, the Apostle Paul, "who was before a blasphemer, and a persecutor, and injurious; but I obtained mercy, because I did it ignorantly in unbelief. . . . Howbeit for this cause I obtained mercy, that in me first Jesus Christ might show forth all longsuffering, for a pattern to them which should hereafter believe on him to life everlasting" (I Tim. 1:13, 16).

The word "speaketh" in Matthew 12:32, and verse 30 of Mark 3 are the keys to the correct interpretation.

7. *Emblems of the Holy Spirit.*

a. *The Dove.* "John bare record, saying, I saw the Spirit decending from heaven like a dove, and it abode upon him" (John 1:32). Upon no other one did the Spirit descend in this manner. In Genesis 1:2 the Holy Spirit is pictured as moving upon the face of the waters, as a dove brooding upon her eggs. The dove is a gentle, clean bird, particular about its food. So are they who are of the Spirit. "Harmless as a dove" (Matt. 10:16). Truly an emblem of the Holy Spirit. The Word pictures to us the wrath of the Son, but never the wrath of the Holy Spirit.

b. *Water.* "I will pour water upon him that is thirsty,

and floods upon the dry ground: I will pour my spirit upon thy seed, and my blessings upon thy offspring" (Is. 44:3). See also John 7:38, 39. What water means to thirsty lips, and what rain means to the parched land, is what the Spirit means to the individual. There is nothing that quenches thirst better than water; there is nothing that satisfies the longing of the heart as the Holy Spirit.

c. *Oil.* "Then Samuel took the horn of oil, and anointed him in the midst of his brethren: and the Spirit of the LORD came upon David from that day forward. So Samuel rose up, and went to Ramah" (I Sam. 16:13). See also Isaiah 61:1; Acts 10:38. When the priest was anointed with oil, it took place in this manner: first, his ear – he was always to hear God's Word; his thumb – his actions were to be for God's glory; his big toe – he was to walk with God.

d. *Wind.* "Then he said unto me, Prophesy unto the wind, prophesy, son of man, and say to the wind, Thus saith the Lord GOD; Come from the four winds, O breath, and breathe upon these slain, that they may live. . . . and [I] shall put my spirit in you, and ye shall live, and I shall place you in your own land: then shall ye know that I the LORD have spoken it, and performed it, saith the LORD" (Ezek. 37:9, 14). See also John 3:3-8. Wind suggests activity. You cannot see the wind, yet is it powerful. Visibility is not the limit of action. The wind also speaks of "cleansing" (Job 37:21).

e. *Fire.* "There appeared unto them cloven tongues like as a fire, and it sat upon each of them" (Acts 2:3). Fire signifies the Spirit of God. It is fire which purifies, consumes, warms, tests, illuminates and energizes. It is the same with the Holy Spirit.

f. *Clothing.* "The Spirit of Jehovah clothed himself with Gideon; and he blew a trumpet; and Abiezer was gathered together after him" (Judg. 6:34, R.V.). Clothing speaks of protection. The Spirit is our Protection.

ANTHROPOLOGY
(The Doctrine of Man)

Outline for Chapter IV

ANTHROPOLOGY

I. Man in His State of Integrity.
   - A. His Origin.
   - B. His Nature.
   - C. His Constitution.
   - D. His Condition.
   - E. His Headship.

II. Man in His State of Sin.
   - A. The Fall of Man.
   - B. The Fallen Sons of Adam.

III. Man in His State of Grace.
   - A. His Standing.
   - B. His State.
   - C. His Two Natures.

Chapter IV

ANTHROPOLOGY

Anthropology comes from the Greek word "anthropos," meaning "man." Anthropology is the doctrine of man. There are many different definitions of man, some comical, some tragic. In this study of anthropology we shall go to the true source – the Scriptures.

Man has always wanted to know *who* he is, where he *came from,* and where he is *going.* God's Holy Word gives the only complete account.

I. Man in His State of Integrity

By this we mean man in his original state of purity, his uprightness.

A. His Origin.

1. *Negative.*

a. *Not by Abiogenesis or Spontaneous Generation.* This theory holds to the belief that there was no creator of man, but that man simply came into being without a cause and began to exist, fulfilling the nursery rhyme, which reads:

> Where did you come from, Baby dear?
> Out of the nowhere, into here!

This argument needs no answer, but in order to forestall criticism, we simply state that if such a thing as abiogenesis were possible, there would be no power to keep it from happening again. There is no record of a second occurrence, and, of course, it never happened in the first place.

b. *Not by Evolution or Natural Developments.* A short definition of evolution is: "That process by which, through some kind of aggregation of matter through many ages and species, by chance or by law, man appears." This concept has held sway for many years, but its adherents are on the decline. Modern science, such as anthropology, is refuting all of its claims. The Bible declares that man is a separate creation of

God, and that the animals were created at a different time, completely apart from man. Evolution teaches that man and animals have a common origin, which branched out into the different species. In refuting this we use the Scriptures and human reasoning as follows:

(1) *It is Opposed to Scripture.* The Scriptures state: "After his kind" (Gen. 1:24). This pins the species down to themselves, forbidding them to evolve into a completely new species.

(2) *There is No Record of Animal Becoming Man.* Surely, in six thousand years, if evolution were true, there would be living examples of it today.

(3) *There is No Evidence that the Missing Link Has Been Found.* Many so-called history books show pictures of the creature they term as the missing link. These pictures are photographs of drawings, and not photographs of real creatures, as none of these exist. The "missing link," we are told, is that creature between man and the ape. Its picture is wholly the imagination of the artist who took a piece of a bone or tooth and built a man around it. It is the same as a man taking a key hole and building a house around it. We would like to quote William Jennings Bryan concerning the "missing link": "If the missing link has been found, why are they still looking for it?"

(4) *There is No Evidence that Primitive Man Differed From Man Today.*

(5) *There Is Proof that Human Blood is One Blood.* (Acts 17:26). World War II has proved this. The blood of a white man can be placed into the veins of a black man, and vice versa, and give life. Blood transfusions have only been in practice during the last hundred years, but God revealed this to us several thousand years ago.

(6) *There is a Great Difference Between the Constitution of Man and Animal.*

(a) *Physically.* Man is an upright being, while animals are on all fours.

(b) *Mentally.* Man has *intellect,* while animals have instinct.

(c) *Morally.* Man is the only creature of God that has moral qualities.

(d) *Spiritually.* Man alone has been created with

spiritual concepts. He alone of all the creatures can worship God.

2. *Positive.* Man is a direct creation of God. "God created man in his own image, in the image of God created he him; male and female created he them" (Gen. 1:27).

B. His Nature.

1. *Original Image of Man.* "God said, Let us make man in our image, after our likeness" (Gen. 1:26a). "Whoso sheddeth man's blood, by man shall his blood be shed: for in the image of God made he man" (Gen. 9:6). See also I Corinthians 11:7; James 3:9.

a. *Seen in Man's Triunity.* "The LORD God formed man out of the dust of the ground, and breathed into his nostrils the breath of life; and man became a living soul" (Gen. 2:7). "The very God of peace sanctify you wholly: and I pray God your whole *spirit* and *soul* and *body* be preserved blameless unto the coming of our Lord Jesus Christ" (I Thess. 5:23).

b. *Seen in Man's Intellectual and Moral Nature.* "Lie not one to another, seeing that ye have put off the old man with his deeds; and have put on the new man, which is renewed in knowledge after the image of him that created him" (Col. 3:9, 10). See also Ephesians 4:24.

c. *Seen in Physical Likeness.* It is true that God is a Spirit (John 4:24); God is invisible (Col. 1:15). Yet God has always had a form in which He manifests Himself: "As for me, I shall behold thy face in righteousness; I shall be satisfied, when I awake with beholding thy form" (Ps. 17:15, R.V.). See also Philippians 2:6, 7; Mark 15:12; John 5:37, R.V.

Christ was not made in the form or image of Adam, but Adam was made in the form, or image of Christ, who was to come: "Nevertheless death reigned from Adam to Moses, even over them that had not sinned after the similitude of Adam's transgression, who is the *figure* of him that was to come" (Rom. 5:14).

2. *Original Innocence of Man.* Some declare that Adam was created in holiness, or righteousness. This is not quite correct. Man was created perfect, yes, but he was created in innocence. There is a vast difference between innocence and righteousness. Innocence is sinlessness that has never faced trial. Righteousness is innocence that has been tested and tried, and has come out victorious.

C. His Constitution.

As we shall see, man is composed of earthly (Gen. 2:7) and spiritual elements (I Thess. 5:23; Heb. 4:12).

1. *Body.* His body was made from the earth. This was the first part of man that was formed. "The LORD God formed man of the dust of the ground, and breathed into his nostrils the breath of life; and man became a living soul" (Gen. 2:7). The body is set forth in Scripture as the house of the inner man. "How much less in them that dwell in houses of clay, whose foundation is the dust, which are crushed before the moth?" (Job 4:19). See also II Corinthians 5:1, 3, 4. The process by which God made man is not known; we leave that up to God. Men give their opinions and speculations, but they remain as such. The word "dust" does not mean clay, or old dirty dirt, but the finest materials of the earth.

a. *Analysis Proves Man's Source.* Modern chemical analysis detects in the body the same elements that are in the earth beneath man's feet; such elements as sodium, carbon, iron, and the like.

b. *Earth Sustains Man's Existence.* The body is sustained by that which grows out of the earth. It is man's body and not his spirit that is sustained. Famine in our modern day has proved that if vegetation is taken away, life is taken away. *Kill vegetation and you kill man.*

c. *Death Substantiates Man's Elements.* At death corruption sets in, and man's body soon returns to the dust from which it was formed. "In the sweat of thy face shalt thou eat bread, till thou return unto the ground; for out of it wast thou taken: for dust thou art, and unto dust shalt thou return" (Gen. 3:19).

2. *Soul.* "The LORD God formed man of the dust of the ground, and breathed into his nostrils the breath of life; and man became a living soul" (Gen. 2:7). See also I Corinthians 15:45. The soul is the seat of the emotions and appetites. Plants, animals and man have bodies; only animals and man have a soul; but only man has a spirit. The soul is that *conscious* life which is in man and animal. Plants have life, but it is *unconscious* life. There is a difference between the souls of men and the souls of animals. The animal's soul is connected with his *body,* while man's soul is connected with his *spirit.* The soul of an animal dies with the animal, but man's soul

never dies, for he was made a "living soul" – a soul that would never die.

As stated, the soul of man is the seat of his emotions and appetites, and the following Scriptures will bring out the degrees of same: *Appetites*: "Thou mayest kill and eat flesh in all thy gates, whatsoever thy soul lusteth after, according to the blessing of the LORD thy God which he hath given thee: the unclean and the clean may eat thereof, as of the roebuck, and as of the hart" (Deut. 12:15). *Desires*: "If any man said unto him, Let them not fail to burn the fat presently, and then take as much as thy soul desireth; then he would answer him, Nay; but thou shalt give it me now: and if not, I will take it by force" (I Sam. 2:16). See also Deuteronomy 12:20; Psalm 107:18; Proverbs 6:30; Isaiah 29:8; I Samuel 18:1. *Hates*: "David said on that day, Whosoever getteth up to the gutter, and smiteth the Jebusites, and the lame and the blind, that are hated of David's soul, he shall be chief and captain. Wherefore they said, The blind and the lame shall not come into the house" (II Sam. 5:8). *Mourns*: "His flesh upon him shall have pain, and his soul within him shall mourn" (Job 14:22). *Is Vexed*: "The man of God said, Let her alone; for her soul is vexed within her: and the LORD hath hid it from me, and hath not told me" (II Kings 4:27b). *Rejoices*: "I will greatly rejoice in the LORD, my soul shall be joyful in my God; for he hath clothed me with the garments of salvation, he hath covered me with a robe of righteousness, as a bridegroom decketh himself with ornaments, and as a bride adorneth herself with her jewels" (Is. 61:10). *Suffers*: "They said one to another, We are verily guilty concerning our brother, in that we saw the anguish of his soul, when he besought us, and we would not hear; therefore is this distress come upon us" (Gen. 42:21). *Sorrows*: "He said unto them, My soul is exceeding sorrowful unto death: tarry ye here, and watch" (Mark 14:34).

Where does man get his soul?

a. *Pre-existence*. This theory teaches that all souls that have ever been in the world, or shall ever be in the world, were created in the beginning. At time of conception, they are united with the body. This was taught by Plato, but it was never accepted by the church, as it is without Scriptural foundation.

b. *Creationism*. This belief holds that after forty days

of conception the soul unites with the body. Roman Catholicism proposes this. If this belief is true, then God is the creator of sinful souls.

c. *Traducianism.* This is the truth which holds that both soul and body are derived from the parents. "Adam lived a hundred and thirty years, and begat a son in his own likeness, after his image; and called his name Seth" (Gen. 5:3). See also Acts 17:24-26.

3. *Spirit.* Here is where man differs from all creatures. In Hebrews 12:9 God is said to be "Father of spirits." This does not mean the Father of angels, but of the spirits of men made perfect. God is never said to be the Father of souls.

"As the body without the spirit is dead, so faith without works is dead also" (Jas. 2:26). When a body dies, the soul departs with the spirit of man. The soul and spirit can be separated "the word of God is quick, and powerful, and sharper than any twoedged sword, piercing even to the dividing asunder of soul and spirit, and of the joints and marrow, and is a discerner of the thoughts and intents of the heart" (Heb. 4:12). However, there is no Scriptural proof that they are ever separated. The rich man of Luke 16 goes to Hades upon death, and he has both soul and spirit with him. See also Matthew 10:28.

The spirit of man is the seat of his intelligence. "What man knoweth the things of a man, save the spirit of man which is in him? even so the things of God knoweth no man, but the Spirit of God" (I Cor. 2:11). Animals do not possess intelligence. "Be ye not as the horse, or as the mule, which have no understanding: whose mouth must be held in with bit and bridle, lest they come near unto thee" (Ps. 32:9).

The word "spirit," both in the Hebrew and Greek, is sometimes translated as "breath," and "wind." The context determines the translation.

The materialists say that the word for spirit should be "breath," and that when man dies he is gone forever.

Some people say that man lost his spirit at the Fall and regains his spirit at conversion. This would make him a dual being however, and this conception has no Scriptural grounds.

4. *Heart.* When we speak of the heart, we do not mean the muscle in the body, but rather the seat of conscience. "Let us draw near with a true heart in full assurance of faith, having

our hearts sprinkled from an evil conscience, and our bodies washed with pure water" (Heb. 10:22). See also I John 3:19, 20; Acts 2:26; 5:3, 5; Matthew 22:37. There is a warning that there may be a profession without a possession, a head knowledge without a heart trust. "Not every one that saith unto me, Lord, Lord, shall enter into the kingdom of heaven; but he that doeth the will of the Father which is in heaven" See also Matthew 7:22, 23.

D. His Condition.

By this we mean man's condition in his state of integrity before he fell.

1. *His Knowledge.* He had immediate knowledge, intuitive knowledge. He was not an adult infant. He named all animals that came from the hand of God; It would take an intelligent man to do this. "Adam gave names to all cattle, and to the fowl of the air, and to every beast of the field; but for Adam there was not found an help meet for him" (Gen. 2:20).

2. *His Fellowship.* He was able to commune with God. "The LORD God commanded the man saying, Of every tree of the garden thou mayest freely eat" (Gen. 2:16). "God said, Behold, I have given you every herb bearing seed, which is upon the face of all the earth, and every tree, in the which is the fruit of a tree yielding seed; to you it shall be for meat" (Gen. 1:29).

3. *His Home.* It was located in a garden. "The LORD God planted a garden eastward in Eden; and there he put the man whom he had formed" (Gen. 2:8). Some men claim that primitive man was a cave man, but this was not so, for he was a garden man. The first records we have of men living in caves are of the persecuted: "Of whom the world was not worthy; they wandered in deserts, and in mountains, and in dens and caves of the earth" (Heb. 11:38), and of the insane: "when he was come out of the ship, immediately there met him out of the tombs a man with an unclean spirit" (Mark 5:2).

This garden is not called Eden, but rather, the Garden in Eden. "Eden" means plains, or plateau. Armenia, no doubt, is the place where man began.

4. *His Companion.* "For Adam there was not found an help meet for him. . . . And the rib, which the LORD God had taken from man, made he a woman, and brought her unto the

man" (Gen. 2:20, 22). The words "help meet" are not a compound word, but two separate ones, meaning "fit for." Eve was "fit for" Adam. Some who laugh at this "rib story" cannot tell us where woman did come from. Why do you suppose God did not make woman from the dust? For the simple reason that God did not want to have two origins of man.

God can make a human being in four ways:

By conception.
Without the aid of a woman, as Eve.
Without a man or woman, as Adam.
Without a man, by a woman, as Christ.

5. *His Work.* "God blessed them, and God said unto them, Be fruitful, and multiply, and replenish the earth, and subdue it: and have dominion over the fish of the sea, and over the fowl of the air, and over every living thing that moveth upon the earth" (Gen. 1:28). "The LORD God took the man, and put him into the garden of Eden to dress it and to keep it" (Gen. 2:15). There was employment in the garden, but no toil. There was work, but not the kind that wears one out. The word "keep" in Genesis 2:15 is best translated "guard." Against whom was Adam to guard the garden? Against wild animals? No, there were none. Against wild men? No, for Adam was the only man. He was put on his guard against the possible appearance of the Devil. Whenever man is placed in a position of trust, God always gives ample warning.

6. *His Food.* "God said, Behold, I have given you every herb bearing seed, which is upon the face of all the earth, and every tree, in the which is the fruit of a tree yielding seed; to you it shall be for meat" (Gen. 1:29). The first man and beast of the field were vegetarians. Their diets included no meat. Man was not carnivorous as evolutionists claim.

7. *His Responsibility.*

a. *To Replenish the Earth With a New Order – Man.* "God blessed them and God said unto them, Be fruitful, and multiply, and replenish the earth, and subdue it" (Gen. 1:28). Adam was the first man: "The first man Adam was made a living soul" (I Cor. 15:45). Eve is the mother of all human beings. "Adam called his wife's name Eve; because she was the mother of all living" (Gen. 3:20).

b. *To Abstain from Eating of the Fruit.* This fruit was of the tree of the knowledge of Good and Evil. "The LORD

God commanded the man saying, Of every tree of the garden thou mayest freely eat: but of the tree of the knowledge of good and evil, thou shalt not eat of it: for in the day that thou eatest thereof thou shalt surely die" (Gen. 2:16, 17).

They were allowed to eat freely, as there was plenty. There was only one tree forbidden them. We do not know what kind of fruit it was. Nothing was wrong with the fruit; there was just God's prohibition behind it. God wanted Adam and Eve to have knowledge, but he did not want them to gain it by disobedience. Remember, man had been placed on his guard; he had been warned of the enemy; Satan did not come in unawares. This being true, why did God allow Adam and Eve to be subjected to the attack of the Devil? Testing always comes before a blessing. Man always has to be tried before he is promoted.

E. His Headship.

The entire human race comes from that one man, Adam. As is the head, so are the descendants.

1. *Ethnography.* This is the branch of anthropology that considers man geographically and descriptively, treating of the subdivision of races, the causes of migration, and related matters. This science points to a common homeland – Armenia.

2. *Comparative Philology.* This is the science of language, and it considers that men all come from the same origin.

3. *Psychology.* This is the science of the mind, and it also indicates that man comes from one origin.

4. *Physiology.* This is the science that deals with the organic structure of the body, and it declares that all men come from the same source, a common origin.

II. Man in His State of Sin

A. The Fall of Man.

Some may say that the fall of man is an old Babylonian fable, but we have only to look upon man and see him toil for his bread, weaken in his diseases, and die in his misery, to realize that he has had a fall. "By one man sin entered into the world, and death by sin; and so death passed upon all men, for that all have sinned" (Rom. 5:12).

1. *The Source of Sin.* "Now the serpent was more subtle than any beast of the field which the Lord God had made. And he said unto the woman, Yea, hath God said, Ye shall not eat of every tree of the garden?" (Gen. 3:1). "I fear, lest by

any means, as the serpent beguiled Eve through his subtlety, so your minds should be corrupted from the simplicity that is in Christ" (II Cor. 11:3). God is not speaking about a beast when He mentions the serpent, but a person. Notice that the Scripture does not say, "more subtle than any *other* beast of the field," but leaves out the word "other," stating only that he is more subtle than *any* beast. This is merely a statement of what God thinks of the Devil. Nowhere in Scripture does it state that the Devil was *in* the serpent, but it does say that the serpent *was* the Devil. "He laid hold on the dragon, that old serpent, which is the Devil, and Satan, and bound him a thousand years" (Rev. 20:2).

2. *The Nature of Sin.* "The serpent said unto the woman, Ye shall not surely die: For God doth know that in the day ye eat thereof, then your eyes shall be opened, and ye shall be as gods, knowing good and evil. And when the woman saw that the tree was good for food, and that it was pleasant to the eyes, and a tree to be desired to make one wise, she took of the fruit thereof, and did eat, and gave also unto her husband with her; and he did eat" (Gen. 3:4-6). Now the fruit was all right; it was good fruit, with only the prohibition of God behind it. Some people may contend that it was a small thing to bring about man's downfall, but we ask the question, "How many steps does it take to fall off a bluff?"

a. *He Doubted God's Love.* In doubting God's love, man denied God's goodness, and acted apart from God and became a sinner. "There is a way which seemeth right unto a man, but the end thereof are the ways of death" (Prov. 14:12). See also Isaiah 55:6.

b. *He Doubted God's Word.* In doubting God's Word, man denied His Truth; denying His Truth, he acted in spite of God and became a criminal. "Whosoever committeth sin transgresseth also the law: for sin is the transgression of the law" (I John 3:4).

c. *He Doubted God's Authority.* In doubting God's authority, man denied God's deity; denying His deity, he became contrary to God. Thus, he became God's enemy and a rebel in God's universe. "The carnal mind is enmity against God: for it is not subject to the law of God, neither indeed can be. So then they that are in the flesh cannot please God" (Rom. 8:7, 8).

The testing was given to see if man would stay true to God. He failed because he wanted to be a god. The Devil himself fell (Is. 14), because he wanted to be like the Most High God. This brought about his downfall, so he planted the same seed of false ambition in Adam and Eve to see if it would bring about their downfall, and it did.

Some may ask, "Was this fair to them?" They were warned and placed on guard against Satan. There was only one prohibition in the garden. They did not need the fruit; they lacked nothing.

3. *The Effects of Sin.*

a. *Immediate Effects Upon Eve.*

(1) *Shame.* "They both were naked, the man and his wife, and were not ashamed. . . . And the eyes of them both were opened, and they knew that they were naked; and they sewed fig leaves together, and made themselves aprons" (Gen. 2:25; 3:7). God Himself is clothed with a garment of light (Ps. 104:2); and when He made man, he made him in His own image and likeness. Thus, we believe that man also was clothed with a garment of light. When man sinned, that clothing of light was lost, and he made himself a fig leaf covering to take the place of that which was lost. Ever since, man has tried to put on what God once gave him, but he has nothing but filthy rags.

(2) *Fear.* "He said, I heard thy voice in the garden, and I was afraid, because I was naked; and I hid myself" (Gen. 3:10). Man still tries to hide from God.

(3) *Separation from God.* There is no doubt that man lost his perfect nature and ended his fellowship with God. There is no such thing as the Fatherhood of God and the brotherhood of man of the *natural* man, the unsaved man.

(4) *Expulsion from the Garden.* "The Lord God sent him forth from the garden of Eden to till the ground from whence he was taken. So he drove out the man; and he placed at the end of the garden of Eden cherubims, and a flaming sword, which turned every way to keep the way of the tree of life" (Gen. 3:23, 24). Man was *driven* out.

(5) *Lost Lordship Over Creation.* In the beginning Adam was indeed the ruler of all earthly creatures: "Thou madest him to have dominion over the works of thy hands; thou hast put all things under his feet: all sheep and oxen,

yea, and the beast of the field; the fowl of the air, and the fish of the sea, and whatsoever passeth through the paths of the sea" (Ps. 8:6-8). This is not true of man today. He has lost that lordship. Christ will return it to man when He comes again (Heb. 2 and Is. 11).

b. *Remote Effects Upon Adam's Posterity.*

(1) *The Spirit is Darkened.* "This I say therefore, and testify in the Lord, that ye henceforth walk not as other Gentiles walk, in the vanity of their mind, having the understanding darkened, being alienated from the life of God through the ignorance that is in them, because of the blindness of their heart" (Eph. 4:17, 18). The darkened room of understanding will remain darkened until the Holy Spirit comes in to illuminate.

(2) *The Soul Is Debased and Corrupt.* Unbelievers, "being past feeling have given themselves over unto lasciviousness to work all uncleanness with greediness" (Eph. 4:19). See also Jeremiah 17:9.

(3) *The Body Is Subjected to Disease and Death.* "The creature itself also shall be delivered from the bondage of corruption into the glorious liberty of the children of God" (Rom. 8:21).

4. *The Effects on Sin.*

a. *The Immediate Expression of God's Judgment.*

(1) *On the Serpent.* "The LORD God said unto the serpent, Because thou hast done this, thou art cursed above all cattle, and above every beast of the field; upon thy belly shalt thou go, and dust shalt thou eat all the days of thy life: and I will put enmity between thee and the woman, and between thy seed and her seed; it shall bruise thy head, and thou shalt bruise his heel" (Gen. 3:14, 15). Satan, in all of his majesty, is considered nothing but a serpent. This is a figure of speech, for we know that snakes do not eat dust. God's decree unto the serpent that he should eat dust all the days of his life, showed the contempt in which He held the Devil.

(2) *On the Woman.* "Unto the woman he said, I will greatly multiply thy sorrow and thy conception; in sorrow shalt thou bring forth children; and thy desire shall be to thy husband, and he shall rule over thee" (Gen. 3:16).

(3) *On Creation.* "Unto Adam he said, Because thou hast hearkened unto the voice of thy wife, and hast eaten of the

tree, of which I commanded thee, saying, Thou shalt not eat of it: cursed is the ground for thy sake; in sorrow shalt thou eat of it all the days of thy life; thorns also and thistles shall it bring forth to thee; and thou shalt eat the herb of the field" (Gen. 3:17, 18).

(4) *On Man.* "In the sweat of thy face shalt thou eat bread till thou return unto the ground; for out of it wast thou taken: for dust thou art, and unto dust shalt thou return" (Gen. 3:19). See also Genesis 5:29.

b. *The Future Expression of God's Judgment.* "The fearful, and unbelieving, and the abominable, and murderers, and whoremongers, and sorcerers, and idolators, and all liars, shall have their part in the lake which burneth with fire and brimstone: which is the second death" (Rev. 21:8).

5. *The Provision for the Sinner.* "I will put enmity between thee and the woman, and between thy seed and her seed; it shall bruise thy head, and thou shalt bruise his heel" (Gen. 3:15). In the hour that man sinned, God promised a Redeemer. The Seed of the woman is no one else but Jesus Christ. "Unto Adam also and to his wife did the LORD God make coats of skin, and clothe them" (Gen. 3:21). When they realized their nakedness, they covered themselves with aprons of fig leaves. God clothed them with animal skins instead. As far as covering their nakedness was concerned, fig leaves were as good as animal skins; however, *blood* had to be spilt – "For without the shedding of blood there is no remission of sin." They had to be covered with that which was slain for their sins. Likewise, the sinner today has to be clothed with the righteousness of Him who died for them.

B. The Fallen Sons of Adam.

1. *Their Standing.*

a. *In Adam.* "Since by man came death, by man came also the resurrection of the dead. For as in Adam all die, even so in Christ shall all be made alive" (I Cor. 15:21, 22). See also I Corinthians 15:45, 47; Romans 5:12-21. There are only two representative men in the world: the first man and the second man; the first Adam and the last Adam. All men are born in Adam; all born-again men are in Christ.

b. *Of Sin and Guilt.* "What then? are we better than they? No, in no wise: for we have before proved both Jews and Gentiles, that they are all under sin, as it is written, There is none righteous, no, not one" (Rom. 3:9, 10). See also Romans 3:19.

2. *Their State.* By their state we mean their spiritual condition; that is, the absence of righteousness in their spiritual life.

a. *Sinful in Nature.* "Behold, I was shapen in iniquity; and in sin did my mother conceive me" (Ps. 51:5). See also Ephesians 2:3; Genesis 6:5; Jeremiah 17:9; Romans 8:7; Galatians 5:19-21.

b. *Sinful in Practice.* "We ourselves also were sometimes foolish, disobedient, deceived, serving divers lusts and pleasures, living in malice and envy, hateful, and hating one another" (Titus 3:3). See also Romans 3:23; Colossians 1:21; Psalm 14:1-3.

c. *Lost in Sin.* "The Son of man is come to seek and to save that which was lost" (Luke 19:10). See also Isaiah 53:6; II Corinthians 4:3, 4.

d. *Spiritually Dead.* "You hath he quickened who were dead in trespasses and sins. . . . Even when we were dead in sins, hath quickened us together with Christ, by grace are ye saved" (Eph. 2:1, 5). God's picture of a sinner is a dead man, a man with all of the organs of movement, but no motion. Likewise, the sinner cannot move in the things of God.

e. *Under God's Wrath.* "The wrath of God is revealed from heaven against all ungodliness and unrighteousness of men, who hold the truth in unrighteousness" (Rom. 1:18). See also John 3:36.

f. *Waits for Death.* "It is appointed unto men once to die, but after this the judgment. . . ." (Heb. 9:27).

g. *Sure of Hell.* "Whosoever was not found written in the book of life was cast into the lake of fire" (Rev. 20:15). See also Revelation 21:8.

III. Man in His State of Grace

A. *His Standing.*

1. *In Christ.* "As in Adam all die, even so in Christ shall all be made alive" (I Cor. 15:22). See also I Corinthians 15:21, 45, 47; Romans 5:12-21.

2. *Of Perfection.* "According as he hath chosen us in him before the foundation of the world, that we should be holy

and without blame before him in love. . . . To the praise of the glory of his grace, wherein he hath made us accepted in the beloved" (Eph. 1:4, 6). There are no charges against the Head; and, as that is so, there can be no charges against the Body.

B. His State.

By this we mean his spiritual condition. This differs from the life of the unbeliever. In the believer's life righteousness is present – the righteousness of the Lord Jesus Christ.

1. *A New Creature.* "If any man be in Christ, he is a new creature: old things are passed away, behold, all things are become new" (II Cor. 5:17). See also II Peter 1:4; Galatians 6:15; John 3:16. Regeneration is a re-creation. Only God can create; only God can re-create.

2. *Saved.* "Who hath saved us, and called us with an holy calling, not according to our works, but according to his own purpose and grace, which was given us in Christ Jesus before the world began" (II Tim. 1:9). See also Ephesians 2:8, 9.

3. *Dead Unto Sin.* "Likewise reckon ye also yourselves to be dead indeed unto sin, but alive unto God through Jesus Christ our Lord" (Rom. 6:11). "Who his ownself bare our sins in his own body on the tree, that we, being dead to sins, should live unto righteousness: by whose stripes ye were healed" (I Peter 2:24).

4. *Child of God.* "As many as received him, to them gave he power to become the sons of God, even to them that believe on his name" (John 1:12). "Ye are all the children of God by faith in Christ Jesus" (Gal. 3:26).

5. *Under God's Favor.* "Blessed be the God and Father of our Lord Jesus Christ, who hath blessed us with all spiritual blessings in heavenly places in Christ" (Eph. 1:3). See also Romans 5:2.

6. *Waits for God and Glory.* "Our conversation is in heaven; from whence also we look for the Saviour, the Lord Jesus Christ: Who shall change our vile body, that it may be fashioned like unto his glorious body, according to the working whereby he is able to subdue all things unto himself" (Phil. 3:20, 21).

7. *Sure of Heaven.* "The Lord shall deliver me from every evil work, and will preserve me unto his heavenly kingdom: to whom be glory for ever and ever. Amen" (II Tim. 4:18). See also I Peter 1:4.

C. His Two Natures.

"The flesh lusteth against the Spirit, and the Spirit against the flesh: and these are contrary the one to the other: so that ye cannot do the things that ye would" (Gal. 5:17). The above Scriptures could not describe anyone but a saved man. The sinner has but one nature; the child of God has two natures. Every true believer has experienced the warfare of which Paul speaks. This warfare is best demonstrated by the household of Abraham. He had two sons – Ishmael, the older; and Isaac, the younger. Ishmael stands for that born of the flesh, while Isaac stands for that born of the Spirit. The trouble started when Isaac came into the household. Trouble comes into a Christian's life when Christ enters in.

1. *The Description of the Old Nature.*

a. *Names and Characteristics.*

(1) *The Flesh.* "That which is born of the flesh is flesh" (John 3:6). See also Romans 7:18, 23; 8:9. By "the flesh" we do not mean "muscles and sinews," which are part of the human body, but rather the carnal nature, which all possess at birth. There is no such thing as our being in the flesh; the flesh is in us. No man has ever begotten an unfallen man. "For I know that in me (that is, in my flesh,) dwelleth no good thing" (Rom. 7:18a). See also John 6:63; Romans 8:8. There is no such thing as a person being born with a "divine spark" within them.

(2) *The Natural Man.* "The natural man receiveth not the things of the Spirit of God: for they are foolishness unto him: neither can he know them, because they are spiritually discerned" (I Cor. 2:14). This is what man is by nature, by his natural birth.

(3) *The Old Man.* "Our old man is crucified with him, that the body of sin might be destroyed, that henceforth we should not serve sin" (Rom. 6:6). See also Ephesians 4:22; Colossians 3:9. This is the man of old – what we once were: corrupt, full of evil desires and lusts.

(4) *The Outward Man.* "Though our outward man perish, yet the inward man is renewed day by day" (II Cor. 4:16).

(5) *The Heart.* "From within, out of the heart of men, proceed evil thoughts, adulteries, fornications, murders, thefts, covetousness, wickedness, deceit, lasciviousness, an evil

eye, blasphemy, pride, foolishness: all these evil things come from within, and defile the man" (Mark 7:21-23). We hear so much of man having a change of heart, but this is impossible, for only God can give a new heart.

(6) *The Carnal Mind.* "The carnal mind is enmity against God: for it is not subject to the law of God, neither indeed can be" (Rom. 8:7).

(7) *Sin.* "By one man *sin* entered into the world, and death by sin; and so death passed upon all men, for that all have sinned" (Rom. 5:12). The word "sin" refers to the fallen nature of man, while "sins" refer to the actions of this nature.

b. *The Character and End.*

(1) *It Is an Adam's Nature.* This means that Adam fell, and his children are, therefore, fallen children of a fallen father.

(2) *It Is an Inherited Nature.* We receive our fallen nature from Adam.

(3) *It Is an Evil Nature.* The eighth chapter of Romans is a commentary on this point.

(4) *It Is an Unchangeable Nature.* "That which is born of the flesh is flesh" (John 3:6a). As long as man lives, that fallen nature remains in him. It will be eradicated only at the resurrection of the dead in Christ, and the transformation of those alive in Christ, at His second appearing.

(5) *Its End Is Death.* "The wages of sin is death" (Rom. 6:23a). See also Romans 8:5-13.

2. *The Description of the New Nature.*

a. *Its Names and Characteristics.*

(1) *Spirit.* "That which is born of the flesh is flesh; and that which is born of the Spirit is spirit" (John 3:6).

(2) *Divine Nature.* There "are given unto us exceeding great and precious promises: that by these ye might be partakers of the divine nature, having escaped the correction that is in the world through lust" (II Peter 1:4). See also I John 3:9; 5:18, 19.

(3) *The New Man.* "Put on the new man, which after God is created in righteousness and true holiness" (Eph. 4:24). See also Colossians 3:10; II Corinthians 5:17.

(4) *The Inward Man.* "Though our outward man perish, yet the inward man is renewed day by day" (II Cor.

4:16). "I delight in the law of God after the inward man" (Rom. 7:22). See also Ephesians 3:16.

(5) *Mind.* "I thank God through Jesus Christ our Lord. So then with the mind I myself serve the law of God: but with the flesh the law of sin" (Rom. 7:25).

b. *Its Character and End.*

(1) *It Is a Christly Nature.*

(2) *It Is an Imparted Nature.*

(3) *It Is a Holy Nature.*

(4) *It Is an Unchangeable Nature.*

(5) *It Is a Non-forfeited Nature.*

Verses 1 and 2 of I John 2 speak of the relation of the saint with the Father. Even when the saint sins it is a family matter.

(6) *Its End is Resurrection and Rapture.* "Behold, I shew you a mystery; we shall not all sleep, but we shall all be changed, in a moment, in the twinkling of an eye, at the last trump: for the trumpet shall sound, and the dead shall be raised incorruptible, and we shall be changed. For this corruptible shall put on incorruption, and this mortal shall put on immortality. . . . But thanks be to God, which giveth *us* the victory through our Lord Jesus Christ" (I Cor. 15:51-53, 57).

3. *The Conflict Between the Two Natures.*

a. *The Believer's Experience.* Every child of God has two natures; the unsaved man has only one nature. The old nature cannot be eradicated while the believer lives in the flesh; therefore, we have the fight between the old and new natures. "The flesh lusteth against the Spirit, and the Spirit against the flesh: and these are contrary the one to the other: so that ye cannot do the things that ye would" (Gal. 5:17). Romans 7:15-25 is another marvelous example illustrating this truth. However, someone may declare that this passage shows the conflict in Paul's life *before* he was saved, but one verse in this passage clearly reveals that this conflict, so vividly described, occurred *after* he was saved: "I delight in the law of God after the inward man" (Rom. 7:22). *No unsaved man ever delights after the law of God.* Also, only the saved man has the *inward man,* which is the new nature.

b. *The Believer's Responsibility.*

(1) *In Relation to the Old Nature.*

(a) *Accept God's Estimate of It.* "Our old man is crucified with him, that the body of sin might be destroyed, that henceforth we should not serve sin. For he that is dead is freed from sin. Now if we be dead with Christ, we believe that we shall also live with him: knowing that Christ being raised from the dead dieth no more; death hath no more dominion over him. For in that he died, he died unto sin once: but in that he liveth, he liveth unto God. Likewise reckon ye also yourselves to be dead indeed unto sin, but alive unto God through Jesus Christ our Lord" (Rom. 6:6-11). This one truth must be pointed out: the old man is never said to be crucified *in* the believer, but is crucified *with Christ.* It is a reality! Accept it! It is not a matter of feeling, but one of faith. All of this truth is according to God's view. As for the believer's view, he knows that the old nature, the old man, is not dead; he is very much alive. The Scripture says, "Reckon ye also yourselves to be dead indeed unto sin." If the old nature were actually dead, the believer would not have to *reckon* him so; he would *know.*

(b) *Make No Provision for the Flesh.* "Put ye on the Lord Jesus Christ, and make not provision for the flesh, to fulfill the lusts thereof" (Rom. 13:14). In other words, do not feed the flesh. Starve it.

(c) *Mortify the Flesh.* "Mortify therefore your members which are upon the earth; fornication, uncleanness, inordinate affection, evil concupiscence, and covetousness, which is idolatry" (Col. 3:5). A stronger term is, "Put to death, therefore, your members." The words "as good as dead" (Heb. 11:12) are the same terminology.

(d) *Never Try to Improve It.* "Neither yield your members as instruments of unrighteousness unto sin: but yield yourselves unto God, as those that are alive from the dead, and your members as instruments of righteousness unto God" (Rom. 6:13).

(e) *Put It Off.* "Put off concerning the form of conversation the old man, which is corrupt according to the deceitful lusts" (Eph. 4:22). The same word is translated "laid down" in Acts 7:58.

(2) *In Relation to the New Nature.*

(a) *Reckon Ourselves to Be Alive.* "Reckon ye also yourselves to be dead indeed unto sin, but *alive* unto God through Jesus Christ our Lord" (Rom. 6:11).

(b) *Walk in Newness of Life.* "We are his workmanship, created unto good works, which God hath before ordained that we should walk in them" (Eph. 2:10). See also Romans 6:14; 7:6.

(c) *Feed and Nourish It.* "As newborn babes, desire the sincere milk of the word, that ye may grow thereby" (I Peter 2:2). We are to feed the new nature by the exposition of the Word, and not by the exhortation of man. We know we have two natures, and it is well to consider that the food for one will starve the other. It is the individual Christian who must decide which man, the old or the new, shall be fed. He cannot feed both at the same time.

(d) *Put On the New Man.* "Put on the new man, which after God is created in righteousness and true holiness" (Eph. 4:24).

(e) *Depend Upon the Indwelling Spirit for Power.* "Grieve not the Holy Spirit of God, whereby ye are sealed unto the day of redemption" (Eph. 4:30). "My brethren, be strong in the Lord, and in the power of his might" (Eph. 6:10). "Not by might, nor by power, but by my spirit, saith the LORD of hosts" (Zech. 4:6b).

HAMARTIOLOGY
(The Doctrine of Sin)

Outline for Chapter V

HAMARTIOLOGY

I. The Origin of Sin.
   - A. The Entrance of Sin into the Universe.
   - B. The Introduction of Sin into the Human Race.

II. The Reality of Sin.
   - A. Scripture Declares the Fact of Sin.
   - B. Nature Proclaims the Fact of Sin.
   - C. Law Discovers the Fact of Sin.
   - D. Experience Proves the Fact of Sin.
   - E. Man Confesses the Fact of Sin.

III. The Nature of Sin.
   - A. The Modern View of Sin.
   - B. The Biblical View of Sin.
   - C. The Scriptural Statement of Sin.
   - D. The Theological Definitions of Sin.
   - E. The Summary of Scripture Concerning Sin.

IV. The Extent of Sin.
   - A. As to the Heavens.
   - B. As to the Earth.

V. The Realm of Sin.
   - A. As an Act.
   - B. As a State.
   - C. As a Nature.

VI. The Penalty of Sin.
   - A. The Natural Penalty.
   - B. The Positive Penalty.

Chapter V

HAMARTIOLOGY

Hamartiology is derived from the Greek word, *hamartia,* meaning "sin." Thus, hamartiology is the doctrine of sin.

I. The Origin of Sin

A. The Entrance of Sin into the Universe.

Turning to Ezekiel 28:11-19 we see that it was Lucifer who brought sin into the universe: "Thine heart was lifted up because of thy beauty, thou hast corrupted thy wisdom by reason of thy brightness: I will cast thee to the ground, I will lay thee before kings, that they may behold thee" (v. 17). There was no sin before Lucifer sinned and became the Devil – Satan. His sin, the first in the universe, was when he chose his will over God's will, desiring to be equal with God. Why did God allow sin to enter into the universe? This is one question God has not answered as yet.

B. The Introduction of Sin into the Human Race.

As there is sin in the human race, there must have been a beginning of sin. If there is no beginning of sin, man was *created* in sin. Thus, God is the creator of sin; but He is not. Sin came into the human race through deception and disobedience, motivated by unbelief. "Adam was not deceived, but the woman being deceived was in the transgression" (I Tim. 2:14). Why did God allow man to sin? The only possible answer we can give is Ephesians 2:7: "That in the ages to come he might shew the exceeding riches of his grace in his kindness toward us through Christ Jesus."

II. The Reality of Sin

A. Scripture Declares the Fact of Sin.

"All have sinned, and come short of the glory of God" (Rom. 3:23). "The Scripture hath concluded all under sin, that the promise by faith of Jesus Christ might be given to them that believe" (Gal. 3:22).

B. Nature Proclaims the Fact of Sin.

"We know that the whole creation groaneth and travaileth in pain together unto now" (Rom. 8:22).

C. Law Discovers the Fact of Sin.

"By the deeds of the law there shall no flesh be justified in his sight: for by the law is the knowledge of sin" (Rom. 3:20). The Apostle Paul thought that he was free from sin until he looked into the mirror of God's law: "Nay, I had not known sin, but by the law: for I had not known lust, except the law had said, Thou shalt not covet" (Rom. 7:7b).

D. Experience Proves the Fact of Sin.

The experiences of Moses, David, Peter and John reveal the facts of sin. Even your own experience substantiates it.

E. Man Confesses the Fact of Sin.

1. *Saints Have Owned Up to It.* It was Job who said, "I am vile, and I abhor myself." Isaiah declared, "Woe is me, for I am undone." Daniel, of whom no breath of sin is mentioned, said, "My comeliness was turned into corruption." Jeremiah confessed, "I am black." Peter cried, "Depart from me, I am a sinful man." Paul stated, "Christ Jesus came into the world to save sinners; of whom I am chief." Luther revealed, "I am afraid more of my heart than the Pope and all the Cardinals." Moody said, "The man I have the most trouble with is the man who walks under my hat."

2. *Sinners Have Owned Up to It.* The Scriptures abound with the confession of the sinner and his sin: Pharaoh declared, "I have sinned this time" (Ex. 9:27b). Achan answered, "Indeed I have sinned" (Josh. 7:20b). Balaam admitted, "I have sinned," (Num. 22:34b). Even Judas, who betrayed the Lord, said, "I have sinned" (Matt. 27:4).

III. The Nature of Sin

A. The Modern View of Sin.

1. *Society Calls It Indiscretion.*
2. *Scholars Label It Ignorance.*
3. *Evolutionists Say It Is the Trait of the Beast.*
4. *Christian Scientists Teach It Is the Absence From Good.*
5. *The Fleshly Man Excuses It As Amiable Weakness.*
6. *The New Theologians Declare It Is Merely Selfishness.*

B. The Biblical View of Sin.

1. *Sin Is Missing the Mark.* "All have sinned, and come short of the glory of God" (Rom. 3:23). See also Romans 5:12, Sin means "to miss the divine aim of God."

2. *Sin Is Transgression.* "Whosoever committeth sin transgresseth also the law: for sin is the transgression of the law" (I John 3:4). Transgression of the law may be deliberate or unintentional. Either is sin. There was *sin* before the law, but there was no transgression. See Numbers 4:15; Joshua 7:11, 15; Isaiah 24:5; Daniel 9:11; Hosea 6:7; 8:1.

3. *Sin Is Bending of That Which Is Right.* "Righteous" means straight. Sin is the bending of that which was once straight. "David spake unto the LORD when he saw the angel that smote the people, and said, Lo, I have sinned, and have done wickedly: but these sheep, what have they done? let thine hand, I pray thee, be against me, and against my father's house" (II Sam. 24:17). See also Romans 1:18; 6:13; II Thessalonians 2:12; II Peter 2:15; I John 5:17.

4. *Sin Is Rebellion Against God.* "Hear, O heavens, and give ear, O earth: for the LORD hath spoken, I have nourished and brought up children and they have rebelled against me" (Is. 1:2). See also II Thessalonians 2:4, 8.

5. *Sin Is a Debt.* "Forgive us our debts, as we forgive our debtors" (Matt. 6:12). See also Luke 11:4. The words "duty" (Luke 17:10), "ought" (John 13:14) and "bound" (II Thess. 2:13) are all from the same Greek word denoting debt.

6. *Sin Is Disobedience.* Sin is a lack of response to God. "In time past ye walked according to the course of this world, according to the prince of the power of the air, the spirit that now worketh in the children of disobedience" (Eph. 2:2). See also Ephesians 5:6; John 3:36, R. V.

7. *Sin Is a Deviation From God's Requirement.* This means a fall; every offense against God is a fall. Sin is always a fall that hurts. "If ye forgive men their trespasses, your heavenly Father will also forgive you" (Matt. 6:14). See also Galatians 6:1; Romans 5:15-20.

8. *Sin Is Unbelief.* "He that believeth on the Son of God hath the witness in himself: he that believeth not God hath made him a liar; because he believeth not the record that God gave of his Son" (I John 5:10).

9. *Sin Is Impiety, or Ungodliness.* "To him that worketh not, but believeth on him that justifieth the ungodly, his faith

is counted for righteousness" (Rom. 4:5). "When we were yet without strength, in due time Christ died for the ungodly" (Rom. 5:6). See also I Timothy 1:9; I Peter 4:18; II Peter 2:5, 7; Jude 4, 15.

10. *Sin Is Iniquity.* By this we mean a wrong doing to the moral order of the universe. "Now the works of the flesh are manifest, which are these; Adultery, fornication, uncleanness, lasciviousness, idolatry, witchcraft, hatred, variance, emulations, wrath, strife, seditions, heresies, envyings, murders, drunkenness, revellings, and such like: of the which I tell you before, as I have also told you in time past, that they that do such things shall not inherit the kingdom of God" (Gal. 5:19-21). See also Colossians 3:5-9; Mark 7:19, 20.

C. The Scriptural Statement of Sin.

"All unrighteousness is sin: and there is a sin not unto death" (I John 5:17). See also I John 3:4; Proverbs 14:21; 21:4; 24:9; Romans 3:23; 6:23; I Samuel 15:23; Jeremiah 3:25; 14:7; James 2:9; 4:17; Romans 14:23.

D. The Theological Definitions of Sin.

1. *Sin is the transgression of, or lack of conforming to the law of God.*
2. *Sin is deficiency of love to God and man.*
3. *Sin is preference of self to God.*
4. *Sin is insubordination.*
5. *Sin is lack of conformity with God or His moral law in act, disposition, or state.*
6. *Sin is that which ought not to be.*

E. The Summary of Scripture Concerning Sin.

1. *Toward God.*

a. *Rebellion.* "Rebellion is as the sin of witchcraft, and stubbornness is as iniquity and idolatry" (I Sam. 15:23a).

b. *Failure to Love God Supremely.* "Thou shalt love the LORD thy God with all thine heart, and with all thy soul, and with all thy might" (Deut. 6:5).

2. *Toward the Divine Law.*

a. *Willful Transgression.* "The soul that doeth ought presumptuously, whether he be born in the land, or a stranger, the same reproacheth the LORD; and that soul shall be cut off from among his people" (Num. 15:30).

b. *Violation Through Ignorance.* "If any soul sin through ignorance, then he shall bring a she goat of the first year for a sin offering" (Num. 15:27). See also Hebrews 9:7.

3. *Toward Man.*

a. *Injustice.* "Thou shalt not defraud thy neighbor, neither rob: the wages of him that is hired shall not abide with thee all night until the morning" (Lev. 19:13).

b. *Failure to Love Him as One's Self.* "Thou shalt not avenge, nor bear any grudge against the children of thy people, but thou shalt love thy neighbor as thyself: I am the LORD" (Lev. 19:18).

4. *Toward Self.*

a. *Selfishness.* "What is a man profited, if he shall gain the whole world, and lose his own soul? or what shall a man give in exchange for his soul?" (Matt. 16:26).

b. *Corruption.* "Behold, I was shapen in iniquity; and in sin did my mother conceive me" (Ps. 51:5).

IV. The Extent of Sin

A. As to the Heavens.

The Scriptures reveal the fact that both sin and salvation began in heaven and came to earth. Sin began in heaven with the fall of Satan (Ezek. 28). Salvation is completed in heaven with the mediatorial work of Christ (Heb. 9:24).

B. As to the Earth.

1. *The Vegetable Kingdom.* "Unto Adam he said, because thou hast hearkened unto the voice of thy wife, and hast eaten of the tree, of which I commanded thee, saying, Thou shalt not eat of it: cursed is the ground for thy sake; in sorrow shalt thou eat of it all the days of thy life; thorns also and thistles shall it bring forth to thee; and thou shalt eat the herb of the field" (Gen. 3:17, 18). Isaiah 53:13 reveals the blessed fact that the curse shall be taken off of the vegetable kingdom when Christ comes: "Instead of the thorn, shall come up the fir tree, and instead of the briar shall come up the myrtle tree: and it shall be to the LORD for a name, for an everlasting sign that shall not be cut off."

2. *The Animal Kingdom.* Before the fall of man there were no man-eating animals. Isaiah 11:6-9 tells us that this curse also shall be removed at Christ's second coming: "The wolf also shall dwell with the lamb, and the leopard shall lie down with the kid; and the calf and the young lion and the fatling together; and a little child shall lead them. And the

cow and the bear shall feed; their young ones shall lie down together: and the lion shall eat straw like the ox. And the sucking child shall play on the hole of the asp, and the weaned child shall put his hand on the cockatrice' den. They shall not hurt nor destroy in all my holy mountain: for the earth shall be full of the knowledge of the LORD as the waters cover the sea."

3. *The Race of Mankind.*

a. *The Universality of Sin.* All men are sinners: "All have sinned and come short of the glory of God" (Rom. 3:23).

b. *The Totality of Sin.* All of man is sinful – his body, soul and spirit. "They are all gone out of the way, they are together become unprofitable: there is none that doeth good, no, not one. . . . there is no fear of God before their eyes. Now we know that what things soever the law saith, it saith to them that are under the law: that every mouth may be stopped, and all the world may become guilty before God" (Rom. 3:12, 18, 19.)

V. The Realm of Sin

A. As An Act.

Man commits sins by his conduct.

B. A State.

Man is void of righteousness.

C. As a Nature.

Man is conceived in sin, born in sin, and is, therefore, a sinner by nature.

VI. The Penalty of Sin

A. The Natural Penalty.

This can best be illustrated by the example of a child who was forbidden to eat of a certain food. He disobeyed and ate too much, with the result that he became sick. The *natural consequence* of his disobedience was his illness. *The natural penalty of sin* is disease, disappointment and physical death.

B. The Positive Penalty.

To continue with the above example, we find that the *natural* penalty was the child's becoming sick. The positive penalty is the spanking he received from his father. The positive penalty of sin is described by the following:

1. *Death.* "The wages of sin is death; but the gift of God is eternal life through Jesus Christ our Lord" (Rom. 6:23).

Death, in Scripture, never means "annihilation" or "complete destruction." There is no place in the Word where the word "annihilation" can be substituted for "death."

a. *Spiritual Death.* "She that liveth in pleasure is dead while she liveth" (I Tim. 5:6).

b. *Eternal Death.* "Death and hell were cast into the lake of fire. This is the second death" (Rev. 20:14). "The Lord Jesus shall be revealed . . . in the flaming fire taking vengeance on them that know not God, and that obey not the gospel of our Lord Jesus Christ: who shall be punished with everlasting destruction from the presence of the Lord, and from the glory of his power" (II Thess. 1:7, 8, 9). See also Revelation 20:12; 21:8. There was no death before sin came into man's life. Man was created to dwell with God forever. Death is said to have "passed upon all men" (Rom. 5:12). The word "passed" is translated "pierced through" in Luke 2:35; "go through" in Matthew 19:24; and "passed through" in I Corinthians 10:1.

2. *Lost.* "While I was with them in the world, I kept them in thy name: those that thou gavest me I have kept, and none of them is *lost,* but the son of perdition; that the scripture might be fulfilled" (John 17:12). The word "lost" is the same as the words "perish" (John 3:16) and "destroy" (Matt. 10:28).

3. *Condemned.* "He that believeth on him is not condemned: but he that believeth not is condemned already; because he hath not believed on the name of the only begotten Son of God" (John 3:18). The word "condemnation" is a legal term, and indicates judicial decision. This same word, "condemnation," is "damnation" in John 5:29, and "judgment" in Matthew 11:22, 24; II Peter 2:4, 9; 3:7; I John 4:17; Jude 6.

4. *Guilt.* "Now we know that what things soever the law saith, it saith to them who are under the law: that every mouth may be stopped, and all the world may become guilty before God" (Rom. 3:19).

5. *Perdition.* "Let your conversation be as it becometh the gospel of Christ: that . . . I may hear . . . that ye stand fast in one spirit. . . in nothing terrified by your adversaries: which is to them an evident token of *perdition,* but to you of salvation, and that of God" (Phil. 1:27, 28). See also John 17:12; II Thessalonians 2:3; Hebrews 10:39; II Peter 3:7; Revelation 17:8, 11. This same word "perdition" is translated

"destruction" in Matthew 7:13: "Enter ye in at the strait gate: for wide is the gate, and broad is the way, that leadeth to destruction, and many there be which go in thereat." See also Romans 9:22; Philippians 3:19; II Peter 3:16. (In the New Testament the word "destruction" means "ruin".) In Matthew 26:8 it is translated "waste": "When his disciples saw it, they had indignation, saying, To what purpose is this *waste?*" The word "perish" in Matthew 9:17 is the same word as "perdition": "Neither do men put new wine into old bottles: else the bottles break, and the wine runneth out, and the bottles *perish*: but they put new wine into new bottles, and both are preserved."

6. *Punishment.* "These shall go away into everlasting punishment: but the righteous into life eternal" (Matt. 25:46). There is a difference between the above Scripture and Hebrews 12:6: "Whom the Lord loveth he chasteneth, and scourgeth every son whom he receiveth." Punishment is for the sinner; chastisement for the saint.

7. *Eternal – Everlasting.* "These shall go away into everlasting punishment: but the righteous into life eternal" (Matt. 25:46). See also Jude 6; II Thessalonians 1:9; Revelation 20:10; 14:11.

Some say that the words "everlasting" and "eternal" mean "a long life, an age, age lasting." In other words, they say that guilty sinners will endure the fires of hell only for an age; after being purified, they shall enjoy eternal bliss with the rest of the saints of God. But this we add, "If hell and punishment are not forever, then there is no such thing as eternal life, nor eternal salvation." The same word "eternal," or "everlasting," is used of God, "How much more shall the blood of Christ, who through the *eternal* Spirit offered himself without spot to God, purge your conscience from dead works to serve the living God?" (Heb. 9:14). "The revelation of the mystery . . . now is made manifest, and by the scriptures of the prophets, according to the commandment of the *everlasting* God, made known to all nations for the obedience of faith" (Rom. 16:26). If the punishment in hell for the damned is not eternal, then salvation is not eternal, and *God is not eternal! But He is!* So is salvation eternal; so is punishment.

SOTERIOLOGY
(The Doctrine of Salvation)

Outline for Chapter VI

SOTERIOLOGY

I. Repentance.
   - A. Citation.
   - B. Explanation.
   - C. Manifestation.
   - D. Condition.
   - E. Definition.

II. Faith.
   - A. Citation.
   - B. Explanation.
   - C. Donation.
   - D. Centralization
   - E. Production.

III. Regeneration.
   - A. Citation.
   - B. Explanation.
   - C. Compulsion.
   - D. Condition.

IV. Justification.
   - A. Citation.
   - B. Explanation.
   - C. Condition.
   - D. Illustration.
   - E. Manifestation.

V. Sanctification.

- A. Citation.
- B. Explanation.
- C. Condition.
- D. Definition.

VI. Adoption.

- A. Citation.
- B. Explanation.
- C. Origination.
- D. Consummation.
- E. Manifestation.

VII. Redemption.

- A. Citation.
- B. Explanation.

VIII. Prayer.

- A. Affirmation.
- B. Delineation.
- C. Explanation.
- D. Stimulation.
- E. Illustration.
- F. Regulation.
- G. Condition.
- H. Limitation.
- I. Mediation.

Chapter VI

SOTERIOLOGY

Soteriology is the doctrine of salvation.

I. Repentance

A. Citation.

"In those days came John the Baptist, preaching in the wilderness of Judaea, and saying, Repent ye: for the kingdom of heaven is at hand" (Matt. 3:1, 2). "Jesus began to preach, and to say, Repent: for the kingdom of heaven is at hand" (Matt. 4:17). Paul testified "both to the Jews, and also to the Greeks, repentance toward God, and faith toward our Lord Jesus Christ" (Acts 20:21). "As many as I love, I rebuke and chasten: be zealous therefore, and repent" (Rev. 3:19). See also Mark 6:12; Luke 24:47; Acts 2:38; 11:18; 26:20; II Peter 3:9.

To those who say that repentance is not to be preached today, and that it is not essential for salvation, we point out that repentance was preached by John the Baptist, the Lord Jesus Christ, and the Apostle Paul. Repentance was proclaimed *before* Pentecost, *at* Pentecost, and *after* Pentecost. "Except ye repent, ye shall all likewise perish" (Luke 13:5).

B. Explanation.

1. *It Is Not Reformation.* Repentance is wholly an inward act of the mind. To many people it means to turn away from their sins, but if that were so, this would be *reformation.* Repentance is not doing something, as an act, for no man is saved because he gives up something. A man can turn away from his sins and still not be a Christian.

2. *It Is Not Contrition.* By this we mean that repentance is not agony of the soul for sin. Many folk in jail are sorry. Are they sorry for their crime? No. They are sorry because they were caught. We believe, however, that in a genuine case of repentance, the sinner will be sorry for his sin. Just being sorry

for sin is not repentance, but it can *lead* to repentance. "Godly sorrow worketh repentance to salvation not to be repented of: but the sorrow of the world worketh death" (II Cor. 7:10).

3. *It Is Not Penance.* Penance is an expression of sorrow (by some act) that is done to pay for sin; it is something like a punishment.

4. *It Is a Change of Mind.* The literal meaning of repentance is "after-thought" or "reconsideration." By "change of mind" we do not mean a "change of opinion"; a "change of mind" is the substitution of a new mind for the old. It is new in character. True repentance is a change of mind which will lead to a change of action, but let us be warned that it is possible to have a change of action without a change of mind. A good example of repentance is found in Mathew 21:28, 29: "But what think ye? A certain man had two sons; and he came to the first, and said, Son, go work today in my vineyard. He answered and said, I will not: but afterward he repented, and went."

Before anyone can be saved there must be repentance. There must be a change of mind about many things: sin, self, God and Jesus Christ. "The servant of the Lord" must instruct "in meekness . . . those that oppose themselves; if God peradventure will give repentance to the acknowledging of the truth" (II Tim. 2:25).

Making it a little stronger, repentance means not only a change of mind; it is the taking of one's stand against himself and the placing of himself on the side of God. Thus, repentance is self-judgment.

C. *Manifestation.*

1. *Change in the Intellect.*
2. *Change of Feeling.*
3. *Change of Will.*
4. *Change of Action.*

D. *Condition.*

1. *Through the Goodness of God.* "Despisest thou the riches of his goodness and forbearance and longsuffering; not knowing that the goodness of God leadeth thee to repentance?" (Rom. 2:4). See also II Peter 3:9.

2. *Through the Gospel of God.* "Now when they heard this, they were pricked in their hearts, and said unto Peter and to the rest of the apostles, Men and brethren, what shall we

do? Then Peter said unto them, Repent and be baptized every one of you in the name of Jesus Christ for [because of] the remission of sins, and ye shall receive the gift of the Holy Ghost. . . . Then they that gladly received his word were baptized: and the same day there were added unto them about three thousand souls" (Acts 2:37, 38, 41).

3. *Through the Scriptural Teaching.* "The servant of the Lord must not strive; but be gentle unto all men, apt to teach, patient, in meekness instructing those that oppose themselves; if God peradventure will give them repentance to the acknowledging of the truth" (II Tim. 2:24, 25).

4. *Through the Chastisements of God.* "Repent; or else I will come unto thee quickly and will fight against them with the sword of my mouth" (Rev. 2:16). See also Revelation 2:5; 3:3; Hebrews 12:6-11.

E. *Definition.*

Repentance is the work of God which results in a change of mind in respect to man's relationship to God. It is neither sorrow nor penance, though penitent sorrow may lead to a change of mind. *Repentance is always an element of saving faith.*

II. Faith

A. *Citation.*

"The gospel of Christ . . . is the power of God unto salvation to every one that believeth. . . . For therein is the righteousness of God revealed from faith to faith: as it is written, the just shall live by faith" (Rom. 1:17). "We conclude that a man is justified by faith without the deeds of the law" (Rom. 3:28). See also Matthew 9:22; Acts 26:18; Romans 4:5; II Corinthians 5:7; Ephesians 2:8; Hebrews 11:6; James 5:15; I Peter 1:5.

B. *Explanation,*

A good definition of faith is: confidence in others; reliance upon testimony. True faith is composed of the following:

1. *Knowledge.* One must be informed before he can have faith. This is true in the things of man, as it is in Christ. It is impossible to have faith in Christ without the Word. "Faith cometh by hearing, and hearing by the word of God" (Rom. 10:17). Sometimes we may ask for *more* faith, but this is out of order. To increase one's faith, one has only to

read more of the Word of God. Before a person can have faith, he must know it exists.

2. *Belief.* The second element of faith is belief. Everyone knows what belief means, that is, to accept it as the truth. People can know that there is a Saviour by the name of Jesus, and believe that He can save. Yet, this is not *saving faith.* To have faith in a chair, one must know that it exists, and believe that it can hold him up. Still this is not complete faith in the chair, until the third element is involved, and that is:

3. *Trust.* Trust is essential to faith in anything. It is most essential in saving faith. It is one thing to know that Christ died, and believe it; it is quite another thing to trust Him, the dying and resurrected Saviour, for salvation. Let us take the chair again for example: One can know that a chair exists, and believe that it can hold him up, but faith in that chair is not exercised until he sits in it. Are you completely *trusting* Christ for *your* salvation?

4. *Recumbency.* This means to wholly rely upon Christ. When one lies upon the bed, he fully relaxes upon it and rests. When we put our trust in Him, we should rely upon Him and rest.

C. Donation.

1. *By God the Father.* "I say, through the grace given unto me, to every man that is among you, not to think of himself more highly than he ought to think; but to think soberly, according as God hath dealt to every man the measure of faith" (Rom. 12:3).

2. *By God the Son.* Jesus is "the author and finisher of our faith; who for the joy that was set before him endured the cross, despising the shame, and is set down at the right hand of the throne of God" (Heb. 12:2).

3. *By God the Holy Spirit.* "To one is given by the Spirit the word of wisdom . . . to another faith by the same Spirit; to another the gifts of healing by the same Spirit" (I Cor. 12:8, 9).

D. Centralization.

The object of faith is Christ, and He alone.

E. Production.

The end of faith is salvation. "By grace are ye saved through faith; and that not of yourselves: it is the gift of God: not of works, lest any man should boast" (Eph. 2:8, 9).

III. Regeneration

A. Citation.

"Jesus answered and said unto him, Verily, verily, I say unto thee, Except a man be born again, he cannot see the kingdom of God. . . . Jesus answered, Verily, verily, I say unto thee, except a man be born of water and of the Spirit, he cannot enter into the kingdom of God" (John 3:3, 5). We are "born again, not of corruptible seed, but of incorruptible, by the word of God, which liveth and abideth forever" (I Peter 1:23). "Whosoever is born of God doth not commit sin; for his seed remaineth in him: and he cannot sin, because he is born of God" (I John 3:9). See also I John 2:29; 5:4, 18.

B. Explanation.

1. *It Is Not Reformation.* Some people think that by turning over a new leaf one becomes a child of God. Some men quit drinking because of a bad heart, not because they know it is sin against God. One could cease from *all* sin; yet this is not regeneration.

2. *It Is Not Conversion.* Many times we speak of regeneration as conversion, but, in reality, "conversion" means to turn around. Saved people can be *converted* (turned around) even after they are saved, as was Peter. He was saved long before the Lord Jesus had declared: "Simon, Simon, behold, Satan hath desired to have you, that he may sift you as wheat: but I have prayed for thee, that thy faith fail not: and when thou art *converted* [turned around], strengthen thy brethren" (Luke 22:31, 32).

3. *It Is Not Confirmation.* Some churches, as they administer a certain ritual of the church, claim that the participants (usually children of twelve or thirteen years of age) receive the Holy Spirit with the anointing of oil. This is a false doctrine. One does not receive the Holy Spirit by any act of man, but upon receiving Christ as Saviour.

4. *It Is Not Water Baptism.* There is no saving faith in all the water of the world. Someone may ask, then, "Why are we commanded to be baptized?" It is the answer of a good conscience toward God (I Peter 3:21b). It is an ordinance depicting the death, burial and resurrection of Christ, and nothing more.

5. *It Is Not Church Membership.* We are told in Hebrews 10:25 not to forsake "the assembling of ourselves together as

the manner of some is." However, this does not bring about change in a sinner's heart. Remember, the word "church" means "a called-out company," or "assembly." Joining a human assembly cannot bring about salvation. Some people believe that the *Church* saves. Now translate this statement correctly: "The assembly saves." Is there an assembly on earth which can give salvation? Is there a called-out company which can make a person a child of God? *No!* There is no assembly that we would trust with the saving of our soul.

6. *It Is Not the Taking of the Lord's Supper.* There is no saving efficacy, or cleansing of sin, in partaking of the elements of the Lord's Supper. The Lord's Supper is taken only in remembrance of Christ and His work upon Calvary. We shall do this in remembrance of Him until He comes.

7. *It Is the New Birth.* "If any man is in Christ, there is a new creation: the old things are passed away; behold, they are become new" (II Cor. 5:17, R.V.). "If ye know that he is righteous, ye know that every one that doeth righteousness is born of him" (I John 2:29).

C. Compulsion.

Ye *must* be born again. It is a necessity declared by the Lord Himself.

1. *As Seen in the Depravity of Man.* "That which is born of the flesh is flesh: and that which is born of the Spirit is spirit" (John 3:6). The words, "Ye must be born again," are better translated, "Ye must be born from above." Man must have a birth from above if he is to live some day in the heavens above.

2. *As Seen in the Universality of Man.* There is not a man anywhere but who has to be born again. "All have sinned, and come short of the glory of God" (Rom. 3:23).

3. *As Seen in the Holiness of God.* If one is to be received and made a child of God by a righteous and holy God, a great change must take place to make him holy. "It is written, Ye shall be holy; for I am holy" (I Peter 1:16, R.V.).

D. Condition.

1. *The Divine Work.* The process of becoming a child of God is not by natural generation. Man cannot regenerate himself. It is not a matter of the human will, but of God. "As many as received him, to them gave he power to become the sons of God, even to them that believe on his name: which

were born, not of blood, nor of the will of the flesh, nor of the will of man, but of God" (John 1:12, 13). Practically speaking, we had nothing to do with our first birth, and we can have nothing to do with the second birth.

2. *The Human Element.* While it is God who regenerates the believing sinner, yet there is one part that man plays; he must *believe!* "By grace are ye saved"; yes, but "through faith." "No man cometh unto the Father but by me." Yes, Jesus is the way, but the sinner must *come!* The sinner must *receive* Christ by his own faith. This is the human part. God does the rest.

IV. Justification

A. *Citation.*

We are "justified by his grace through the redemption that is in Christ Jesus" (Rom. 3:24). "The righteousness of Christ shall be imputed to us, if we believe on him that raised up Jesus our Lord from the dead; who was delivered for our offences, and was raised again for our justification" (Rom. 4:24, 25). "Being justified by faith, we have peace with God through our Lord Jesus Christ" (Rom. 5:1). "Such [thieves, covetous, drunkards, and the like] were some of you: but ye are washed, but ye are sanctified, but ye are justified in the name of the Lord Jesus, and by the Spirit of our God" (I Cor. 6:11). See also Romans 3:26; 5:9; Galatians 2:16, 17; Titus 3:7.

B. *Explanation.*

To justify is "to reckon, to declare, or to show righteous." To justify does not mean to make righteous. God declares the believer to be righteous; He does not make him righteous. Justification is a legal term: a good standing.

In the human law courts, the law is over the judge. If the judge is an honest and just judge, he can show no mercy. He must declare the defendant guilty, or not guilty, according to the law. In God's law court, the believer, a guilty man, is brought before the judgment bar of God and is declared not guilty. God is over His law.

In a human law court, a guilty person may be pardoned, the crime forgiven but not paid. In God's law court this is not so. All sins must be paid for, and the sinner punished. Three things are incorporated in God's justification.

1. *Forgiveness.* "He, whom God raised again, saw no

corruption. Be it known you, therefore, men and brethen, that through this man is preached unto you the forgiveness of sins: and by him all that believe are justified from all things, from which ye could not be justified by the law of Moses" (Acts 13:37-39).

A Christian is not a pardoned criminal; he is a righteous man. God declares him so. He is one who has paid for his sins by another, his substitute, the Lord Jesus Christ. God never pardons apart from Christ.

2. *Imputation.* "Blessed is the man unto whom the Lord imputeth not iniquity, and in whose spirit there is no guile" (Ps. 32:2). "Blessed is the man to whom the Lord will not impute sin" (Rom. 4:8). "Until the law sin was in the world: but sin is not imputed when there is no law" (Rom. 5:13).

Imputation means to "put something against." Therefore, the righteousness of Christ is put to the sinner's account. All of the believer's sins were put to Christ's account – He paid them in full. In turn, His righteousness was put to the believer's account, and he stands there, declared to be righteous.

3. *Fellowship.* "One God and Father of all, who is above all, and through all, and in you all" (Eph. 4:6). This is the fellowship of God and the believer as Father and Son. Remember, God is Father only of His children, not of unbelievers.

C. *Condition.*

1. *Negative.*

a. *Not By Works.* "Now to him that worketh is the reward not reckoned of grace, but of debt. But to him that worketh not, but believeth on him that justifieth the ungodly, his faith is counted for righteousness" (Rom. 4:4, 5). See also Romans 11:6.

b. *Not By the Deeds of the Law.* "That no man is justified by the law in the sight of God, it is evident: for, The just shall live by faith" (Gal. 3:11). See also Romans 3:20; Galatians 2:16.

2. *Positive.*

a. *By God.* God set forth Christ Jesus "to declare . . . his righteousness: that he might be just, and the justifier of him which believeth in Jesus" (Rom. 3:26). See also Romans 8:33.

b. *By Grace.* "Being justified by his grace, we should

be made heirs according to the hope of eternal life" (Titus 3:7). See also Romans 3:24.

c. *By Blood.* "Being now justified by his blood, we shall be saved from wrath through him" (Rom. 5:9). See also Romans 3:24, 25.

d. *By Faith.* "Being justified by faith, we have peace with God through our Lord Jesus Christ" (Rom. 5:1).

e. *By Resurrection.* Faith shall be imputed to us for righteousness "if we believe on him that raised up Jesus our Lord from the dead; who was delivered for our offences, and was raised again for our justification" (Rom. 4:24, 25).

D. *Illustration.*

1. *Abraham* (Rom. 4:1-5).
2. *David* (Rom. 4:6-8).
3. *Noah* (Heb. 11:7).

E. *Manifestation.*

1. *In Works.* "Was not Abraham our father justified by works, when he had offered Isaac his son upon the altar? Seest thou how faith wrought with his works, and by works was faith made perfect? And the scripture was fulfilled which saith, Abraham believed God, and it was imputed unto him for righteousness: and he was called the Friend of God" (Jas. 2:21-23). The evidence of salvation is gratitude, which is good works. Many times the good works are very, very weak, but God accepts the will that is behind them.

2. *In Experience.* "Being justified by faith, we have peace with God through our Lord Jesus Christ: by whom also we have access by faith into this grace wherein we stand, and rejoice in hope of the glory of God. And not only so, but we glory in tribulation also: knowing that tribulation worketh patience; and patience, experience; and experience, hope: and hope maketh not ashamed; because the love of God is shed abroad in our hearts by the Holy Ghost which is given unto us" (Rom. 5:1-5).

V. Sanctification

This is one phase of salvation which is very much confused today. The Bible student will be surprised at what God has to say about sanctification. Much is said about experience, and we believe in experience; but let us be cautious and let the Word of God interpret our experience, rather than our experience interpret the Word of God.

A. Citation.

"This is the will of God, even your sanctification, that ye should abstain from fornication. . . . For God hath not called us unto uncleanness, but unto holiness" (I Thess. 4:3, 7). "Unto the church of God which is at Corinth, to them that are sanctified in Christ Jesus, called to be saints, with all that in every place call upon the name of Jesus Christ our Lord, both theirs and ours: Grace be unto you and peace" (I Cor. 1:2). "Both he that sanctifieth and they that are sanctified are all of one: for which cause he is not ashamed to call them brethren" (Heb. 2:11). "Follow peace with all men, and holiness, without which no man shall see the Lord" (Heb. 12:14). See also I Peter 1:2; John 17:17; Exodus 13:2; Jeremiah 2:3; Ephesians 1:1. The words "sanctification, holiness, and saints" all come from the same root.

B. Explanation.

1. *It Is Not a Betterment of the Flesh.* Never does it say in Scripture that the work of the Holy Spirit is to improve the old nature. The natural man cannot understand the Holy Spirit. How could the natural man be improved by the Spirit? This is hard to say, but nevertheless, it is true, that the flesh of the believer is no better than the flesh of the sinner. The Scriptures say, "Mortify the deeds of the flesh."

2. *It Is Not the Eradication of the Sinful Nature.* There are those who contend that a believer may have a purifying experience that will burn out all carnality, thus rendering him sinless, incapable of committing sin. We do not deny such an experience, but we caution the believer to prove his experience by the Word, rather than trying to prove the Word by his experience. Even though the Old Testament is written in the Hebrew, and the New Testament is written in the Greek, the words "sanctification," "holy," and "saint" all have the same root meaning.

To those who hold that sanctification is an experience by which the sinful nature is eradicated, let us turn to the Word and see how sanctification is used: "Thou shalt anoint the altar of the burnt-offering, and all his vessels, and sanctify the altar: and it shall be an altar most holy" (Ex. 40:10). Where is the eradication here? Did the altar have a sinful nature? Here is another example: "Moses said unto the LORD, The people cannot come up to mount Sinai: for thou chargedst us, saying,

Set bounds about the mount, and sanctify it" (Ex. 19:23). Did Mount Sinai have a sinful nature? "Let the priests also, which come near to the LORD, sanctify themselves, lest the LORD break forth upon them" (Ex. 19:22). How could priests eradicate their own sinful natures? "Say ye of him, whom the Father hath sanctified, and sent unto the world, Thou blasphemest; because I said, I am the Son of God" (John 10:36). Here Christ Himself is spoken of as being sanctified. There is no sinful nature here! "For their sakes I sanctify myself, that they also might be sanctified through the truth" (John 17:19). Does this mean eradication of the sinful nature? Of course not. "The unbelieving husband is sanctified by the wife, and the unbelieving wife is sanctified by the husband: else were your children unclean; but now are they holy" (I Cor. 7:14). Is it possible that believing wives can eradicate the sinful nature from their unbelieving husbands? If sanctification means eradication from the sinful nature, explain the following: "Sanctify the Lord God in your hearts: and be ready always to give an answer to every man that asketh you a reason of the hope that is in you with meekness and fear" (I Peter 3:15). Carnal Christians are sanctified; this does not speak of the eradication of the sinful nature (I Cor. 1:1, 2 with 3:1, 3).

3. *It Is Not Sanctimoniousness.* Sanctification is not an affected, or hypocritical devoutness; neither is it false saintliness. Sanctification is not marked by the wearing of a beard, or black stockings, and the like. You can tell whether saintliness is real or false.

4. *It Is Not a Second Blessing.* In II Corinthians 1:15 Paul speaks of wanting to give the Church a second benefit, not a second blessing. This epistle was written to people who were already sanctified (I Cor. 1:2 and 6:11).

5. *It Is "To Be Set Apart."* The root idea always means "to be set apart," or "separation." To sanctify always means to set apart for a purpose, whether in respect to saint or sinner. Unsaved men can separate, or sanctify themselves unto sin. "They that sanctify themselves, and purify themselves in the gardens behind the tree in the midst, eating swine's flesh and the abomination, and the mouse, shall be consumed together, saith the LORD" (Is. 66:17). Jesus sanctified Himself; to say He made Himself sinless is blasphemous. The Sabbath was sanctified, and we know that the Sabbath had no sinful nature.

Again we emphasize that the words "holiness," "sanctification," and "saint" all come from the same word meaning "set apart," "separation." The word "sanctify" in Exodus 13:2, and the word "holiness" in Psalm 29:2, and the word "saints" of Psalm 34:9 are the same word. The word "sanctify" of John 17:17, and the word "saint" of Philippians 1:1, and the word "holiness" of Hebrews 12:10 are all from the same word.

Sanctification, being set apart, is spoken of in three ways:

a. *Positional.* "Such were some of you: but ye are washed, but ye are sanctified, but ye are justified in the name of the Lord Jesus, and by the Spirit of our God" (I Cor. 6:11). We are sanctified the very moment we believe. The above Scripture declares that we are sanctified before we are justified, thus ruling out the second and third works of grace. "We are bound to give thanks alway to God for you, brethren beloved of the Lord, because God hath from the beginning chosen you to salvation through sanctification of the Spirit and belief of the truth" (II Thess. 2:13). Sanctification is first in order, absolutely. See also I Peter 1:2. God never allows us to work up to a position; He first places us in a position set apart to Him, and tells us to be true to that position. A saint truly is God's man.

b. *Practical.* "Having therefore these promises, dearly beloved, let us cleanse ourself from all filthiness of the flesh and spirit, perfecting holiness in the fear of God" (II Cor. 7:1). "Grow in grace, and in the knowledge of our Lord and Saviour Jesus Christ. To him be glory both now and forever. Amen" (II Peter 3:18).

This is our present state of sanctification. A saint never grows up to sanctification, but grows *in* sanctification. Every believer is a saint; however, some believers do not act like saints. The living Christian still has the flesh in him and obeys it at times. Then God, by Jesus Christ, through the Holy Spirit, metes out chastisement. See John 17:17; I Thessalonians 4:3; Hebrews 12:10; II Corinthians 3:18.

c. *Final.* Perfect sanctification will occur in the future at Christ's second coming. "The Lord make you to increase and abound in love one toward another, and toward all men, even as we do toward you: to the end he may stablish your hearts unblameable in holiness before God, even our Father, at the coming of our Lord Jesus Christ with all his saints" (I Thess. 3:12, 13).

C. Condition.

1. *The Divine Side.*

a. *Through God the Father.* "Sanctify unto me all the firstborn, whatsoever openeth the womb among the children of Israel, both of man and of beast: it is mine" (Ex. 13:2).

b. *Through Jesus Christ the Son.* "Jesus also, that he might sanctify the people with his own blood, suffered without the gate" (Heb. 13:12).

c. *Through the Holy Spirit.* "We are bound to give thanks alway to God for you, brethren beloved of the Lord, because God hath from the beginning chosen you to salvation through sanctification of the Spirit and belief of the truth" (II Thess. 2:13).

2. *The Human Side.*

a. *Faith in the Redemptive Work of Christ.* "Of him [God] are ye in Christ Jesus, who of God is made unto us wisdom, and righteousness, and sanctification, and redemption" (I Cor. 1:30).

b. *Study of and Obedience to the Word of God.* "Now ye are clean through the word which I have spoken unto you" (John 15:3).

c. *Through Yieldedness.* "I speak after the manner of men because of the infirmity of your flesh: for as ye have yielded your members servants to uncleanness and to iniquity unto iniquity; even so now yield your members servants to righteousness unto holiness" (Rom. 6:19).

d. *Through Chastening.* "Whom the Lord loveth he chasteneth, and scourgeth every son whom he receiveth. . . . Now no chastening for the present seemeth to be joyous, but grievous: nevertheless, afterward it yieldeth the peaceable fruit of righteousness unto them which are exercised thereby" (Heb. 12:6, 11).

D. Definition.

1. Sanctification is the work of Christ for the believer, which sets him apart for God.

2. Sanctification is that work of God in the believer, through the Spirit and the Word, which changes him into the image of Christ progressively.

3. Sanctification is the work of God which perfects the believer in the likeness of Christ by His appearing in glory.

VI. Adoption

A. Citation.

"Not only they [the whole creation], but ourselves also, which have the firstfruits of the Spirit, even we ourselves groan within ourselves, waiting for the adoption, to wit, the redemption of our body" (Rom. 8:23). There are four other places in the New Testament where the word "adoption" is mentioned: Romans 8:15; 9:4; Galatians 4:4, 5; Ephesians 1:5.

B. Explanation.

The English word "adoption" has an entirely different meaning than the Greek word or the Oriental custom. The English word means to take a person from another family and make him legally one's own son or daughter. The Greek word, however, means "placing as a son."

In New Testament times, when the boy or girl was a minor, he or she differed little from a slave. (Gal. 4:1). Upon the day appointed by the father, at the age from twelve to fourteen, a celebration was held declaring the child of age. Thus the boy or girl was made a son or daughter. A boy or girl was born into the family as a child; upon reaching majority, the boy or girl was declared a son or daughter. The same is true in the case of the believer. He is not adopted into the family of God; he is born into the family of God. By birth, he is a child of God; by adoption he *shall be* a son of God.

C. Origination.

"He hath chosen us in him before the foundation of the world, that we should be holy and without blame before him in love: having predestinated us unto the adoption of children by Jesus Christ to himself, according to the good pleasure of his will" (Eph. 1:4, 5).

D. Consummation.

We are now only the *children* of God. "Ye are all sons of God, through faith, in Christ Jesus" (Gal. 3:26, R. V.). We will become *sons* of God at the day appointed by the Father. At that time He will openly present us as the sons of God. We do not look like sons of God now, but some day the world will be able to recognize us as the sons of God. This will take place at the second coming of Christ. "Not only they, but ourselves also, which have the firstfruits of the Spirit, even we ourselves groan within ourselves, waiting for the adoption to wit, the redemption of our body" (Rom. 8:23).

E. *Manifestation.*

1. *Delivered From a Slavish Fear of God.* "Ye have not received the spirit of bondage again to fear; but ye have received the Spirit of adoption, whereby we cry, Abba, Father" (Rom. 8:15).

2. *Made Possessors of Sonship.*

3. *Made Subject to Both Privileges and Responsibility of Adult Sonship.*

VII. Redemption

The Bible is full of redemption. It is God's character to save. He can destroy, but He loves to save. The theme of the Bible is Jesus Christ. The message of the Word is *redemption.*

A. *Citation.*

"If thy brother be waxen poor, and hath sold away some of his possession, and if any of his kin come to redeem it, then shall he redeem that which his brother sold. . . . And if a sojourner or stranger wax rich by thee, and thy brother that dwelleth by him wax poor, and sell himself unto the stranger or sojourner by thee, or to the stock of the stranger's family: after that he is sold he may be redeemed again; one of his brethren may redeem him" (Lev. 25:25, 47, 48). "Zion shall be redeemed with judgment, and her converts with righteousness" (Is. 1:27). "In whom we have redemption through his blood, the forgiveness of sin, according to the riches of his grace" (Eph. 1:7). See also Nehemiah 5:8; Colossians 1:4; Galatians 3:13; I Corinthians 1:30; Romans 8:23.

B. *Explanation.*

There are four Hebrew words in the Old Testament that pertain to redemption, and all mean "to set free." The word "goel" is used two ways: first, the One who redeems; second, the act of redeeming. The "goel" was always a near kinsman. While the word "redemption" means "to set free," it incorporates the meaning "to buy back, to purchase."

The redemption of the child of God is by his Near Kinsman, the Lord Jesus Christ, who alone has the redemptive price — His own precious blood!

1. *Redemption Declared.*

a. *Is Wholly of God* (John 3:16).

b. *Is Through a Person—Christ* (I Peter 1:18, 19).

c. *Is By Blood* (Heb. 9:12).

d. *Is By Power* (I Cor. 1:30).

2. *Redemption Perfected.* The use of the word "redemption" is presented in the following three ways:

a. *To Buy or Purchase in a Slave Market.* The Lord Jesus Christ came down into this slave market of sin and bought us, who were upon the slave block.

b. *To Purchase Out of the Market.* After one purchased a slave, the master took him out of the market. We are looking for our Master to come and take us out of this slave market.

c. *To Loose or Set Free.* The Lord Jesus is not a slave trader; neither is He a slave holder. One day the Lord Jesus shall set us free from the bondage of corruption and sin, and we shall know the perfect liberty of being the *sons* of God.

In Israel a man could not be a slave forever against his will. After becoming a slave, he could be set free by redemption through a near kinsman, or by waiting for the Sabbatical year or the year of Jubilee, when all slaves were set free. Should he love his master, however, and not care to be set free under any circumstances, he could go to his master, who in turn would bore a hole in his ear and make him a bondslave for life (Ex. 21:6). Paul said that he was a bondslave of Jesus Christ—a bondslave for life. He was *bought* by blood, *bound* by love. The Christian should have his ear bored, figuratively speaking, yea, his hands, his all. He should recognize that he is crucified with Christ.

VIII. Prayer

Prayer is the essential element of Christian character which is lacking in most believers today. One reason for this is that prayer is misunderstood. Prayer is mostly thought of as asking and receiving. It is that; however, it is much more. We fail to see the value of prayer as communion with our God (Is. 43:21, 22; 64:6, 7 R.V.; Zeph. 1:46; Dan. 9:13, 14 with Hos. 7:13, 14; 8:13, 14).

A. Affirmation.

1. *It Is Sin to Neglect Prayer.* "As for me, God forbid that I should sin against the Lord in ceasing to pray for you: but I will teach you the good and the right way" (I Sam. 12:23).

2. *It Is Appointed by God.* "Ask, and it shall be given you; seek, and ye shall find; knock, and it shall be opened unto you: for everyone that asketh receiveth; and he that seeketh findeth; and to him that knocketh it shall be opened. Or what man is there of you, whom if his son ask bread, will he give him a stone? Or if he ask a fish, will he give him a serpent? If ye then, being evil, know how to give good gifts unto your children, how much more shall your Father which is in heaven give good things to them that ask him?" (Matt. 7:7-11).

3. *It Is Commanded by God.* "Pray without ceasing" (I Thess. 5:17). "Continue steadfastly in prayer, watching therein with thanksgiving" (Col. 4:2, R.V.).

4. *It Is Necessary to Ask.* "Ye have not, because ye ask not" (Jas. 4:2c).

B. Delineation.

1. *Abraham Prays for Sodom* (Gen. 18).

2. *Jacob Prays the First Personal Prayer* (Gen. 32:9-12). See other personal prayers (Deut. 26:1-16; Ex. 5:22).

3. *Joshua and Judges Cry Unto the Lord* (Josh. 7:6-9; Judg. 10:14).

4. *Samuel Prays As an Intercessor* (I Sam 7:5, 12).

5. *David Prays With Thanksgiving* (II Sam. 7).

6. *Believers Pour Out Their Hearts to God* (Ps. 42:4; 62:8).

C. Explanation.

1. *Presbyterian Catechism.* "Prayer is the offering up of our desires to God, for things agreeable to His will in the name of Christ with confession of our sins and thankful acknowledgment of his mercy."

2. *Scriptural Definition.*

a. *As a Child Going to the Father.* "Ye have not received the spirit of bondage again to fear; but ye have received the Spirit of adoption, whereby we cry Abba, Father" (Rom. 8:15).

b. *As a Child Crying to the Father.* "Lord, what wilt thou have me to do?" (Acts 9:6).

c. *As a Child Desiring to Be With the Father.* "Jabez called on the God of Israel, saying, Oh that thou wouldest bless me indeed, and enlarge my coast, and that thine hand might be with me, and that thou wouldest keep me from evil, that it may not grieve me! And God granted him that which he requested" (I Chron. 4:10).

d. *As a Child Petitioning the Father.* "When heaven is shut up, and there is no rain, because they have sinned against thee; if they should pray toward this place, and confess thy name, and turn from their sin, when thou afflictest them: then hear thou in heaven" (I Kings 8:35, 36).

e. *As a Child Asking Intercession of the Father.* "When he had taken the book, the beast and four and twenty elders fell down before the Lamb, having every one of them harps, and golden vials full of odours, which are the prayers of the saints" (Rev. 5:8). See also Revelation 8:34.

f. *As a Child Waiting in Silence Before God.* "LORD, thou hast heard the desire of the humble: thou wilt prepare their heart, thou wilt cause thine ear to hear" (Ps. 10:17).

3. *Human Experience.* By this we mean that the saints of God have found these truths through prayer.

a. *It Is a Fervent Mind Settled On God.*

b. *It Is Laborious in Its Task* (Col. 4:12).

c. *It Is a Business.*

D. *Stimulation.*

1. *Abundant Testimony of Christians Proves That God Answers Prayer.*

2. *Universality of Phrases in Scripture: Whosoever, Whatsoever, Whensoever.*

3. *The Wealth of the Promises by God to Praying Believers.*

4. *The Confidence of Access Through Jesus Christ.* "Having therefore, brethren, boldness to enter into the holy place by the blood of Jesus, by the way which he dedicated for us, a new and living way through the veil, that is to say, his flesh; and having a great priest over the house of God; let us draw near with a true heart in fulness of faith, having our hearts sprinkled from an evil conscience: and having our bodies washed with pure water" (Heb. 10:19-22, R.V.).

5. *The Assurance of Help by the Holy Spirit.* "The Spirit helpeth our infirmities: for we know not what we should pray for as we ought: but the Spirit itself maketh intercession for us with groanings which cannot be uttered" (Rom. 8:26).

6. *The Revelation of God by Christ.* "No man hath seen

God at any time; the only begotten Son, which is in the bosom of the Father, he hath declared him" (John 1:18).

7. *The Limitless Supply of Grace in Christ.* "My God shall supply all your need according to his riches in glory by Christ Jesus" (Phil. 4:19).

8. *The Unlimited Possibility of Faith.* "Jesus said unto him, If thou canst believe, all things are possible to him that believeth" (Mark 9:23).

9. *The Abundant Ability of God.* "Now unto him that is able to do exceeding abundantly above all that we ask or think, according to the power that worketh in us, unto him be glory" (Eph. 3:20).

E. *Illustration.*

1. *Abraham Interceding for Sodom* (Gen. 18:22, 23; 19:29).
2. *Prayer of Abraham's Servant* (Gen. 24:12).
3. *Personal Prayer of Jacob* (Gen. 32:9-12).
4. *Moses' Intercession for Israel* (Ex. 32:11-14, 30-34; Num. 14:11-21).
5. *Samuel Interceding for King and People* (I Sam. 12:6-25).
6. *Elijah Praying for Fire and Water* (I Kings 18:25-41; James 5:17, 18).
7. *Nehemiah's Prayer for Jerusalem* (Neh. 2:4).
8. *Joshua's Prayer for Discernment* (Josh. 7:7-9).
9. *Samson's Prayer for Renewed Strength* (Judg. 16:28).
10. *Hannah's Prayer for a Child* (I Sam. 1:10, 11).
11. *David's Prayer of Penitence* (Ps. 51).
12. *Solomon's Prayer for Wisdom* (I Kings 3:5-9).
13. *Solomon's Prayer of Dedication* (I Kings 8:25-53).
14. *Jonah's Prayer for Deliverance* (Jonah 2).
15. *Habakkuk's Prayer of Praise* (Hab. 3).
16. *Paul's Intercession for the Saints* (Eph. 1:15-23; 3:14-21; Col. 1:9-14).
17. *The Malefactor's Prayer for Forgiveness* (Luke 23: 42, 43).
18. *Stephen's Prayer of Submission* (Acts 7:59, 60).
19. *The Lord Jesus' Prayer for Strength* (Matt. 26:27-46).
20. *The Bible's Last Prayer* (Rev. 22:20).

F. *Regulation.*

1. *As to the Posture of the Body.* There is much sup-

position concerning the posture of the body while in prayer. Some contend that prayer is not prayer unless one is on his knees, believing it to be blasphemous to pray while walking, and the like. According to the following Scriptures there is *no* set rule as to the position of the body in prayer:

a. *Christ on His Face.* "He went a little farther, and fell on his face, and prayed, saying, O my Father, if it be possible, let this cup pass from me: nevertheless not as I will, but as thou wilt" (Matt. 26:39).

b. *Solomon on His Knees.* "It was so, that when Solomon had made an end of praying all this prayer and supplication unto the LORD, he arose from before the altar of the LORD, from kneeling on his knees with his hands spread up to heaven" (I Kings 8:54).

c. *Peter on the Water.* "Lord, save me" (Matt. 14:30c).

d. *Thief on the Cross.* "Lord, remember me when thou comest into thy kingdom" (Luke 23:42).

e. *Elijah With Face Between His Knees.* "So Ahab went up to eat and to drink. And Elijah went up to the top of Carmel; and he cast himself down upon the earth, and put his face between his knees" (I Kings 18:42).

f. *David on His Bed.* "I am weary with my groaning; all the night make I my bed to swim; I water my couch with my tears" (Ps. 6:6).

2. *As to Time.* Many poems have been written suggesting the time to pray. We do know that the Christian should select a time when it is the most convenient for him to be alone with the Lord. Here again there is no regulation stipulated. Notice the following examples:

a. *Daniel: Three Times a Day.* "Now when Daniel knew that the writing was signed, he went into his house; and his windows being open in his chamber toward Jerusalem, he kneeled upon his knees three times a day, and prayed, and gave thanks before his God as he did aforetime" (Dan. 6:10).

b. *Christ: Early in the Morning.* "In the morning, rising up a great while before day, he went out, and departed into a solitary place, and there prayed" (Mark 1:35).

c. *Peter and John: Hour of Prayer* (3 P.M.). "Now Peter and John went up together into the temple at the hour of prayer, being the ninth hour" (Acts 3:1).

3. *As to Place.* Where is the place God meets man today? The Lord Jesus said, "Woman, believe me, the hour cometh, when ye shall neither in this mountain, nor yet at Jerusalem, worship the Father. . . . But the hour cometh, and now is, when the true worshippers shall worship the Father in spirit and in truth; for the Father seeketh such to worship him" (John 4:21, 23). Here, too, we see that no definite place is commanded:

a. *Christ in the Garden*: "Then cometh Jesus with them unto a place called Gethsemane, and said unto the disciples, Sit ye here, while I go and pray yonder" (Matt. 26:36).

b. *Christ on the Grass.* "He commanded the multitude to sit down on the grass, and took the five loaves, and the two fishes, and looking up to heaven, he blessed, and brake, and gave the loaves to his disciples, and the disciples to the multitude" (Matt. 14:19).

c. *Christ on a Mountain.* "It came to pass in those days, that he went out into a mountain to pray, and continued all night in prayer to God" (Luke 6:12).

d. *Paul in a Storm on Board Ship* (Acts 27). Where is the place the Christian should pray? Christ said, "Thou, when thou prayest, enter into thy closet, and when thou hast shut thy door, pray to thy Father, which is in secret; and thy Father which seeth in secret shall reward thee openly" (Matt. 6:6). Where is the closet, and how may one close the door? The closet is any place where the believer may closet himself from the outside world. It may be on a bus, walking on the street, or it may be in a closed room. It is a place where he and God are alone together.

G. Conditions.

What will it take to get our prayers answered? The Christian is one who asks to receive. The following truths guarantee answers to prayer.

1. *Confidence.* "Without faith it is impossible to please him: for he that cometh to God must believe that he is, and that he is a rewarder of them that diligently seek him" (Heb. 11:6).

2. *Earnestness.* "I say unto you, Ask, and it shall be given you; seek, and ye shall find: knock, and it shall be opened unto you" (Luke 11:9). *Ask*: Matthew 7:7; *seek*: James 5:17; *knock*: Acts 12:5.

3. *Definiteness.* "If ye then, being evil, know how to give good gifts unto your children, how much more shall your Father which is in heaven give good gifts to them that ask him" (Matt. 7:11).

4. *Persistence.* "Continue in prayer, and watch in the same with thanksgiving" (Col. 4:2). See also Luke 18:1-8.

5. *Faith.* "I say unto you, What things soever ye desire, when ye pray, believe that ye receive them, and ye shall have them" (Mark 11:24).

6. *Submission.* "This is the confidence that we have in him, that, if we ask anything according to his will he heareth us: and if we know that he hear us, whatsoever we ask, we know that we have the petitions that we desire of him" (I John 5:14, 15). When we ask according to His will, then *two* have agreed, thus assuring that prayer will be answered. "Again I say unto you, That if two of you shall agree on earth as touching anything that they shall ask, it shall be done for them of my Father which is in heaven" (Matt. 18:19).

H. Limitation.

1. *Through Spiritual Profanation.* This is well illustrated in the life of Esau. Paul bids us to look diligently "lest there be any fornicator, or profane person, as Esau, who for one morsel of meat sold his birthright. For ye know how that afterward, when he would have inherited the blessing, he was rejected: for he found no place of repentance though he sought it carefully with tears" (Heb. 12:16, 17). Esau gave away the blessings that went with the birthright. That which he sold was gone forever. In the Christian life lost days and lost opportunities are gone. Yesterday is gone forever.

2. *Through Judicial Penalties.* "Speak unto them, and say unto them, Thus saith the Lord GOD; Every man of the house of Israel that setteth up his idols in his heart, and putteth the stumblingblock of his iniquity before his face, and cometh to the prophet; I the LORD will answer him that cometh according to the multitude of his idols" (Ezek. 14:4). See also Deuteronomy 3:25-27; Jeremiah 15:1.

3. *Through Lack of Action.* "The LORD said unto Moses, Wherefore criest thou unto me? speak unto the children of Israel, that they *go forward*" (Ex. 14:15). To be sure there is a time to "stand still and see the salvation of the LORD," but there is also the time to go forward.

4. *Through Insincerity.* "When thou prayest, thou shalt not be as the hypocrites are, for they love to pray standing in the synagogue and in the corner of the streets, that they may be seen of men. Verily I say unto you, They have their reward" (Matt. 6:5).

5. *Through Carnal Motives.* "Ye ask, and receive not, because ye ask amiss, that ye may consume it upon your lust" (Jas. 4:3).

6. *Through Unbelief.* "Let him ask in faith, nothing wavering. For he that wavereth is like a wave of the sea driven with the wind and tossed. For let not that man think that he shall receive anything of the Lord" (Jas. 1:6, 7).

7. *Through Cherished Sin.* "If I regard iniquity in my heart, the Lord will not hear me" (Ps. 66:18).

8. *Through Failure to Ask.* "Ye have not, because ye ask not" (Jas. 4:2c). Some find a conflict with the above verse and Matthew 6:8: "Be not ye therefore like unto them: for your Father knoweth what things ye have need of, before ye ask him." They reason that if the Father knows what we have need of, why then should they pray? This has hurt the prayer life of many Christians. It should not. It is true that our Father knows everything we have need of; if He didn't He would not be God. His knowledge, however, is not a guarantee that we shall have the needed things: "Ye have not, because ye ask not." Yes, the Father knows what we need, but we have to pray for it. We are warned, nevertheless, that we cannot fool God and ask for things we do not need.

I. Mediation.

"There is one God, and one mediator between God and men, the man Christ Jesus" (I Tim. 2:5). "In whom we have boldness and access with confidence by the faith of him" (Eph. 3:12). See also John 16:24-26. "Through him we both have access by one Spirit unto the Father" (Eph. 2:18). This is the Scriptural formula for the presentation of prayers: To the Father, through the Son, by the Spirit.

Prayers should contain the following:

1. *Adoration.*
2. *Thanksgiving.*
3. *Confession.*
4. *Supplication.*
5. *Intercession.*

ECCLESIOLOGY
(The Doctrine of the Church)

Outline for Chapter VII

ECCLESIOLOGY

I. The Meaning of the Word.

II. The Use of the Word.

III. What the Church Is Not.

IV. What the Church Is.
   - A. A Mystery.
   - B. A Body.
   - C. A Building.
   - D. A Bride.

V. The Gifts to the Body.

VI. The Local Church.

VII. Discipline in the Church.

VIII. Ordinances in the Church.
   - A. Baptism.
   - B. Lord's Supper.

Chapter VII

ECCLESIOLOGY

Ecclesiology is the doctrine of the Church.

I. The Meaning of the Word

The word "church" does not mean the building in which the congregation meets; neither is it as the Catholics say, the Papal system. Others contend that it is a company, or a club, just an organization. The Church is not an organization, but an *organism.*

The following may surprise most students of the Word, but nevertheless, it is true. The word "church" cannot be found in the New Testament. The word "church," is a *rendition,* and not a translation. This same word "church" is a rendition of the word *ecclesia,* which means a called-out company, or assembly. If we should call Bible things by Bible names correctly, we would call it the assembly of God in Christ, instead of the Church of God in Christ.

The word *ecclesia* always means a called-out company, or assembly. It refers to all classes of people; it is not limited to believers in Christ. There are three references in the Bible that refer to three different kinds of people. None of them are related, yet they are called-out companies, or assemblies.

A. *A Mob.*

"When Paul would have entered in unto the people, the disciples suffered him not. And certain of the chief of Asia, which were his friends, sent unto him, desiring him that he would not adventure himself to the theater. Some therefore cried one thing, and some another: for the *assembly* [ecclesia: that is a mob, and not believers] was confused; and the more part knew not wherefore they were come together. . . . And when the townclerk had appeased the people, he said. . . . Ye have brought hither these men, which are neither robbers of churches [this word means temple; it is not from the word *ecclesia*], nor yet blasphemers of your goddess. . . . But if ye inquire anything concerning other matters, it shall be determined in a lawful *assembly* [this is the same word *ecclesia,* and does not mean believers] . . . . And when he had thus spoken, he dismissed the *assembly* [again the word *ecclesia*]" (Acts 19:30-32, 35, 37, 39, 41).

B. The Children of Israel.

Certainly the children of Israel were a called-out company from Egypt, but we know that they were not the body of Christ. Christ had not been manifested in the flesh as yet. "This is he, that was in the church in the wilderness with the angel which spake to him in the mount Sina, and with our fathers who received the lively oracles to give unto us" (Acts 7:38).

C. The Body of Christ.

By this we mean the body of believers in the Lord Jesus. The New Testament abounds with references to the *ecclesia,* the called-out company, or assembly, from the world to Christ. The following are a few: God "hath put all things under his feet, and gave him to be the head over all things to the *church* [*ecclesia,* meaning called-out company, or assembly], which is his body, the fulness of him that filleth all in all" (Eph. 1:22, 23). "Husbands, love your wives, even as Christ also loved the *church* [*ecclesia,* meaning called-out company or assembly], and gave himself for it. . . . This is a great mystery: but I speak concerning Christ and the *church* [*ecclesia,* meaning called-out company, or assembly]" (Eph. 5:25, 32).

II. The Use of the Word

Knowing that the word "church" is a rendition from the Greek, *ecclesia,* meaning called-out company, or assembly, we shall turn our attention to those portions of Scripture dealing with the body of believers. The word *ecclesia* is used in the following ways:

A. A Local Assembly (church).

"Paul, and Silvanus, and Timotheus, unto *the church* of the Thessalonians . . ." (I Thess. 1:1). "Unto the *church* of God which is at Corinth . . ." (I Cor. 1:2).

B. Local Assemblies (churches).

This has reference to several local bodies. "Paul . . . and all the brethren which are with me, unto the churches of Galatia: Grace be to you and peace" (Gal. 1:1-3).

C. The Body of Living Believers (unnumbered).

We must explain that by this we mean a group of believers, living in a certain section, without reference to a local assembly, and without number. For instance, a minister may speak of the Church of Chicago, the Church of Denver, etc. we immediately know that he is referring to all Christian believers in these cities. The best illustration in the Word is: "Ye have heard of my conversation in time past in the Jews' religion, how that beyond measure I persecuted the *church* of God, and wasted it" (Gal. 1:13). Saul (Paul) did not limit his persecution to one certain assembly, or several local assemblies. He went *everywhere,* hailing into prison, and voting the death penalty for the early Christians. He considered all Christians as *The Church.*

D. The Complete Body of Christ.

The complete body of Christ is called the *Church,* and is composed of all believers from Pentecost to the Rapture. "Husbands, love your wives even as Christ also loved the *church,* and gave Himself for it" (Eph. 5:25).

III. What the Church Is Not

A. The Church Is Not Israel.

"Give none offence, neither to the Jews, nor to the Gentiles, nor to the church of God" (I Cor. 10:32). Here is revealed that there are three classes of people today: Jew, Gentile and Church. When a Jew is saved, he ceases to be a Jew, and becomes a Christian. When a Gentile accepts Christ, he ceases to be a Gentile, and becomes a Christian. "As many of you as have been baptized into Christ have put on Christ. There is neither Jew nor Greek, there is neither bond nor free, there is neither male nor female: for ye are all one in Christ Jesus" (Gal. 3:27-29). The Church (Body of Christ) is not spiritual Israel: "He is our peace, who hath made both one, and hath broken down the middle wall of partition between us; having abolished in his flesh the enmity, even the law of commandments contained in ordinances; for to make in himself of twain *one new man,* so making peace" (Eph. 2:14, 15). The Body of Christ (Church) is a *new man,* and not Israel, whether spiritual Israel or revived Israel.

B. The Church Is Not the Kingdom.

Church	Kingdom
1. No heirs of the Church.	1. The Church is heir of the kingdom.
2. No receiver of the Church.	2. The Church is the receiver of the kingdom.
3. There are elders of the Church.	3. No elders of the kingdom.
4. No sons of the Church.	4. Sons of the kingdom.
5. Church called a temple (Eph. 2:21).	5. Kingdom never called a temple.
6. Church is here.	6. Kingdom is not here, for the King is not present (Matt. 6:10).
7. Church was never a subject of prophecy (Eph. 3:5, 9).	7. Kingdom is the one subject of prophecy.
8. Church is to be built up (Eph. 4:12).	8. Kingdom is to be set up (Acts 15:16).

IV. What the Church Is

A. It Is a Mystery.

"By revelation he made known unto me the mystery; (as I wrote afore in few words, whereby, when ye read, ye may understand my knowledge in the mystery of Christ) which in other ages was not made known unto the sons of men, as it is now revealed unto his holy apostles and prophets by the Spirit; that the Gentiles should be fellow heirs, and of the same body, and partakers of his promise in Christ by the gospel. . . . And to make all men see what is the fellowship of the mystery, which from the beginning of the world hath been hid in God, who created all things by Jesus Christ" (Eph. 3:3-6,9). A "mystery" in Scripture means a "truth revealed for the first time." In the above verses, the Holy Spirit shows us that *The Church* (Body of Christ) was first revealed to the Apostle Paul, and that it was not known by the Old Testament prophets. The truth of The Church was not hidden in Old Testament writings, but was hid in God.

B. It Is the Body of Which Christ Is the Head.

"As the body is one, and hath many members, and all the members of that one body, being many, are one body: so also is (the) Christ. For by one Spirit are we all baptized into one body, whether we be Jews or Gentiles, whether we be bond or free; and have been all made to drink into one Spirit. For the body is not one member, but many. . . . That there should be no schism in the body; but that the members should have the same care one for another. And whether one member suffer, all the members suffer with it; or one member be honored, all the members rejoice with it. Now ye are the body of Christ, and members in particular" (I Cor. 12:12-14, 25-27).

The Body is an organism composed of many members. All members do not have the same function. The Church is not a physical body, but a spiritual body. Believers in Christ are made members of that spiritual body by the Spirit's baptism. There are those who hold that I Corinthians 12:13 is speaking of water baptism, but this argument can easily be refuted by another Scripture. I Corinthians 12:13 says that we are made members of the Body by *baptism* (Spirit's), while Ephesians 3:6 declares we are made members of that Body by the *Gospel.* Both are correct. If I Corinthians 12:13 speaks of water baptism, then water baptism is an essential part of the Gospel of Ephesians 3:6. We know, however, that water baptism has no part in the Gospel whatsoever. *The Gospel is the death, burial and resurrection of Jesus Christ* (I Cor. 15:1-4).

As is true of the physical body, so it is of the spiritual Body; when one member of the Body suffers, all members suffer with it. Not one Christian can suffer persecution without the whole Body hurting also. One member cannot grieve, but that the whole Body grieves with it. When the Body suffers, the Head also suffers. When we are persecuted, Christ is also persecuted: "Saul, Saul, why persecutest thou me?" (Acts 9:4).

Remember that the Body is an organism and must be considered as such. A building, for example, can be repaired by replacing old doors and windows, and the like, with new ones, but when part of a body is removed, such as an arm, leg, eye, and the like, the part can never be replaced. If it were possible for a member of the Body of Christ to lose his salvation, then the Body of Christ would be mutilated, and this could never happen. The following are four characteristics of the Body of Christ:

1. *Oneness.* A body is one, a complete whole, an organic unity, So is the Body of Christ.

2. *Deathlessness.* The Body of Christ will never die, for it is connected with a living Head.

3. *Manifestation.* The one purpose of the Body of Christ is to manifest, or reveal Christ. "To me to live is Christ, and to die is gain" (Phil. 1:21). "I am crucified with Christ: nevertheless I live; yet not I, but Christ liveth in me: and the life which I now live in the flesh, I live by the faith of the Son of God, who loved me, and gave himself for me" (Gal. 2:20).

4. *Service.* The thoughts and the plans of the head are to be carried out by the body. Likewise, the Body of Christ is to carry out the will of its Head, the Lord Jesus Christ. What He commands we must do. His will shall govern our movements.

C. It Is a Building.

"Ye are no more strangers and foreigners, but fellow citizens with the saints, and of the household of God; and are built upon the foundation of the apostles and prophets, Jesus Christ himself being the chief cornerstone; in whom all the building fitly framed together groweth unto a holy temple in the Lord: in whom ye also are builded together for an habitation of God through the Spirit" (Eph. 2:19-22).

The apostles and New Testament prophets are the foundation of the Building (Church). They were the first ones to believe in the Lord Jesus, and they were the first ones to proclaim the Lord Jesus.

"Ye also, as lively stones, are built up a spiritual house, an holy priesthood, to offer up spiritual sacrifices, acceptable to God by Jesus Christ" (I Peter 2:5). We believers are living stones of this new building of God. When the temple of old was erected, there was no sound of hammer, chisel, or saw. All materials were formed beforehand. So are we, for we were selected before the foundation of the earth was laid. The inside stones of the temple could not be seen, for they were covered with cedarwood and gold. Only the gold could be seen. We, the living stones of the Building of God, are not to be seen. Christ only is to be seen.

The building was erected of different colored stones; even so the Building of God is composed of black, red, yellow and white races. God dwelt in the temple, and He abides in us.

D. It Is the Bride.

Some have contended that the Bride of Christ is the same

as the Wife of Jehovah, who is Israel. However, there is one Scripture which disproves this theory, and that is Revelation 22:17: "The Spirit and the bride say, Come. And let him that heareth say, Come. And let him that is athirst come. And whosoever will, let him take the water of life freely." The above passage declares that the Spirit and the Bride are extending the invitation to sinners to believe in the Lord Jesus Christ. If the Bride is Israel, then it is the Spirit and Israel extending the invitation. We know that is not true, for the greater part of Israel is in unbelief today. Who is inviting, or urging people to accept Christ? It is the Church, not Israel. Therefore, the Bride is the Church, the Body of believers.

Ephesians 5:25-32 clearly points to the fact that husband and wife have the same relationship as that of Christ and His Bride, the Church. Especially we see this in verses 28-30: "So ought men to love their own wives as their own bodies. He that loveth his wife loveth himself. For no man ever yet hateth his own flesh; but nourisheth and cherisheth it, even as the Lord the Church: For we are members of his body, of his flesh, and of his bones."

1. *The Bride Is Purchased By Christ.* "Husbands, love your wives, even as Christ also loved the church, and *gave himself* for it" (Eph. 5:25). See also I Corinthians 6:19, 20. In the Orient men purchased their wives; the price became her dowry. Christ bought His Church with His own precious blood. His blood is her dowry forever!

2. *The Bride Is Espoused to Christ.* "I am jealous over you with godly jealousy: for I have *espoused* you to one husband, that I may present you as a chaste virgin to Christ" (II Cor. 11:2). The Oriental marriage differs greatly from marriage as we know it. The Eastern custom of marriage took place after the following manner: First, the bride was bought (we have been bought by Christ); second, the ceremony was performed, inaugurating the espousal period, which lasted about a year. During this time the bride was considered the wife of her husband, yet they did not live together. The one year waiting period was protection of the future home. If there were any blemishes against the character and conduct of the bride, they would come to light during this time. The Bride of Christ is now in her espousal period. During this interval the blemishes of the Bride, if any, will certainly manifest

themselves. History has proved that there have been many who have had the form of godliness, but have denied the power thereof. These blemishes (these men) vanish away; finally comes the consummation of the marriage.

3. *The Bride Is Married to Christ.* "Let us be glad and rejoice, and give honour to him: for the marriage of the Lamb is come and his wife hath made herself ready. And to her was granted that she should be arrayed in fine linen, clean and white: for the fine linen is the righteousness of saints" (Rev. 19:7, 8). "Then shall the Realm of heaven be compared to ten maidens who took their lamps and went out to meet the bridegroom and the bride" (Matt. 25:1 – Moffatt). This is the consummation of Christ's marriage to His Church. The espousal period is over; she is now with her husband, and so shall she ever be with Him (I Thess. 4:17).

V. The Gifts to the Body

"Unto every one of us is given grace according to the measure of the gift of Christ. Wherefore he saith, When He ascended up on high, he led captivity captive, and gave gifts unto men. . . . And he gave some apostles; and some, prophets; and some, evangelists; and some, pastors and teachers" (Eph. 4:7, 8, 11).

A. *Apostles.*

This was the first gift to the Church (Body). Upon the Apostles was built the early Church. The word "apostle" in the Greek is the same as the word "missionary" in Latin, meaning "the sent one." Of course, the Church has missionaries (sent ones) today, but no apostles.

B. *Prophets.*

To these men God gave His revelations. At the first, the Church did not have the New Testament, yet it needed to know the doctrines of God; therefore, God gave to men His unwritten Word; these in turn gave it to the people. The Church has no prophets today for we have God's complete revealed truth, the New Testament.

C. *Evangelists.*

Another gift to the Church was evangelists. These men fervently heralded the Gospel. They were men of humility, burdened for the lost. The pastor is told to do the work of an evangelist (II Tim. 4:5). The day of the evangelist is *not* over, and will not be until Christ comes to reign upon the earth.

D. Pastors and Teachers.

The word "pastor" means "shepherd." The pastor is to be the shepherd of his sheep, looking after his flock, weeping and rejoicing with them. The crying need of the Church today is for pastors. Blessed is the man who has a pastor's heart. A pastor is not only called to preach three sermons a week, but he is called to pastor, shepherd, look after, care for, visit, love, protect, instruct the sheep. Every pastor, while doing the work of an evangelist, which is winning souls, should also be one who is able to *teach* the Word to his flock. Where will the church members get the Word if not from the pastor? All of the truth some people will get will be at a Sunday service.

Some distinguish between the pastor and the teacher, believing that there are those who are called only to be teachers. This may be so, but we know that all pastors are to be teachers also. All teachers may not be pastors, but all pastors *must* be teachers.

VI. The Local Church

While we believe that the Body of Christ is composed of all believers from Pentecost to the Rapture, we do stress the importance of the *local* church, or assembly. The local assembly is the physical body by which the Body (Church) is manifested. God stresses the importance of the local church by giving it officers and ordinances. He who is ashamed of the local assembly is ashamed of that which was established at Pentecost. The local church, as well as the Body of Christ, was established at Pentecost.

A. Its Organization.

The Scriptures indicate that there was some organization, but not as that today. It was not copied after the synagogue. It was entirely different.

B. Its Officers.

1. *Deacons.* I Timothy 3:8-13 gives the requirements for deacons. The deacons were not chosen to run the church, but to minister to the church.

2. *Bishops and Elders.* There is a vast difference between the early Church and that of today as to bishops. The early Church had *many* bishops in one local church; today, we have *one* bishop over many local churches. The elders were called

by that name because they were the oldest in the family. If the father were dead, the first son took his place. An elder was an elderly man. Titus 1:5-7 says, "For this cause I left thee in Crete, that thou shouldest set in order the things that are wanting, and ordain elders in every city, as I appointed thee: if any be blameless, the husband of one wife, having faithful children not accused of riot or unruly. For a bishop must be blameless, as the steward of God; not self-willed, not soon angry, not given to wine, no striker, not given to filthy lucre." According to this, the elder and bishop were the same. The word "elder" refers to the person, while the word "bishop" refers to the office. Every bishop was an elder, but every elder was not a bishop. The word "bishop" means "overseer." The "overseers" of the local churches were old men. This group of bishops composed what is known as the presbytery (I Tim. 1:4).

C. Its Purpose.

The purpose of the Church is to glorify God in the building up of the Body of Christ in the holy faith; and to spread the Gospel to the ends of the earth, winning, baptizing, teaching.

VII. Discipline in the Local Church

Even though it is true that the Church is under grace rather than law, the flesh is still in the believer, and the Lord has laid down rules of discipline for His local church. There were three steps in Church discipline, and they are as follows:

A. Judgment By Self.

"If we would judge ourselves, we should not be judged" (I Cor. 11:31). The believer knows when he has sinned and should immediately confess it to God (I John 1:9). If he confesses that sin, he has judged himself. It is forgiven, and he shall never be judged for it again. Let us stress the word "confess" however. Confess does not mean to admit it, that is, to own up to it; that is implied, but it goes deeper than that. It means to take one's stand against.

B. Judgment By the Church.

If a sinning brother will not judge himself, then he must be judged by the local church. I Corinthians 5:11, 12 says "I have written unto you not to keep company, if any man that is called a brother be a fornicator, or covetous, or an idolator, or a railer, or a drunkard, or an extortioner; with such an one no not to eat. For what have I to do to judge them also that are without? do not ye judge them that are within?" Yes, fellowship in the local church should be withheld from the erring brother as judgment. Some term this "back-door revival." This extreme judgment should be meted out only after the effort to restore him. "Brethren, if a man be overtaken in a fault, ye which are spiritual, restore such an one in the spirit of meekness: Considering thyself, lest thou also be tempted" (Gal. 6:1).

C. *Judgment By God.*

If the fallen brother does not judge himself, and the Church will not judge him, then God will judge him through chastisement (Heb. 12:5-13).

VIII. Ordinances in the Local Church

The Church has two ordinances: baptism and the Lord's Supper. Baptism is observed at the beginning of the Christian life; the Lord's Supper is taken all during the Christian life. We emphasize the fact that these are ordinances of the Church, and not sacraments.

A. *Baptism.*

Baptism is from the Greek word *baptizo,* meaning to dip, to plunge, to immerse for the purpose of dying. It can never mean sprinkling, or pouring.

1. *Obligation* (Matt. 28:18-20; Rom. 6:1-6; Col. 2:12). All believers are obliged to be baptized. One does not have to pray about it to seek God's will in the matter. The Lord has commanded it.

2. *Administration.* Nearly every denomination, with the exception of some local Baptist groups, demands that their ministers, who administer the ordinance of baptism, must be ordained.

3. *Explanation.* Baptism is a public declaration of faith in Christ by the believer before man. It is his outward demonstration of an inward act, and is a picture of the death, burial and resurrection of the Lord Jesus Christ. Immersion fully portrays the place of death; there are some people, even today, who have met actual physical death after coming up out of the baptismal waters. Those who have come out of other religions evaluate the ordinance of baptism more highly than those who

have been raised in Christian homes. Not only does baptism show the death, burial and resurrection of the Lord Jesus Christ, but it also shows the believer's identification *with* Christ. Baptism is his full declaration of his own death in Christ (II Cor. 5:14): dead to sin, dead to self and dead to the old life. It is also his declaration of being raised with Christ, after burying the old life, to walk in newness of life with Him.

The baptism of all believers, as recorded in the Word, pictures the death, burial and resurrection of Christ. The baptism of John the Baptist looked *forward* to Christ's death and resurrection, and our baptism today looks *back* to the death and resurrection of our Lord.

It is not a saving ordinance. Man is saved by faith alone. This occurs *before* baptism. It is true, however, that baptism is a public declaration of faith before man, and God looks not upon the baptismal waters, but upon the heart of man.

4. *Participation.* Who should be baptized? I believe *only* the believer! "He that believeth and is baptized shall be saved; but he that believeth not shall be damned" (Mark 16:16). Faith is first, then baptism. Again the question arises, "Does man have to be baptized to be saved?" No, for this Scripture says that he that *believeth not* shall be damned. *If* water baptism were essential, the Lord would have added these words, "He that is not baptized is damned." The Apostle Paul, in writing to the Corinthians said, "I thank God that I baptized none of you, but Crispus and Gaius. . . . For Christ sent me not to baptize, but to preach the gospel: not with wisdom of words, lest the cross of Christ should be of none effect" (I Cor. 1:14, 17). If baptism were necessary for salvation, Paul would not have boasted in the fact that he had baptized so few. He plainly states that baptism had nothing to do with the Gospel (Rom. 1:16), for Christ had sent him not to baptize, but to preach.

It is impossible to baptize an unbeliever, for if he is an unbeliever *before* he is immersed, he will be an unbeliever when he comes out of the baptismal waters.

What is the age limit for baptism? Some parents contend that twelve years of age is the youngest age at which a child should be baptized. This has no Scriptural foundation whatsoever. It may be a carry-over from the Jewish custom of adoption. The Word clearly states that baptism is for *all believers,* regardless of age or sex.

B. Lord's Supper.

"I have received of the Lord that which also I delivered unto you, that the Lord Jesus the same night in which he was betrayed took bread: and when he had given thanks, he brake it, and said, Take, eat: this is my body, which is broken for you: this do in remembrance of me. After the same manner also he took the cup, when he had supped, saying, This cup is the New Testament in my blood: this do ye, as oft as ye drink it, in remembrance of me. For as often as ye eat this bread, and drink this cup, ye do shew the Lord's death till he come. Wherefore whosoever shall eat this bread, and drink this cup of the Lord, unworthily, shall be guilty of the body and blood of the Lord. But let a man examine himself, and so let him eat of that bread, and drink of that cup" (I Cor. 11:23-28).

1. *Origination.* From the above Scriptures little doubt is left as to who instituted the Lord's Supper. There is no record of this ordinance being held *before* the Lord Jesus inaugurated it. We, as it were, take the bread and the cup from His own precious hands. The theory that Christ never lived is exploded by the Lord's Supper. It is His, and His only.

2. *Obligation.* The words "this do" are a command of the Lord, and the words "all of it" (Matt. 26:27) are better translated "all of you." This ordinance is for the entire Body of Christ.

3. *Participation.*

a. *Who?* No one but a baptized child of God should participate in the Lord's Supper. Those who sat with Him at the last supper had been baptized. Baptism is the symbol of the commencing of the new life, and the Lord's Supper is a symbol of the sustenance of that life.

b. *How often?* Some churches observe the Lord's Supper every Sunday; some, once a month; others, four times a year; and still others, once a year; some never observe the Lord's Supper. What is the Scriptural stipulation for this observance? "As often" (I Cor. 11:26): there is no set, rigid rule.

c. *In What Manner?* Some believers are very confused concerning their fitness to partake of the Lord's Supper after reading I Corinthians 11:27-29. They notice the word "unworthily," and immediately they review their past mistakes, ever since they became a Christian, and fear that they shall be eating and drinking damnation to themselves if they partake. Let us point out that the word "unworthily" is an adverb, and modifies the word "drink," which means to drink in an "unworthy manner." As far as being worthy is concerned, which one of us can call himself worthy? No one! This has reference to the *act* of participation. The context will give a perfect explanation. In the early church love feasts were held; the rich brought their store of food and wine, while the converted slaves brought nothing. As the feast progressed, the rich believer, keeping his food and drink to himself, soon became drunk. The poor slave, of course, had nothing, and remained sober. The Lord's Supper was observed at the conclusion of the feast. The drunken believer could not appreciate the Lord's Supper. In his drunkenness, the cup of the Lord's Supper meant nothing more to him than another drink of wine. He could not discern the Lord's body and blood; thus, he drank it "unworthily." This fact led to many untimely deaths in the Corinthian Church: "For this cause many are weak and sickly among you, and many sleep" (I Cor. 11:30).

If the Christian feels unworthy, it is a good indication that he *is* worthy, and vice versa. The man who finds some personal quality in himself to make him worthy to partake of the Lord's Supper had better stay away. The table is not spread for the righteous, but for the unrighteous, who are justified by faith.

4. *Constitution.* The elements of the Lord's Supper are bread and fruit of the vine. The bread was unleavened, as it was used in the observance of the Passover, from which the Lord inaugurated the Lord's Supper.

5. *Interpretation.*

a. *Transubstantiation.* This interpretation is held by the Roman Catholic Church. It declares that by the consecration of the priest the bread and wine cease to remain, as such, and become the actual body and blood of the Lord Jesus Christ. This Faith contends that when the Lord said, "Verily, verily, I say unto you, Except ye eat the flesh of the Son of man, and drink his blood, ye have no life in you" (John 6:53), he meant the actual flesh and blood of Christ. Therefore, the Mass is that ritual which turns the bread and wine into the actual flesh and blood of Christ. The priest alone drinks the wine, as not one drop of Christ's blood must be spilt. The bread is in the form of a wafer, so that not a crumb of His body should be lost. In answer to this we ask, "How could Christ, while being in His perfect body, hold part of His body in His hand when he said, 'This is my body'?"

b. *Consubstantiation.* The Lutherans and the Church of England believe this interpretation, which states that, while the bread remains bread, and the wine remains wine, the body and blood is present in a spiritual sense; the body and blood are present only at the moment when they are partaken of, and after being taken, cease to be the body and blood of Christ.

c. *Symbolism.* This is the true interpretation, which states that the bread and wine are only symbols of Christ's body and blood, which were offered upon Calvary's cross for the remission of sins. "This do in *remembrance* of me"; it is observed in blessed memory, and that is where it ends.

6. *Limitation.* How long should the Church continue this observance? Till He comes again. What is our answer to the scoffer who jeers at the Second Coming, and who asks, "Where is the promise of His coming?" We point to the Lord's Table and reply, "There is the promise of His coming."

7. *Evaluation.*

a. *Its Value Doctrinally.*

(1) *The Person of Christ.*

(a) *His Humanity.* His humanity is as real as His Deity. The symbols speak of His actual human body and blood, and it is most essential that it is human, as the atonement must be in the nature of that which sinned ("Christ died for *us*").

(b) *His Deity.* His Deity is expressed in the words "Lord's Supper." All titles of Deity are in this one word, "Lord."

(2) *The Work of Christ.*

(a) *His Death.* The elements of the Lord's Supper portray this fact, for the body and blood are together in life, but separated in death.

(b) *His Resurrection and Second Coming.* "Till I come" does not mean "till I come from the grave", but "till I come from heaven."

(3) *The Way of Salvation.*

(a) *It Assumes Our Guilt and Helplessness.*

(b) *It Emphasizes Substitution.* ("Broken for you")

(c) *It Reminds Us That Salvation Is Free.* (Given for you)

(d) *It Declares the Gift of Salvation Must Be Accepted.* (Take, eat and drink)

b. *Its Value Devotionally.*

(1) *We Come With Confession.*

(2) *We Come With Prayer.*

(3) *We Come With Consecration.*

(4) *We Come With Humility.*

(5) *We Come With Thanksgiving.*

(6) *The Whole Man Is Engaged.*

(a) *Ears to Hear His Invitation.*

(b) *Eyes to See Its Symbol.*

(c) *Hands That Handle the Elements.*

(d) *Mouth Which Eats the Elements.*

(e) *Body Which Assimilates the Element – Becomes Part of Us.*

c. *Its Value Practically.*

(1) *It Is a Means of Grace.*

(2) *It Is a Means of Testimony.*

(3) *It Is a Means of Strengthening Faith.*

(4) *It Is a Means to Promote Our Love Toward Him.*

(5) *It Is a Means to Promote Love Toward One Another.*

(6) *It Is a Means to Promote Fellowship.* This fellowship is one with another in Christ around the Lord's Table, He being the center.

(7) *It Is a Means to Stimulate Holiness.*

d. *Its Value Prophetically.* If the Lord Jesus is not coming the second time, why celebrate the Lord's Supper? *He is coming!* Remember, in answer to those who ask, "Where is the promise of His coming?", we point to the Lord's Supper.

ANGELOLOGY
(The Doctrine of Angels)

Outline for Chapter VIII

ANGELOLOGY

I. Definition.
  A. Expression.
  B. Explanation.
  C. Designation.

II. Description.
  A. Their Personality.
  B. Their Origination.
  C. Their Enumeration.
  D. Their Habitation.
  E. Their Characterization.
  F. Their Perfection – Attributes.
  G. Their Gradation.
  H. Their Division.

III. Delineation.
  A. Good Angels.
  B. Bad Angels.

IV. Satan.
  A. The Names and Descriptive Titles of Satan.
  B. The Personality of Satan.
  C. The Origin of Satan.
  D. The Career of Satan.
  E. The Location of Satan.
  F. The Character of Satan.
  G. The Work of Satan.
  H. The Limitation of Satan.
  I. Our Attitude Toward Satan.

Chapter VIII

ANGELOLOGY

Angelology is the doctrine of angels.

I. Definition

A. Expression.

"Who maketh his angels spirits; his ministers a flaming fire" (Ps. 104:4). "The angel of the Lord encampeth round about them that fear him, and delivereth them" (Ps. 34:7). "What is man, that thou art mindful of him? and the son of man, that thou visitest him? For thou madest him a little lower than the angels, and hast crowned him with glory and honor" (Ps. 8:4, 5). "Behold, I will send my *messenger,* and he shall prepare the way before me" (Mal. 3:1a). "Then shall he say also unto them on the left hand, Depart from me, ye cursed, into everlasting fire, prepared for the devil and his angels" (Matt. 25:41). See also Genesis 19:1, 15; 24:7; 28:12; Psalm 103:20; Hebrews 1:7, 14; Matthew 11:10; Luke 7:27.

B. Explanation.

1. *Translation.* The Old Testament Hebrew and the New Testament Greek translate the word "angel" as "ambassador, messenger, deputy, and ministers."

a. *For Human Messengers.* From one human to another: "When the *messengers* of John were departed, he began to speak unto the people concerning John" (Luke 7:24a).

b. *For Human Messengers Bearing a Divine Message.* "Then spake Haggai the Lord's *messenger* in the Lord's message unto the people, saying, I am with you, saith the Lord" (Hag. 1:13). See also Galatians 4:14.

c. *For Impersonal Providence.* This may be some physical deformity. "Lest I should be exalted above measure through the abundance of the revelations, there was given to me a thorn in the flesh, the *messenger* of Satan to buffet me, lest I should be exalted above measure" (II Cor. 12:7).

d. *For Bishops or Preachers.* "Unto the *angel* of the

church of Ephesus write; These things saith he that holdeth the seven stars in his right hand, who walketh in the midst of the seven golden candlesticks" (Rev. 2:1). See also Revelation 1:20; 2:8, 12, 18; 3:1, 7, 14.

e. *For Demons Without Bodies.* "When the Pharisees heard it, they said, This fellow doth not cast out devils [demons], but by Beelzebub the prince of the devils [demons]" (Matt. 12:24; 25:41).

f. *For Heavenly Beings.* See Genesis 18.

g. *For One Pre-eminent Angel: The Angel of the Lord.* "The angel of the LORD appeared unto him in a flame of fire out of the midst of a bush: and he looked, and, behold, the bush burned with fire, and the bush was not consumed" (Ex. 3:2).

2. *Notation.* The term "angel" is not a personal name, but rather a title describing an office.

C. *Designation.*

There are three angels whose personal names we know:

1. *Lucifer.* This is the unfallen name of the Devil. Satan is his fallen name. "How art thou fallen from heaven, O Lucifer, son of the morning! how art thou cut down to the ground, which did weaken the nations!" (Is. 14:12).

2. *Michael—The Archangel.* According to the Scriptures there is only one archangel. He is mentioned in the books of Daniel and Revelation. Michael has to do with the resurrection; it is he who shall sound the trumpet, and not Gabriel. "Yet Michael the archangel, when contending with the devil he disputed about the body of Moses, durst not bring against him a railing accusation, but said, The Lord rebuke thee" (Jude 9). "The Lord himself shall descend from heaven with a shout, with the voice of the archangel [*Michael*], and with the trump of God: and the dead in Christ shall rise first" (I Thess. 4:16).

a. *Prince of Daniel's People, the Jews.*

b. *Head of the Heavenly Army of Angels.*

3. *Gabriel.* This name is found in Daniel and Luke. "I heard a man's voice between the banks of Ulai which called, and said, Gabriel, make this man to understand the vision" (Dan. 8:16). "The angel answering said unto him, I am Gabriel, that stand in the presence of God; and am sent to speak

unto thee, and to shew thee these glad tidings" (Luke 1:19). See also Daniel 9:21-27; Luke 1:26, 27.

II. Description

A. Their Personality.

They are personal beings, and not impersonal influences, such as thoughts, ideas, etc. Paul writes that "peradventure" God will give "those that oppose themselves" "repentance to the acknowledging of the truth . . . that they may recover themselves out of the snare of the devil, who are taken captive by him at his will" (II Tim. 2:25, 26). See also II Samuel 14: 20; Revelation 12:9, 12; 22:8, 9.

B. Their Origination.

They are created beings and superior to man, but they are not as the artist paints them, having wings, and the like. No doubt they have bodies, but not like our bodies. If our eyes were not blinded by the fall of man, we might be able to see them. Eve saw Satan as an angel of light. Angels are not *eternal* beings. While they will live forever, yet they have not lived forever, because they are *created* beings. They were created like man, but not as human beings. A Christian does not become an angel when he dies, but, in Christ, he is greater than angels can ever be. "By him were all things created, that are in heaven, and that are in earth, visible and invisible, whether they be thrones, or dominions, or principalities, or powers: all things were created by him, and for him" (Col. 1:16). See also Nehemiah 9:6; Genesis 18:8; Luke 24:37.

C. Their Enumeration.

"Ye are come into mount Sion, and unto the city of the living God, the heavenly Jerusalem, and to an innumerable company of angels" (Heb. 12:22). "Thinkest thou that I cannot now pray to my Father, and he shall presently give me more than twelve legions of angels?" (Matt. 26:53). Six thousand composed a legion; the Lord could have called for seventy-two thousand angels for aid had he so desired. See also Daniel 7:10; Psalm 68:17.

D. Their Habitation.

A great many angels dwell in the heavenlies. "In the resurrection they neither marry, nor are given in marriage, but are as the angels of God in heaven" (Matt. 22:30). See also Matthew 18:10; Luke 2:13-15; John 1:15; Galatians 1:8; Revelation 5:11; 7:11.

E. Their Characterization.

1. *Angels Are Spirits.* "Of the angels he saith, Who maketh his angels spirits, and his ministers a flame of fire" (Heb. 1:7). See also Hebrews 1:14; Psalm 104:4.

2. *Angels are Corporeal.* Although being spirit, they have bodies of some kind and perform bodily acts. Mary "seeth two angels in white sitting, the one at the head, and the other at the feet, where the body of Jesus had lain" (John 20:12). See also Genesis 18:1-8; 19:1-3; Judges 6.

3. *Angels Are Masculine.* It is an error to say they are sexless. They are always manifested in the form of man. Masculine pronouns are always used in connection with them. "And entering into the sepulchre, they saw a young man sitting on the right side, clothed in a long white garment; and they were affrighted. And he saith unto them, Be not affrighted: ye seek Jesus of Nazareth, which was crucified: He is risen; he is not here: behold the place where they laid him" (Mark 16:5, 6). See also Matthew 28:2-4; Luke 1:26.

4. *Angels are Celibates.* There is no record of angels ever marrying angels. "In the resurrection they neither marry nor are given in marriage, but are as the angels of God in heaven" (Matt. 22:30). The quoted Scripture does not mean that we will be sexless, but that we will not marry.

F. Their Perfection – Attributes.

1. *They Are Deathless.* They will never die, or cease to exist. They do not grow old. "They which shall be accounted worthy to obtain that world, and the resurrection from the dead, neither marry, nor are given in marriage: neither can they die any more: for they are equal unto the angels; and are the children of God, being the children of the resurrection" (Luke 20:35, 36).

2. *They are Immutable.* There is no matter in them that can change.

3. *They Are Illocal.* They are not subject to limitation, or space. We are (Acts 17:26). However, they are not omnipresent.

4. *They Are Mighty.* They are not omnipotent (almighty). They are mightier than we are, but are inferior to God. "To you who are troubled rest with us when the Lord Jesus shall

be revealed from heaven with his mighty angels" (II Thess. 1:7). See also Acts 5:19; 12:5-11, 23; Psalm 103:20; II Peter 2:10, 11.

5. *They Are Wise.* They possess super-human intelligence, yet they are not omniscient (all-wise). One of the purposes of Paul's preaching was "to the intent that now unto the principalities and powers in heavenly places might be known by the church the manifold wisdom of God, according to the eternal purpose which he purposed in Christ Jesus our Lord" (Eph. 3:10, 11). See also II Samuel 14:17-20; Matthew 24:36; Mark 13:32; I Peter 1:10-12.

6. *They are Subordinate.* They are always subject to God. Even the Devil is in this category. There is nothing he can do, but by the will of God. "[Jesus Christ] is gone into heaven, and is on the right hand of God; angels and authorities and powers being made subject unto him" (I Peter 3:22). See also Hebrews 1:4-8, 13, 14.

G. *Their Gradation.*

1. *The Angel of the Lord.* This angel is presented as no other angel in the Scriptures. He possesses a position no other angel could occupy. He is the Lord Jesus Christ himself. He presented himself to Hagar, Abraham and Gideon.

2. *The Cherubim.* This is the plural of cherub. They are mighty beings, always connected with the throne of God. They were present in the garden of Eden. They were placed there to keep Adam and Eve from re-entering the garden. According to Scripture, they seem to be more than just angelic beings, for they are connected with God as a symbol of God himself. Images of cherubims were made of gold and overlooked the mercy seat. The mercy seat is a type of Christ; thus, the cherubims are pictured as overlooking the work of Christ in love and light.

3. *The Anointed Cherub.* No doubt this was Satan in his unfallen estate. "Thou are the anointed cherub that covereth; and I have set thee so: thou wast upon the holy mountain of God; thou hast walked up and down in the midst of the stones of fire" (Ezek. 28:14).

4. *The Seraphim.* These angelic beings are mentioned only in Isaiah. They are attentive unto the LORD of Hosts. "In the year that king Uzziah died I saw also the Lord sitting upon a throne, high and lifted up, and his train filled the

temple. Above it stood the seraphims: each one had six wings . . . . Then flew one of the seraphims unto me, having a live coal in his hand, which he had taken with tongs from off the altar" (Is. 6:1, 2, 6).

5. *Archangel.* "Michael the archangel, when contending with the devil he disputed about the body of Moses, durst not bring against him a railing accusation, but said, The Lord rebuke thee" (Jude 9). See also I Thessalonians 4:16.

6. *Throne.* "By him were all things created, that are in heaven, and that are in the earth, visible, and invisible, whether they be *thrones,* or dominions, or principalities, or powers: all things were created by him, and for him" (Col. 1:16).

7. *Dominion.* God set Christ "at his own right hand in the heavenly places, far above all principality, and power, and might, and *dominion,* and every name that is named, not only in this world but also in that which is to come" (Eph. 1:20, 21). See also Colossians 1:16.

8. *Principalities.* "I am persuaded, that neither death, nor life, nor angels, nor principalities, nor powers, nor things present nor things to come, nor heighth, nor depth, nor any other creature, shall be able to separate us from the love of God, which is in Christ Jesus our Lord" (Rom. 8:38, 39). See also Colossians 1:16; Ephesians 6:12.

9. *Powers.* "Unto the principalities and *powers* in heavenly places might be known by the church the manifold wisdom of God" (Eph. 3:10). See also Colossians 1:16; Ephesians 1:21.

10. *Mighty.* "God standeth in the congregation of the mighty; he judgeth among the Gods" (Ps. 82:1). See also Psalm 89:6.

11. *Authorities.* "[Jesus Christ] is gone into heaven, and is on the right hand of God; angels and *authorities* and powers being made subject unto him" (I Peter 3:22).

12. *Dignities.* "These filthy dreamers defile the flesh, despise dominion, and speak evil of *dignities*" (Jude 8). See also II Peter 2:10.

H. Their Division.

Angels are divided into two great moral realms or spheres:

1. *Holy Angels — Angels of God.* "Jacob went on his way, and the angels of God met him. And when Jacob saw them, he said, This is God's host: and he called the name of that

place Mahanaim" (Gen. 32:1, 2). See also Matthew 25:31; Daniel 4:13.

2. *Fallen Angels – Angels of Satan.* "There was war in heaven: Michael and his angels fought against the dragon; and the dragon fought and his angels, and prevailed not; neither was their place found any more in heaven. And the great dragon was cast out, that old serpent, called the Devil, and Satan, which deceiveth the whole world: he was cast out into the earth, and his angels were cast out with him" (Rev. 12:7-9). See also II Peter 2:4-6; Jude 6, 7.

These are called the angels of Satan; they were not created by him; they became his by choice. All angels were created in holiness; possessing a free will, they could choose either to serve God or Satan. "A God very terrible in the council of the holy ones, and to be feared above all them that are round about him" (Ps. 89:7, R.V.). See also Matthew 18:10; 13:9; Mark 8:38; John 8:34; II Peter 2:4; Jude 6; I John 5:18.

III. Delineation

A. *Good Angels.*

1. *Their Adoration.* "Again, when he bringeth in the first begotten into the world, he said, And let all the angels of God worship him" (Heb. 1:6). See also Isaiah 6:3; John 12:41; Revelation 5:11, 12. We are told in Colossians 2:18 never to worship angels.

2. *Their Ministration.*

a. *Angelic Revelation.* They are able to carry the will of God to man. "If the word spoken by angels was stedfast, and every transgression and disobedience received a just recompence of reward; how shall we escape, if we neglect so great salvation" (Heb. 2:2). Also Daniel 8:16, 17; Luke 1:11-13; Acts 1:9-11.

b. *Angelic Preservation.* They are sent to help the saints of God. "He answered and said, Lo, I see four men loose, walking in the midst of the fire, and they have no hurt; and the form of the fourth is like the Son of God" (Dan. 3:25). See also II Kings 6:15-18; Hebrews 1:14.

c. *Angelic Stimulation.* They are sent to encourage the child of God. "For there stood by me this night the angel of God, whose I am, and whom I serve, saying, Fear not, Paul; thou must be brought before Caesar: and, lo, God hath given thee all them that sail with thee. Wherefore, sirs, be of good cheer: for I believe God, that it shall be even as it was told me" (Acts 27:23-25).

d. *Angelic Emancipation.* They are sent to deliver the child of God. "The angel of the Lord by night opened the prison doors, and brought them forth, and said, Go, stand and speak in the temple to the people all the words of this life" (Acts 5:19, 20).

e. *Angelic Sustentation.* "The devil leaveth him, and, behold, angels came and ministered unto him" (Matt. 4:11). See also Luke 22:43.

f. *Angelic Conduction.* "The angel of the Lord spake unto Philip, saying, Arise, and go toward the south unto the way that goeth down from Jerusalem unto Gaza, which is desert" (Acts 8:26). See also Genesis 24:7; Exodus 23:20-23; Numbers 20:16; Acts 10:3-8.

g. *Angelic Administration.* They execute the will of God. "Bless the LORD, all ye hosts; ye ministers of his, that do his pleasure. Bless the LORD all his works in all places of his dominion: bless the LORD, O my soul" (Ps. 103:21, 22).

(1) *In Judgment.* "Let them be as chaff before the wind: and let the angel of the LORD chase them" (Ps. 35:5). See also I Chronicles 21:15; II Kings 19:35.

(2) *In Guarding the Saved.* "At that time shall Michael stand up, the great prince which standeth for the children of thy people" (Dan. 12:1a). See also Hebrews 1:14.

(3) *In Guarding the Dead.* "And it came to pass, that the beggar died, and was carried by the angels into Abraham's bosom: the rich man also died, and was buried" (Luke 16:22).

(4) *In Communicating the Law.* "Wherefore then serveth the law? It was added because of transgression, till the seed should come to whom the promise was made; and it was ordained by angels in the hand of a mediator" (Gal. 3:19). See also Hebrews 2:2.

(5) *In Accompanying Christ.* "To you who are troubled rest with us, when the Lord Jesus shall be revealed from heaven with his mighty angels" (II Thess. 1:7).

(6) *In Regathering Israel.* "When the Son of man shall come in his glory, and all the holy angels with him, then shall he sit upon the throne of his glory" (Matt. 25:31).

(7) *In Harvesting at the End of the Age.* "Let both grow together until the harvest: and in the time of harvest I will say to the reapers, Gather ye together first the tares, and bind them in bundles to burn them: but gather the wheat into my barn" (Matt. 13:30).

B. Evil Angels.

These are the angelic followers of the Devil. These are they for whom hell is prepared.

1. *Their Designation.* They are evil spirits; seductive, unclean, demons. "When he was come to the other side into the country of the Gergesenes, there met him two possessed with devils [demons] coming out of the tombs, exceeding fierce, so that no man might pass by that way" (Matt. 8:28). See also Matthew 9:33; 10:1; 12:43; Mark 1:26; 5:2-5; 9:17, 20; Luke 6:18; 9:39.

2. *Their Division.*

a. *Fallen and Free.*

b. *Fallen and Chained.* "God spared not the angels that sinned, but cast them down to hell and delivered them into chains of darkness, to be reserved unto judgment" (II Peter 2:4). See also Ephesians 6:12; Jude 6.

3. *The Free Angels.*

a. *Their Activities.*

(1) *They Obtain Possession of the Bodies of Men.* "They also which saw it told them by what means he that was possessed of the devils [demons] was healed" (Luke 8:36).

(2) *They Voluntarily Vacate the Bodies of Men.* "When the unclean spirit is gone out of a man, he walketh through dry places, seeking rest, and findeth none" (Matt. 12:43).

b. *Their Energies.*

(1) *They Threw a Man Down and Didn't Hurt Him.* "Jesus rebuked him, saying, Hold thy peace, and come out of him. And when the devil [demon] had thrown him in the midst, he came out of him, and hurt him not" (Luke 4:35).

(2) *They Threw a Man Down and Tore Him.* "As he was yet a coming, the devil [demon] threw him down, and tare him. And Jesus rebuked the unclean spirit, and healed the child, and delivered him again to his father" (Luke 9:42).

(3) *They Drove a Man Into the Wilderness.* "He had commanded the unclean spirit to come out of the man. For

oftentimes it had caught him: and he was kept bound with chains and in fetters; and he brake the bonds, and was driven of the devil [demon] into the wilderness" (Luke 8:29).

c. *Characteristics.*

(1) *Some Are Deaf.* "When Jesus saw that the people came running together, he rebuked the foul spirit, saying unto him, Thou dumb and deaf spirit, I charge thee, come out of him, and enter no more into him" (Mark 9:25).

(2) *Some Are Dumb.* "One of the multitude answered and said, Master, I have brought unto thee my son, which hath a dumb spirit" (Mark 9:17).

(3) *Some Are Lying.* "The LORD said unto him, Wherewith? And he said, I will go forth, and will be a lying spirit in the mouth of all his prophets. And he said, Thou shalt persuade him, and prevail also: go forth, and do so" (I Kings 22:22).

(4) *Some are Foul.* "When Jesus saw that the people were running together, he rebuked the foul spirit" (Mark 9:25a).

(5) *Some Are Seducing.* "Now the Spirit speaketh expressly, that in the latter times some shall depart from the faith, giving heed to seducing spirits, and doctrines of devils [demons]" (I Tim. 4:1).

d. *Their Power.* It is tremendous.

(1) *They Control the Bodies of Both Men and Beasts* (Mark 5:8-13).

(2) *They Inflict Physical Infirmities.* "Ought not this woman, being a daughter of Abraham, whom Satan hath bound, lo, these eighteen years, be loosed from this bond on the sabbath day?" (Luke 13:16).

(3) *They Inflict Mental Maladies.* "Always, night and day, he was in the mountains, and in the tombs, crying, and cutting himself with stones" (Mark 5:5).

(4) *They Produce Moral Impurity.* "When he was come up out of the ship, immediately there met him out of the tombs a man with an unclean spirit" (Mark 5:2). See also Matthew 10:1.

e. *Their Existence.* The word "devil" is best translated "demon." There is only one Devil, but many demons, the Devil being the prince over them. There is such a thing as demon possession today. Missionaries to foreign countries attest to this fact. Demon-possessed men have super-human strength; they are fully controlled by demons.

It is good to point out that the demons always spoke through the mouths of those they possessed. The demons in these people recognized the Lord Jesus, and he distinguished between the demon and the man. Demons do not like to be disembodied; they prefer to be cast into a herd of swine (Mark 5:1-20).

f. *Their Evidence.* Demonism was not limited to the time of Christ. There was evidence that it was in existence before His first advent:

(1) The four Gospels introduced demonism as the thing that was known.

(2) The people showed no surprise at demon possession.

(3) The Jews claimed to cast out demons by their power. (Matt. 12:27).

(4) After the time of Christ, the early Apostolic Fathers came in contact with demonism (Matt. 10:1; Mark 16:17; Acts 8:7).

(5) Demonism is seen today in modern missionary annals (Eph. 2:2; 6).

4. *The Imprisoned Angels.*

a. *Their Sins.* "God spared not the angels that sinned, but cast them down to hell, and delivered them into chains of darkness to be reserved unto judgment" (II Peter 2:4). The above Scripture plainly shows that these angels were not in the original rebellion with Satan. The casting out of Satan occurred before the time of Adam; the angels referred to sinned since the time of Adam.

Surely these must be the "sons of God," who married the "daughters of men." "It came to pass, when men began to multiply on the face of the earth, and daughters were born unto them, that the sons of God saw the daughters of men that they were fair; and they took them wives of all which they chose. . . . There were giants in the earth in those days; and also after that, when the sons of God came in unto the daughters of men, and they bare children to them, the same became mighty men which were of old men of renown" (Gen. 6:1, 2, 4).

There are those who hold that the "sons of God" were the

sons of Seth, and that the "daughters of men" were the daughters of Cain. This is refuted simply by asking, "How could Seth beget sons of God?"

Others contend that the "sons of God" were regenerated men, who married unregenerated women, called the "daughters of men." We see the same things happening even today, but there are no giants born because of this unequally yoked union.

To be safe and sure as to the correct interpretation, let us find out who the "sons of God" could be. There are several persons called the "sons of God" in Scripture:

1. Jesus Christ – *the* Son of God – by relationship.
2. Adam – a son of God – by creation (Luke 3:38).
3. Angels – sons of God – by creation (Job 1, 2).
4. Regenerated men – sons of God – by regeneration and adoption.

Remember, we are only children of God now by regeneration; we shall be declared to be sons at our adoption – "to wit the redemption of our body."

By simple elimination we find out who the "sons of God" were: Christ is eliminated, and Adam also, as he had been dead for a long time. They could not be regenerated men because adoption of sonship had not occurred yet. This leaves only the angels.

The question naturally arises, "Do not the Scriptures teach that angels cannot marry?" They do not teach this; they teach that they do not marry in heaven. Man marries here, but he will not marry in heaven. Then how did they marry the daughters of men? We do not know, but the following verses prove, without a doubt, that they did. We have already quoted Jude 6, but we will do so again, adding verse seven. This substantiates our claim: "And the angels which kept not their first estate [principality, their own being as angels], but left their own habitation [heaven], he hath reserved in everlasting chains under darkness unto the judgment of the great day. Even as Sodom and Gomorrah, and the cities about them in like manner, giving themselves over to fornication and going after strange flesh, are set forth for an example, suffering the vengeance of eternal fire" (Jude 6, 7). Thus, I believe it is positively proved that the angels sinned after the similitude of Sodom and Gomorrah.

This union brought about a race of giants – giants in stature, and giants in sin. They were destroyed by the flood.

Demon possession was prolific before the flood; and the Lord Jesus has revealed, "But as the days of Noe were, so shall also the coming of the Son of man be" (Matt. 24:37). Demon possession shall be in full control during the Great Tribulation (Rev. 12), before the revelation of Christ at His second coming.

b. *Their Position.* They are cast down into Tartarus, the innermost prison of Hades, chained in darkness, awaiting their day of judgment (II Peter 2:4).

IV. Satan

A. *The Names and Descriptive Titles.*

1. *Satan.* This name means "adversary, hater, and accuser." "*Satan* stood up against Israel, and provoked David to number Israel" (I Chron. 21:1).

2. *Devil.* This name means "Slanderer, Accuser, Deceiver." "He laid hold on the dragon, that old serpent, which is the *Devil,* and Satan, and bound him a thousand years" (Rev. 20:2).

3. *Beelzebub.* This is the prince of demons. Originally it meant "Lord of Flies"; the Jews later changed it to mean "Lord of the Dung Hill." "The scribes which came down from Jerusalem said, He hath *Beelzebub,* and by the prince of the devils [demons] casteth he out devils [demons]" (Mark 3:22).

4. *Belial.* This means "good-for-nothing." "Certain men, the children of *Belial,* are gone out from among you, and have withdrawn the inhabitants of their city, saying, Let us go and serve other gods, which ye have not known" (Deut. 13:13).

5. *The Wicked One.* He is the evil one, who has no reverence for Christ. "I have written unto you, fathers, because ye have known him that is from the beginning. I have written unto you, young men, because ye are strong, and the word of God abideth in you, and ye have overcome the *wicked one*" (I John 2:14). See also I John 2:13; Matthew 6:13, R.V.

6. *Prince of This World.* World politics, business and society are under his domain. The Lord Jesus did not deny this when he was accosted by the Devil in the wilderness (Matt. 4; Luke 4). "Now is the judgment of this world: now

shall the *prince of this world* be cast out" (John 12:31). See also John 14:30; 16:11.

7. *The God of This Age.* "If our gospel be hid, it is hid to them that are lost: in whom the *god of this world* [*age*] hath blinded the minds of them which believe not, lest the light of the glorious gospel of Christ, who is the image of God, should shine unto them" (II Cor. 4:4).

8. *Prince of the Power of the Air.* "You hath he quickened, who were dead in trespasses and sins; wherein in time past ye walked according to the course of this world, according to the *prince of the power of the air,* the spirit that now worketh in the children of disobedience" (Eph. 2:2).

9. *That Old Serpent.* "The great dragon was cast out, *that old serpent,* called the Devil, and Satan, which deceiveth the whole world: he was cast out into the earth, and his angels were cast out with him" (Rev. 12:9). See also Revelation 12:3; 20:2.

10. *Dragon.* "He laid hold on the *dragon,* which is the Devil, and Satan, and bound him a thousand years" (Rev. 20:2).

11. *The Evil One.* "We know that whosoever is begotten of God sinneth not; but he that was begotten of God keepeth himself, and *the evil one* toucheth him not" (I John 5:18, R.V.).

12. *Angel of Light.* "Satan himself is transformed into an *angel of light*" (II Cor. 11:14).

13. *Father of Lies.* "Ye are of your father the devil, and the lust of your father ye will do. He was a murderer from the beginning, and abode not in the truth, because there is no truth in him. When he speaketh a lie, he speaketh of his own: for he is a *liar,* and the *father of it*" (John 8:44).

14. *Murderer.* "He was a murderer from the beginning, and abode not in the truth, because there is no truth in him" (John 8:44b). See also I John 3:12-15.

15. *Roaring Lion.* "Be sober, be vigilant; because your adversary, the devil, as a *roaring lion,* walketh about seeking whom he may devour" (I Peter 5:8).

16. *Ruler of Darkness.* "For we wrestle not against flesh and blood, but against principalities, against powers, against the *rulers of the darkness* of this world, against spiritual wickedness in high places" (Eph. 6:12).

B. The Personality of Satan.

There is a general denial that the Devil is a person. To deny such is to deny the Word of God. The Scriptures teach that he is as much a person as the Lord Jesus Christ.

C. The Origin of Satan.

Satan was a created being (Ezek. 28:15). His position was the greatest of all the angelic hosts, "Thou art the anointed cherub that covereth" (Ezek. 28:14). He was one of the cherubim that overlooked the mercy seat of the temple in heaven.

His name, Lucifer, means "Son of the Morning." He was created in perfect beauty (Ezek. 28:12, 17). Some hold that he was the choir leader of heaven, as the tabrets and pipes were prepared in him the day that he was created (Ezek. 28:13). Others may ask, "Isn't the twenty-eighth chapter of Ezekiel speaking about the King of Tyre?" Yes, to begin with but the inspired writer goes beyond the King of Tyre, and speaks about a person that no human person could possibly fulfill. "Thou hast been in Eden" (Ezek. 28:13). Who could this be but Satan? He was perfect in his ways (Ezek. 28:15) until sin was found in him.

D. The Career of Satan.

What was the sin that caused Satan to be? What was it that changed Lucifer into the Devil? It was the original sin of the universe: pride. "I will ascend above the heights of the clouds; I will be like the most High" (Is. 14:14). The sin of pride was caused by choosing his own will above the will of God. "I will" became the original sin of the universe.

He appeared in the garden of Eden and thrust the human race into sin and death. He came to Job and wrought misery in his life. He tempted David to number the people. He tempted Christ (Matt. 4) and Peter (Luke 22:32). He hindered Paul in his great work (I Thess. 2:18). He snatches the Word from people's hearts (Mark 4:15).

E. The Location of Satan.

He does have access to the throne of God, for he accused Job, and we are told that he accuses the brethren daily. "The accuser of our brethren is cast down, which accused them before our God day and night" (Rev. 12:10c). It is an error to think of the Devil living in a palace in hell; his location is in the heavenlies.

F. The Character of Satan.

1. *Has Great Dignity.* His titles show this. "Now is the judgment of this world: now shall the prince of this world be cast out" (John 12:31). See also Jude 8, 9; II Corinthians 4:4.

2. *Has Great Power.* God (Jesus) sent Paul to the Gentiles "to open their eyes, and to turn them from darkness to light, and from the power of Satan unto God, that they may receive forgiveness of sins, and inheritance among them which are sanctified by faith that is in me" (Acts 26:18). See also Job 1:10-12; Luke 11:14, 18; Ephesians 6:11, 12. The whole world without Christ is under him.

3. *Has Great Cunning and Deceit.* "Satan himself is transformed into an angel of light" (II Cor. 11:14). See also Matthew 24:24; II Corinthians 2:11.

4. *Has Great Malignity.* "He that committeth sin is of the devil; for the devil sinneth from the beginning. For this purpose the Son of God was manifested, that he might destroy the works of the devil" (I John 3:8). See also II Corinthians 4:4.

5. *Has Great Fear.* "Submit yourselves therefore to God. Resist the devil, and he will flee from you" (Jas. 4:7).

G. The Work of Satan.

1. *He Is the Author of Sin and Tempts Men to Sin.* "Then was Jesus led up of the spirit into the wilderness to be tempted of the devil" (Matt. 4:1.)

2. *He Produces Sickness and Has Power of Death.* "Forasmuch then as the children are partakers of flesh and blood, he also himself likewise took part of the same; that through death he might destroy him that had the power of death, that is, the devil" (Heb. 2:14). See also Luke 13:16; Acts 10:38.

3. *He Lays Snares for Men.* "God peradventure will give them repentance to the acknowledging of the truth . . . that they may recover themselves out of the snare of the devil, who are taken captive by him at his will" (II Tim. 2:26).

4. *He Takes the Word Out of Hearts.* "When anyone heareth the word of the kingdom, and understandeth it not, then cometh the wicked one, and catcheth away that which was sown in his heart. This is he which received seed by the wayside" (Matt. 13:19).

5. *He Puts Wicked Purposes Into Hearts.* "Neither give place to the devil" (Eph. 4:27).

6. *He Blinds Minds.* "The God of this world hath blinded the minds of them which believe not, lest the light of the glorious gospel of Christ, who is the image of God, should shine unto them" (II Cor. 4:4).

7. *He Harasses Men.* "Lest I should be exalted above measure through the abundance of the revelations, there was given to me a thorn in the flesh, the messenger of Satan to buffet me, lest I should be exalted above measure" (II Cor. 12:7).

8. *He Accuses Men Before God.* "The accuser of our brethren is cast down, which accused them before our God day and night" (Rev. 12:10c).

9. *He Enters Into Men.* "Supper being ended, the devil having now put into the heart of Judas Iscariot, Simon's son, to betray him . . . [Jesus] riseth from supper" (John 13:2).

10. *He Sows Tares Among God's People.* "The field is the world; the good seed are the children of the kingdom; but the tares are the children of the wicked one; the enemy that sowed them is the devil; the harvest is the end of the world; and the reapers are the angels" (Matt. 13:38, 39).

11. *He Gives Power to the Lawless Ones.* "To whom ye forgive anything, I forgive also: for what I also have forgiven if I have forgiven anything, for your sakes have I forgiven it in the presence of Christ; that no advantage may be gained over us by Satan: for we are not ignorant of his devices" (II Cor. 2:10, 11, R.V.).

12. *He Resists God's Servants.* "He shewed me Joshua the high priest standing before the angel of the LORD, and Satan standing at his right hand to resist him" (Zech. 3:1). See also Daniel 10:13.

13. *He Hinders God's Servants.* "We would fain have come unto you, even I Paul, once and again; but Satan hindered us" (I Thess. 2:18, R.V.).

14. *He Sifts God's Servants.* "The Lord said, Simon, Simon, behold, Satan hath desired to have you, that he may sift you as wheat" (Luke 22:31).

15. *He Holds the World.* "We know that we are of God, and the whole world lieth in the evil one" (I John 5:19, R.V.).

H. The Limitation of Satan.

1. *He Is Not Omnipresent.* He can be at only one place at a time. He is a created being, and a created being cannot be in two places at the same time. He is not everywhere, but his followers (demons) are. He can move rapidly to the aid of his agents (Luke 10:18).

2. *He Is Not Omniscient.* He is wise; too wise for us, but he is not all-wise. The Devil would know less if we would tell him less. Spiritism is not all trickery. It is demonism, controlled by the Devil. No one can communicate with the dead, but the Devil and his angels know about the dead and communicate this knowledge to their mediums.

3. *He Is Not Omnipotent.* He is not all-powerful, though he has more power than we do. He is subject to the Word of God. A good example of this is found in Job 1 and 2.

I. Our Attitude toward Satan.

1. *Redemptive Rights Are to Be Claimed by the Believer.* "They overcame him by the blood of the Lamb, and by the word of their testimony; and they loved not their lives unto the death" (Rev. 12:11). See also Ephesians 6:16, R.V.; Hebrews 2:14, R.V.; Colossians 2:15: I John 3:8.

2. *Full Equipment Is to Be Appropriated by the Believer.* "Finally, my brethren, be strong in the Lord, and in the power of his might. Put on the whole armour of God, that ye may be able to stand against the wiles of the devil" (Eph. 6:10, 11). See also Ephesians 6:12-18.

3. *Strict Self Control Is to Be Maintained.* "Neither give place to the devil" (Eph. 4:27).

4. *Vigilance Is to Be Exercised by the Believer.* "Be sober, be vigilant; because your adversary the devil, as a roaring lion, walketh about, seeking whom he may devour" (I Peter 5:8). See also II Corinthians 2:11.

5. *Resistance Is to Be Made by the Believer.* "Submit yourselves therefore to God. Resist the devil, and he will flee from you" (Jas. 4:7). See also I John 2:14.

ESCHATOLOGY
(The Doctrine of Last Things)

Outline for Chapter IX

ESCHATOLOGY

I. Physical Death.
   A. Death Is Not a Cessation of Being.
   B. Death Is Not Soul Sleep.
   C. Death Means Separation.

II. The Bodily Resurrection.
   A. The Fact of Resurrection.
   B. The Nature of the Resurrection.
   C. The Time of the Resurrection.

III. The Intermediate State.
   A. Before the Cross.
   B. At the Time of the Cross.
   C. After the Cross.

IV. The Second Coming of Christ.
   A. The Importance of the Doctrine.
   B. The Meaning of the Second Coming.
   C. The Events of the Second Coming.

V. The Antichrist.
   A. His Person.
   B. His Titles.
   C. His Forerunners.
   D. His Work.
   E. His Career.
   F. His Time.
   G. His Appearance.
   H. His End.

VI. The Tribulation.
   A. The Tribulation of the Body of Christ.
   B. The Tribulation of Israel.
   C. The Great Tribulation.

VII. The Battle of Armageddon.
   A. What It Is Not.
   B. What It Is.

VIII. The Millennium.
   A. The Fact of the Millennium.
   B. The Description of the Millennium.
   C. The Types of the Millennium.
   D. The Conditions During the Millennium.

IX. The Judgments.
   A. Judgments of the Christian.
   B. Judgment of the Nations.
   C. Judgment at the Great White Throne.

X. After the Millennium.
   A. Satan Loosed.
   B. Nations Gathered.
   C. Army Destroyed.
   D. Satan Doomed.

XI. The Future of the Wicked.
   A. The Scriptural Teaching.
   B. The Terms Used.
   C. The Theories Proposed.

XII. Heaven.
   A. First Heaven.
   B. Second Heaven.
   C. Third Heaven.

Chapter IX

ESCHATOLOGY

Eschatology is the doctrine of last things.

I. Physical Death

The Bible always gives sufficient information for the faith of the believer. The Bible was never proposed merely for his curiosity. God teaches finite beings to walk by faith in the unexplained infinite.

A. *Death Is Not a Cessation of Being.*

Thirty-five hundred years ago Job asked, "If a man die, shall he live again?" This question has been asked for millenniums. It is still a universal question. It is a subject of perennial interest. That those whom we love should die and be buried does not seem right; and it is not! God never made man to die; He created him to live and to have fellowship with Himself. But sin brought death and the grave, thus separation from God.

Should the Lord tarry, everyone reading these words, the author included, shall die, for death has passed upon all men (Rom. 5:12).

A poem lasts longer than the poet; the voice on the recording tape can be heard years after the recording artist is dead; pictures of dead loved ones remain, even after the loved ones are gone.

Things on this earth are not equal. The rich have always oppressed the poor; the wicked have always prospered over the righteous. Human justice demands an equalization of all things in a life after death. We are living in a changing world. The robins build their nests, even as they did in the garden of Eden, and animals possess the same characteristics as they did at the beginning. However, man does not live as he used to, even as he did twenty-five years ago. Although this be true, the inquiring mind of man remains the same, still asking the question, "If a man dies, will he live again?"

There is a universal belief in a life after death. If you go to the darkest part of Africa, where Christ has never been preached, you find that people there believe in a life after death. Why do some heathens burn their wives? Why do some bury food with the corpse? They believe that the departed one must have a companion and food on his journey beyond the grave. The Egyptians furnished a charter, a book for the journey, and placed it with the corpse. Why do the birds fly south? Instinct in them proves there is a southland. The heart of man, and his inward instinct are proofs that there is a life hereafter. Both physiology and philosophy maintain there must be a life after death.

There are two great reservations:

1. *Reservation for the Christian.* "Our Lord Jesus Christ . . . hath begotten us . . . to an inheritance incorruptible, and undefiled, and that fadeth not away, *reserved* in heaven for you" (I Peter 1:4). In Philippians 1:23 the Apostle Paul used the word "depart" as describing death. By this he did not mean that he would cease to exist. Depart means "to depart." Did he mean to depart to the grave with Christ? Of course not, for Christ is not in the grave; He is in heaven. II Corinthians 5:8 makes the meaning of departure even clearer when it says, "We are confident . . . and willing . . . to be absent from the body, and to be present with the Lord" The word "present" means "to be at home with." The death of a Christian, therefore, is pictured as a ship pulling up anchor and setting sail for home; in other words, the death of a Christian means "going home."

2. *Reservation for the Ungodly.* "The Lord knoweth how to deliver the godly out of temptations, and to reserve the unjust unto the day of judgment to be punished" (II Peter 2:9).

B. Death Is Not Soul Sleep.

The word "sleep" in Scripture, concerning the dead in Christ, means "rest." It does not mean "unconsciousness." The body may die, but the soul and spirit will never die. In the resurrection it is the body that is raised, not the soul and spirit. The Scriptures clearly state that the soul is absent from the body, present with the Lord; and that the souls and spirits are fully awake and aware of things round about them. A perfect illustration of the above truth is found in Revelation 6:9, 10: "When he had opened the fifth seal, I saw under the altar the *souls* of them that were slain for the word of God, and for the testimony which they held: and they cried with a loud voice, saying, How long, O Lord, holy and true, dost thou not judge and avenge our blood on them that dwell on the earth?" Here we see the disembodied souls, alive, and reasoning with God.

The Apostle Paul says, "For to me to live is Christ, and to die is gain" (Phil. 1:21). "To live" meant that Paul had perfect fellowship with the living Christ. If death were the end, why would Paul say, "and to die is gain?"

C. Death Means Separation.

Death in Scripture always means "separation." *Physical death* is the separation of the soul and spirit from the body. *Spiritual death* is the eternal, complete, final separation from God (Rev. 21:8).

Life means "union" (John 3:16). Death means "separation" (Rom. 8:35-39). The *ego,* the "I," lives in the house of flesh. You are not a body, having a soul and spirit, but you are a soul and spirit possessing a body. Scientists used to tell us that the bodies in which we live change every seven years; now they say that they change every seven days. Our bodies may change, but we ourselves, that is, our ego, never changes. People cannot see *us,* the ego, but only the house, or tent, in which we dwell. Death is the departure from this house (II Peter 1:13, 14; Phil. 1:21, 24; Gal. 2:20; II Cor. 5:6, 7; Job 19:26; Luke 16:26; II Tim. 4:6; II Cor. 12:2). People have been burying bodies for six thousand years; just the bodies, not the persons.

The soul is the seat of feeling and appetite; from Scripture we believe it is the exact counterpart of the body. The spirit is the seat of man's intelligence. When Samuel was called up by the request of Saul, it was his spirit that appeared, not his body. Death, then, is not a circle, or a square. We shall not be formless if we depart this life, but our souls and spirits shall be fully conscious, existing in the same form and shape as our bodies.

Memory may be seated in the brain, but the brain is not the source of thought. We may remember things that happened ten years ago, but we do not have the same brain that we had ten years ago. I *possess* a brain, but the brain is not

I. Death simply means, "*I* have departed"; *I* am separated from my body.

II. The Bodily Resurrection

A. The Fact of the Resurrection.

1. *Anticipated in the Old Testament.* Such terms as "in the latter days," "awake and live," are indications of a resurrection. The Old Testament contains many types of the resurrection. Joseph was counted dead, but he came back to his father; Jonah was in the belly of the fish for three days and three nights, and then was released; Daniel was placed in the lion's den, a place of death, but came out alive; Israel died in the wilderness, and a new Israel went in Canaan. All of these are figures of the resurrection. The following Scriptures verify the resurrection. "Thy dead men shall live, together with my dead body shall they arise. Awake and sing, ye that dwell in dust: for thy dew is as the dew of herbs, and the earth shall cast out the dead" (Is. 26:19). See also Job 19:26, 27; Psalm 16:9, 11; Daniel 6:23; 12:2; Matthew 12:40.

2. *Revealed In the New Testament.* "As in Adam all die, even so in Christ shall *all* be made alive" (I Cor. 15:22). "[I] have hope toward God, which they themselves also allow, that there shall be a resurrection of the dead, both of the just and unjust" (Acts 24:15). See also Matthew 22:30-32; Luke 14:13, 14; 20:35, 36; John 5:28, 29; 6:39, 40, 44, 54; I Thessalonians 4:14-16; II Timothy 1:10. Christ did not come to save my soul only, but all of me: my soul, spirit, and body. *All of me* is to be saved.

B. The Nature of the Resurrection.

Death is never set forth as the hope of the believer. In Corinth (I Cor. 15) some had declared that there was no bodily resurrection, but in the above chapter Paul rebukes them for this false doctrine and proves to them that there is a resurrection (by Christ's own resurrection): if one does not believe in man's resurrection, then it is impossible to believe in Christ's resurrection; and if Christ had no resurrection, there is no Gospel, and if no Gospel, we are not saved.

Satan has always been against the Word, and he has many weapons trained on it. The revelation he most despises is that of the resurrection. Materialism denies the resurrection altogether. Spiritualism denies the bodily resurrection. We are never to doubt the resurrection. "I forgot God when I said, How can this be?" Whether man believes, or understands the resurrection means little; it is true, nevertheless.

Some people cannot believe that flesh and bones shall be perfect. When speaking of Christ's resurrection, they maintain that it was a spiritual resurrection. We know by this statement that they do not know what they are talking about. Jesus Christ's spirit was not put in the tomb; only His body was. The Roman soldiers were not stationed at the sepulcher to guard His spirit, but to guard His body. It was His *body* they guarded; it was His *body* which arose from the dead!

One Scripture used by those who believe only in a spiritual resurrection is I Corinthians 15:44: "It is sown a natural body; it is raised a *spiritual* body. There is a natural body, and there is a *spiritual* body." Notice that the verse does not say "a *spirit* body," but "a *spiritual* body." The natural body is controlled by the soul; the spiritual body shall be controlled by the Spirit; hence, a spiritual body.

1. *Theories Proposed.*

a. *Germ Theory.* This is an old Jewish belief found in the Talmud. According to it, in man there is a little bone, called a "luz," which death can not destroy, and out of that germ the body will be resurrected. Some Christians hold to this theory, using I Corinthians 15:36, 37 for support.

b. *Identity Theory.* This is the belief that the body in the resurrection will be raised just as it was buried. A body buried with an arm missing, will be raised with an arm missing; an infant buried will be an infant raised; a lunatic buried, a lunatic raised. The Mohammedans hold to this theory. If this be true, we will not be like Jesus.

c. *Reincarnation Theory.* This idea supposes that when a man dies he goes immediately into another body. If this should occur, we would not be "at home" with the Lord. When a person dies, he is not a complete human being; he can only be so by a bodily resurrection (I Thess. 5:23).

d. *Intermediate Body Theory.* This theory contends that the believer receives his resurrected body immediately upon his death. It is based on II Corinthians 5:1-4: "We know that if our earthly house of this tabernacle were dissolved, we have a building of God, an house not made with hands, eternal in the heavens. For in this we groan, earnestly desiring to be clothed upon with our house which is from heaven: if so be that being clothed we shall not be found naked. For we that are in this tabernacle do groan, being burdened: not for that we would be unclothed, but clothed upon, that mortality might be swallowed up of life." But the above Scripture refers only to those believers who are *living* when Christ comes.

2. *Truth Believed.* The resurrection is by *Divine Power!* "God giveth a body as it has pleased him, and to every seed his own body" (I Cor. 15:38). Jesus Christ's own resurrected body was proved to be flesh and bone. When Christ appeared unto the disciples, He remarked, "Behold my hands and my feet, that it is I myself: handle me, and see; for a spirit hath not flesh and bones, as ye see me have" (Luke 24:39). Christ did not say that there were no spirits, but that a spirit does not have flesh and bones. Ezekiel 37 pictures the resurrection of Israel; flesh, bones and spirit are mentioned, but no blood. The law demanded the shedding of blood, and Christ shed his blood to pay for that demand. In the resurrection, all will be raised without blood; life will be in the spirit of man.

"[The Lord Jesus Christ] shall change our vile body, that it may be fashioned like unto his glorious body, according to the working whereby he is able even to subdue all things unto himself" (Phil. 3:20, 21). Our bodies, the *same ones* that may be planted in death, will pass under a great transformation and be raised. If we should plant a lily, a lily will come up; if we plant wheat, wheat will come up; if we plant tares, tares will come up; if we plant human bodies, glorified human bodies will come up. God looks upon the cemeteries as nothing but harvest fields. The seeds in these harvest fields are the bodies of the dead, and the harvest is the resurrection.

"And we shall be changed" (I Cor. 15:52c). Yes, a great transformation will take place, but it will be the same body, for the resurrected body of Christ proves that it will be the same body, as He bore in His resurrected body the print of the nails.

I Corinthians 15:42-44 describes fully the resurrection of the just (*God tells nothing of the bodies of the damned in their resurrection*): "It is sown in corruption; it is raised in incorruption." A dead body is a corruptible body. A live body is a mortal body. Nothing is ever said in Scripture of planting a mortal body. A corruptible body is subject to decay and dust, but one day it will be raised in incorruption, a body fit for heaven, that can never be subject to corruption again. "It is sown in dishonour; it is raised in glory." These vile bodies have been dishonored by sin, but one day they will be raised in glory like unto the glorious body of our Lord. "It is sown in weakness; it is raised in power." Sin has made us weak, also. The weakest thing in the world is a dead body. In order for a dead man to move, he must *be moved.* He has eyes that cannot see and ears that cannot hear; he makes no protest about being put in a coffin and placed in a grave. There is no resistance in a dead body. These same weak bodies shall be raised with great power. Notice what man can do for the eyes today, but think what God *will* do. The resurrected believer will be able to see spiritual beings. Mortal man has the microscope and telescope, but, oh, what eyesight our new bodies will have! Today we have limits of speed, but in the resurrection there will be no limit. Do not make present standards the limit of our future standards. "It is sown a natural body; it is raised a spiritual body." The natural body is our animated body, containing flesh, bones and blood. Our resurrected spiritual bodies shall not be spirit-bodies, but spiritual; they will be bodies composed of only flesh and bone, no blood, dominated by our spirits.

C. The Time of the Resurrection.

"As in Adam all die, even so in Christ shall *all* be made alive" (I Cor. 15:22). All men shall be raised from the dead, but not all at the same time. The Scriptures plainly declare that there are *two* resurrections, and *not* a general resurrection. They are the first, and the last resurrection (Rev. 20:5, 6).

1. *The First Resurrection.* The first resurrection includes Christ, and all believers of all ages. Their resurrection occurs at different intervals. Christ at one time; the Church at the Rapture (before the Tribulation); and the Old Testament saints and Tribulation saints *after* the Tribulation.

a. *Christ the Firstfruits.* "Now is Christ risen from the dead, and become the first-fruits of them that slept" (I Cor. 15:20). The firstfruits was God's pledge that the entire harvest would come later. Christ's being the Firstfruits is God's pledge that the harvest will be coming later. "Because I live, ye shall live also" (John 14:19b). There are records of others being raised from the dead, but these were "resuscitations," or restorations; they died again. Christ liveth to die no more! "Behold, I am alive for evermore" (Rev. 1:18b).

b. *The Saints at Christ's Resurrection.* "The graves were opened; and many bodies of the saints which slept arose, and came out of the graves after his resurrection, and went into the holy city, and appeared unto many" (Matt. 27:52, 53). On one occasion, the Lord Jesus said, "Except a corn of wheat fall into the ground and die, it abideth alone: but if it die, it bringeth forth much fruit" (John 12:24). Christ did die and was planted as a corn of wheat, but when He was raised from the dead, He brought forth much fruit with Him. This fruit was the saints who arose immediately after His resurrection. We do not know how many were raised, nor do we know where they went. They may have gone up to heaven with him, for remember, he was the Firstfruits, and we know that in the Feast of Firstfruits, a *sheaf* of the wave offering was waved before the Lord. There was more than one grain in the sheaf. Thus, we are led to believe that there were more people in the firstfruits to go to heaven than just Christ.

c. *The Body of Christ* (*The Church*). The Church will have a resurrection of its own. "The dead in Christ shall rise first" (I Thess. 4:16). The Church was never known in the Old Testament (See Chapter VII). Therefore, the Old Testament prophets saw nothing of its Spiritual baptism, rapture, resurrection and transformation. The Church was a mystery hid in God; it was first revealed to the Apostle Paul (Eph. 3:1-9). However, the old Testament saints did know of their own resurrection, which shall occur *after* the Tribulation (Dan. 12:2, 13).

The resurrection of the Church was revealed to the Apostle Paul; it will occur *before* the Tribulation. "Because thou hast kept the word of my patience, I also will keep thee from the hour of temptation, which shall come upon all the world, to try them that dwell upon the earth" (Rev. 3:10). See also I Thessalonians 1:10.

There has been over nineteen hundred years since Christ the Firstfruits has been raised. The time of the resurrection of the Church is not known.

d. *Old Testament and Tribulation Saints.* This phase

of the first resurrection takes place after the Tribulation, at least seven years after the Church is raised. It includes all saints who do not belong to the Body of Christ. "Go thy way till the end be: for thou shalt rest, and stand in thy lot at the end of the days" (Dan. 12:13). See also Daniel 12:1, 2.

2. *The Last Resurrection.* The last (or second) resurrection occurs after the Millennium, and shall include all the wicked dead. They shall be raised to stand before the Great White Throne. "The rest of the dead lived not again until the thousand years were finished. This is the first resurrection. Blessed and holy is he that hath part in the first resurrection: on such the second death hath no power, but they shall be priests of God and of Christ, and shall reign with him a thousand years" (Rev. 20:5, 6).

III. The Intermediate State

Where are the dead? is the question on the lips of all mankind. The only true and correct answer is given by the Word of God. Other answers, such as those given by spiritualism, are nothing but a babel of voices. Various cults have preyed upon unsuspecting souls, taking them captive at the Devil's will.

The following are things to remember as we explain the intermediate state, the state of man between death and resurrection: Death is the separation of the soul and spirit from the body. The soul and spirit are together in death. The soul is the seat of the appetite, and the spirit is the seat of knowledge, and they both function in death, as shown by the example of the rich man in hades. He was in torment; he had feelings. He reasoned; thus, his spirit and soul were together.

The word "Sheol" and the word "Hades" are the same. "Sheol" is the Old Testament Hebrew word. "Hades" is the New Testament Greek word. We know they are the same, for the Apostle Peter, at Pentecost, quoted from Psalm 16, saying, "Thou wilt not leave my soul in hell [hades], neither wilt thou suffer thy Holy One to see corruption" (Acts 2:27). Psalm 16 uses the word "Sheol" for hell [Hades]. Thus, Hades and Sheol are the same. This is the place of departed souls and spirits. The mistranslation of the words "Sheol" and "Hades" by the King James translators has caused much trouble in the Church today. They translated these words to mean hell (the place of everlasting punishment), grave, pit, and the like. The wrong translation has led people to believe that the grave is the only hell. Sheol and Hades are the names of the same place for the departed spirits of man.

1. These words are never found in the plural.
2. Sheol and Hades are never located on the face of the earth.
3. The Bible never speaks of an individual's Sheol.
4. Man never puts anyone in it, as the grave.
5. Man never digs or makes a Sheol, or Hades.
6. The Bible never speaks of a man touching Sheol.
7. The Bible never speaks of a *body* going into Sheol, but with one exception, and the exception proves the rule. Korah (Num. 16:28-33) defied the leadership of Moses and the priesthood of Aaron, and influenced many in Israel against them. God showed His displeasure by causing the earth to open up its jaws and swallow Korah and his family. The King James Version says that he went down alive into the *pit,* which should be translated "Sheol" (Num. 16:33).

In Luke 16:19-31 we have the true account of Lazarus and the rich man both dying and existing in the intermediate state. There are some who claim that this story was only a parable. The Word does not so state. In all of His parables, the Lord never mentioned proper names, as He does here. If it were a parable, it would be true, for every parable that He spoke was built upon the truth (Matt. 13:3).

The following is a common interpretation of this so-called parable:

Rich man – the Jewish nation, rich in what God has given him.

Lazarus – the Gentiles – poor at the door of the rich man.

Both died – end of the dispensation, when both are blessed by the Gospel.

Why say this refers to Jew and Gentile, when the Scriptures do not say so? Why did the Lord use the rich man in picturing the Jewish nation, when in the preceding passages he was warning the rich? The idea of the Jews ever requesting aid of the Gentiles is farfetched.

There is no gulf between the Jew and the Gentile. No Gentile nation has ever begged from the Jews as Lazarus begged bread from the rich man.

If the Jewish nation died (pictured by the rich man), who were the five brethren who were left? We still contend that this is a true account of two men who died and went to Hades.

A. Before the Cross.

The Cross is the dividing line of many Scriptural truths. We shall discuss the question, where did men go at death before Christ died upon the Cross? We shall show that they all went to the same place – Hades (Sheol) – but in different parts.

From Numbers 16:33 we learn that Sheol, or Hades, is somewhere inside the earth. "They, and all that appertained to them went down alive into Sheol, and the earth closed upon them: and they perished from among the congregation." From Luke 16:19-31 we see that Hades was in two compartments: Abraham's Bosom, the place of the departed righteous, where Lazarus went; and the place of torment, where the rich man went. A great gulf separated these two sections.

Since we know that Sheol (Hades) is somewhere in the earth, and that it is composed of two compartments, we turn to the Lord Himself to find the exact location. "For as Jonas was three days and three nights in the whale's belly; so shall the Son of man be three days and three nights in the *heart* of the *earth*" (Matt.12:40). Ephesians 4:9, 10 makes this clearer still. "Now that he ascended, what is it but that he also descended first into the *lower parts of the earth.* He that descended is the same also that ascended up far above all heavens, that he might fill all things." Philippians 2:9, 10 says, "God . . . hath highly exalted him . . . that at the name of Jesus every knee should bow, of things in heaven, and things in earth, and things *under the earth.*" This speaks of the future adoration of Christ by all creation. However, we want to call attention to the above underlined words. To go "under the earth" means to submerge, as a submarine which goes under water. Thus, we conclude that Sheol (Hades) is in the heart of the earth, composed of two sections, one part for the righteous dead and the other for the unrighteous dead, with a great gulf fixed between them. By the Lord's revelation of the rich man and Lazarus, which occurred before He died on the Cross, we see where all men, whether righteous, or unrighteous, went after death, before the Cross.

B. At the Time of the Cross.

Under this heading we shall deal with only two persons, the Lord Jesus, and the penitent thief. Upon death, the Lord Jesus went to Hades. We know this from Psalm 16:10, which says, "Thou wilt not *leave* my soul in Sheol; neither wilt thou suffer thine holy one to see corruption." The Apostle Peter, on the day of Pentecost, quoted from this same passage, but, of course, he used the Greek word "Hades," instead of "Sheol." These words describe the resurrection of Christ, while fully stating that he went to Hades. We see this by the use of the word "leave." The Holy Ghost would not have employed the word "leave" if He had not gone there. As to the thief on the cross, he went to Hades with Jesus, into the compartment reserved for the righteous dead. "Today shalt thou be with me in paradise" (Luke 23:43b). How many days was Jesus in Hades? Three days. On the first of the three days, the thief was to be with Jesus in paradise; therefore, we learn that paradise was another name given to Abraham's Bosom, which was the place of the righteous dead.

C. After the Cross.

Now where do the departed go at death? The unrighteous still go to Sheol (Hades), awaiting the last judgment.

The righteous, praise the Lord, go at once to heaven to be with the Lord. "We are confident . . . and willing rather to be absent from the body, and to be present with the Lord" (II Cor. 5:8). When Christ arose from the dead "he led captivity captive" (Eph. 4:8). Christ emptied Hades (Sheol) of all the righteous, and took them and paradise with him to glory. Paradise was, at one time, in the heart of the earth; now it is in the third heavens. "I knew a man in Christ about fourteen years ago (whether in the body, I cannot tell; or whether out of the body, I cannot tell: God knoweth;) such an one caught up to the third heaven. And I knew such a man (whether in the body, or out of the body, I cannot tell: God knoweth;) how that he was caught up into *paradise,* and heard unspeakable words which is not lawful for a man to utter" (II Cor. 12:2-4).

IV. The Second Coming of Christ

A. The Importance of the Doctrine.

It is said that one out of every twenty-five verses of the New

Testament speaks of the Second Coming, while in the Old Testament there are eight verses concerning the Second Coming to every verse concerning the First Coming. In the promise of a Redeemer (Gen. 3:15), the Second Coming is mentioned before the First Coming. "It shall bruise thy head [occurs at the Second Coming], and thou shalt bruise his heel [occurred at the First Coming, upon the Cross]."

1. *Testimony of Our Lord.* "If I go and prepare a place for you, I will come again, and receive you unto myself; that where I am, there ye may be also" (John 14:3). See also Matthew 24, 25; Mark 13; Luke 21.

2. *Testimony of Angels.* "Ye men of Galilee, why stand ye gazing up into heaven? this same Jesus, which is taken up from you into heaven, shall so come in like manner as ye have seen him go into heaven" (Acts 1:11).

3. *Testimony of Peter.* "He shall send Jesus Christ, which before was preached unto you" (Acts 3:20). See also I Peter 5:4; II Peter 1:16.

4. *Testimony of Paul.* "I thank my God always on your behalf . . . that in every thing ye are enriched by him . . . so that ye come behind in no gift; waiting for the coming of our Lord Jesus Christ" (I Cor. 1:4-7). See also Romans 11:26: I Corinthians 15:23; II Corinthians 5; Philippians 3:20; Colossians 3:4; I Thessalonians (all); II Thessalonians 1:7, 10; I Timothy 6:14; II Timothy 4:8; Titus 2:11-14; Hebrews 9:28.

5. *Testimony of James.* The prophets, quoted by James, represent the Lord as saying, "After this I will return, and will build again the tabernacle of David, which is fallen down; and I will build again the ruins thereof, and I will set it up" (Acts 15:16). See also James 5:7.

6. *Testimony of John.* "Beloved, now are we the sons of God, and it doth not yet appear what we shall be: but we know that, when he shall appear, we shall be like him; for we shall see him as he is" (I John 3:2). See also I John 2:28, and the Book of Revelation.

7. *Testimony of Jude.* "Enoch also, the seventh from Adam, prophesied of these, saying, Behold, the Lord cometh with ten thousands of his saints" (Jude 14).

B. The Meaning of the Second Coming.

1. *Negative.*

a. *It Is Not Death.* Death is the departing of the saint,

not the coming of the Lord. The Lord *will* come, but death may never come.

b. *It Is Not the Fall of Jerusalem.* Luke 21:20-24, and I Thessalonians 4:13-18 did not occur when Jerusalem fell. The second coming of Christ is connected with the *gathering* of Israel, not the scattering.

c. *It Is Not the Coming of the Holy Spirit.* Christ said that He would send another (John 14:16). I Thessalonians 4: 13-18 did not occur when the Holy Spirit came. Notice that all of the Epistles which speak of the Second Coming were written *after* Pentecost.

d. *It Is Not the Conversion of a Sinner.* If this is true, He has come millions of times. According to I Corinthians 15:51-57, the dead would have to be raised every time a soul was saved, and then get back into the grave, waiting for another to be saved.

e. *It Is Not the Diffusion of Christianity.* By this some mean the spreading of the Gospel. But remember, this same Jesus, a personal Christ, is to come again.

f. *It Is Not the End of the World.* When Christ comes, the world will not be destroyed, for He will reign a thousand years after He appears.

2. *Positive.*

a. *It Will Be a Personal Coming.* John 14:3 says, "I will come." We are not to expect a spirit, but a Spirit in a body. I Thessalonians 4:16, 17 uses the word "himself." Acts 1:11 declares "this same Jesus"; not some other person or thing is expected, but Christ Himself.

b. *It Will Be a Visible Coming.* "As the lightning cometh out of the East, and shineth even unto the West; so shall also the coming of the Son of man be" (Matt. 24:27). See also Zechariah 12:10; Revelation 1:7.

c. *Meaning of the Words Used.*

(1) *Parousia.* This means the personal presence, the coming presence. It is spoken not only of the coming of the Lord, but of the coming of other men (I Cor. 16:17; II Cor. 7:6, 7; Philippians 1:26). Concerning the coming of the Lord, it is at that moment, when absence ceases and presence begins (Matt. 24:3, 27; I Cor. 15:23; I Thess. 2:9; Jas. 5:8).

(2) *Epiphaneia.* This simply means "appearing." It is

used of both advents (II Tim. 1:10; II Thess. 2:8; I Tim. 6:14; II Tim. 4:1, 8; Titus 2:13).

(3) *Apokalupsis.* The literal meaning is "unveiling revelation." It emphasizes the visibility of the Lord's return (II Thess. 1:7; I Peter 1:7, 13; 4:13. It is used also for men: Romans 8:19; II Thessalonians 2:3, 6, 8).

d. *It Is a Coming in Two Phases.*

(1) *When Christ Comes for His Saints in the Air.* "We beseech you, brethren, by the coming of our Lord Jesus Christ, and by our gathering together unto him" (II Thess. 2:1). The promise of Christ's return of Acts 1:9-20 was given before the Rapture was revealed. Hebrews 9:28 has nothing to do with the Rapture.

(2) *When Christ Comes with His Saints to Earth.* "Enoch also, the seventh from Adam, prophesied of these, saying, Behold, the Lord cometh with ten thousands of his saints" (Jude 14).

(3) *These Two Phases Are Vastly Different.*

(a) *Different in Character.* "For His people" is an act of faith; "with His people" is an act of judgment.

(b) *Different in Manner.* One is secret, the other is a manifestation.

(c) *Different in Place.* "For His people"—in the air (I Thess. 4:17); "with His people"—to the earth (Zech. 14:14).

(d) *Different as to Time.* "For His people" occurs before the Tribulation (Jacob's trouble); "with His people" occurs after the Tribulation (Jacob's trouble). We are never told in Scripture to look for signs preceding His coming *for* His saints, but men are told to look for signs before He comes *with* His saints (Compare II Thess. 2:1-3 with Is. 13:6-9).

(e) *Different as to Dispensations.* Coming "for His saints" occurs at the beginning of the dispensation of Tribulation; coming "with His saints" occurs at the beginning of the dispensation of the Millennium.

(f) *Different as to Purpose.* Coming "for His saints" fulfills His promise to gather His people (John 14:3); coming "with His saints" as a man of war, His promise to overthrow His enemies (Jude 14).

(g) *Different as to Relation.* "For His saints" is

the adoption of the children of God; "with His saints" the time that the sons of God are manifested to the world. (Rom. 8:19, 23).

C. The Events of the Second Coming in Relation to the Body of Christ.

As we deal with the Rapture of the Church, we recognize the fact that the word "rapture" is not a Scriptural word. The Rapture is, however, a Scriptural fact.

1. *The Resurrection of the Dead in Christ.* "The Lord Himself shall descend from heaven with a shout, with the voice of the archangel, and with the trump of God: and the dead in Christ shall rise first" (I Thess. 4:16). The very first thing that happens is the resurrection of the body of Christ. Certainly this will include all who die before reaching the age of accountability, such as babes, the mentally retarded, and the like. If Christ does not come, there will be no resurrection, and if no resurrection, then man shall be an eternal spirit. If diamonds can be made from soot, sapphire from clay, and opals from sand, what will God make out of our bodies? It will be wonderful, will it not?

2. *The Renovation of the Living in Christ.* "Behold, I shew you a mystery; we shall not all sleep, but we shall all be changed. . . . and we shall be changed. . . . And this mortal must put on immortality" (I Cor. 15:51-53). The Christian is one who is not looking for death, but for the conqueror of death. The words "we shall not all sleep" mean "we shall not all die." What a glorious hope this is! What a shout that will be that day! "O death, where is thy sting? O grave, where is thy victory?" (I Cor. 15:55). Isn't it a blessed hope that it is possible for us to go without dying? No man, not even a Christian, wants to die. That is natural. The Christian, however, is one who is not afraid to die. The Christian is the only person who has a hope of never seeing death. Yes, we know the Scripture says, "It is appointed unto men once to die." But the Scripture does not only say *all* men! The changing of us who are alive and remain at His coming is not death, for we shall not all die!

3. *The Rapture of All in Christ.* "Now we beseech you, brethren, by the coming of our Lord Jesus Christ, and by our gathering together unto him, that ye be not soon shaken in mind . . . as that the day of the Lord is at hand" (II Thess.

2:1, 2). The above Scripture, and the phrase, "we all shall be changed," eliminates the possibility of a partial rapture. The entire Body of Christ will be raptured (caught up); it will be a rapture, and not a rupture. The Body of Christ will be complete. No member of His Body will be left to go through the Tribulation. Some say, "How can this be?" God took Elijah up without death; He can take a million, or ten million up just as easily.

The Rapture of the Church will cause a great separation. All unbelievers will be left here to go through the Tribulation. The Rapture of the Church will be the means of a great reunion. "Then we which are alive and remain shall be caught up *together* with them in the clouds, to meet the Lord in the air: and so shall we ever be with the Lord" (I Thess. 4:17). What a great word is "together"; all of our loved ones in Christ "together" once more.

"We should live soberly, righteously, and godly . . . looking for that blessed hope, and the glorious appearing of the great God and our Saviour Jesus Christ" (Titus 2:13). What do we mean by "looking for Christ"? It does not mean that we believe that He may come at any moment, but that we are looking for Him to come. Are you looking for Him today? Are you looking for Him tonight? That is what the Scripture means by "looking for Him."

V. The Antichrist

"I will put enmity between thee and the woman, and between thy seed and her seed; it shall bruise thy head, and thou shalt bruise his heel" (Gen. 3:15). While this verse speaks of Christ as the seed of the woman, it also prophetically declares the Antichrist as being the seed of the serpent. The seed of the serpent, the Antichrist, is mentioned first in the first book of the Bible, and described fully in the last book of the Bible; it can be traced in between as well. This is very significant.

A. His Person.

The Early Church taught that Nero was the Antichrist, and that when he died he would be raised from the dead. In the eleventh century the Waldenses, Hussites and Wycliffites declared that the Roman Catholic Church was the Antichrist. The Roman Catholic Church, in turn, declared that Napoleon was the Antichrist. During World War I Kaiser Wilhelm of Germany was thought to be the Man of Sin. Many men will be proposed for this office, but it is useless to speculate, for he will not be revealed until after the Rapture of the Church (II Thess. 2:1-12).

He Is a Man! "Here is wisdom. Let him that hath understanding count the number of the beast: for it is the *number of a man*; and his number is six hundred three score and six" (Rev. 13:18). Notice the Scripture says he has the number of a man. Man's number is 6. God says his number is 6-6-6: he is a *man;* he is a *man*; he is a *man!* He is not the Roman Catholic Church; he is not a system; he is a man. He will rule in Jerusalem, and not in Rome.

1. *He Will Be a Jew.* "Neither shall he regard the God of his fathers" (Dan. 11:37a). "God of his fathers" means Abraham, Isaac and Jacob. "I am come in my Father's name, and ye receive me not: if *another* shall come in his own name, him ye will receive" (John 5:43). The word "another" implies "another Jew." The name Antichrist is a Jewish title, and the Jews will not accept a Gentile as their Messiah.

2. *He Will Be a Genius.* He will be the most remarkable man the world has ever seen apart from Jesus Christ.

a. *An Intellectual Genius.* "In the latter time of their kingdom, when the transgressors are come to the full, a king of fierce countenance, and understanding dark sentences, shall stand up" (Dan. 8:23). See also Ezekiel 28:3.

b. *An Oratorical Genius.* "He shall come in peaceably, and obtain the kingdom by flatteries" (Dan. 11:21b). He shall be a mockery and an imitation of Him of whom it is said, "Never man spake like this man."

c. *A Governmental Genius.* He rises from obscurity to power. He is the "little horn" spoken of in Daniel 7 and 8, and the "beast" of Revelation 13 and 14. All kings will give their power to him.

d. *A Commercial Genius.* No one will be able to buy or sell without his seal. "No man might buy or sell, save he that had the mark, or the name of the beast, or the number of his name" (Rev. 13:17).

e. *A Military Genius.* "I saw, and behold a white horse; and he that sat on him had a bow; and a crown was given unto him: and he went forth conquering, and to conquer"

(Rev. 6:2). "Who is like unto the beast? who is able to make war with him?" (Rev. 13:4b).

f. *A Religious Genius.* He demands to be worshiped as God. "Who opposeth and exalteth himself above all that is called God, or that is worshiped; so that he as God sitteth in the temple of God, shewing himself that he is God" (II Thess. 2:4).

g. *A Financial Genius.* "He shall have power over the treasures of gold and silver, and over all the precious things of Egypt: and the Libyans and the Ethiopians shall be at his steps" (Dan. 11:43). See also Ezekiel 28:4, 5.

B. *His Titles.*

1. *Man of Sin.* This is the most important and most terrible of all his titles. All the sins of man will be embodied and headed up in him. "Let no man deceive you by any means: for that day shall not come, except there come a falling away first, and that *man of sin* be revealed, the son of perdition" (II Thess. 2:3).

2. *Son of Perdition.* The above Scripture declares him to be the *son of perdition,* also (II Thess. 2:3).

3. *The Lawless One.* "Then shall that Wicked [lawless one] be revealed, whom the Lord shall consume with the spirit of his mouth, and shall destroy with the brightness of his coming" (II Thess. 2:8). Christ is the *righteous* one; the Antichrist is the *lawless one.*

4. *The Lie.* "God shall send them strong delusion, that they should believe a [the] lie" (II Thess. 2:11). Jesus Christ is the Truth; the Antichrist is the *Lie.* John 8:44 says that the Devil is a liar "and the father of it." "It" refers to "the lie."

5. *The Antichrist.* "Little children, it is the last time: and as ye have heard that *antichrist* shall come, even now are there many antichrists; whereby we know that it is the last time" (I John 2:18).

6. *King of Babylon.* Babylon is always the seat of Satan. Babylon shall be revived in the last days, and the Antichrist shall reign over it (Rev. 17 and 18).

7. *The Little Horn.* "Out of one of them came forth a *little horn* which waxed exceeding great, toward the south, and toward the east, and toward the pleasant land. . . And in the latter time of their kingdom, when the transgressors are come to the full, a king of fierce countenance, and understanding

dark sentences, shall stand up" (Dan. 8:9, 23). See also Daniel 7:8.

8. *The Wilful King.* "The king shall do according to his will; and he shall exalt himself, and magnify himself above every god, and shall speak marvelous things against the God of gods, and shall prosper till the indignation be accomplished: for that that is determined shall be done" (Dan. 11:36).

9. *The Assyrian.* "O *Assyrian*, the rod of mine anger, and the staff in their hand is mine indignation" (Is. 10:5). See also Isaiah 10:12, 24.

10. *The Beast.* (Rev. 13, 17, 19).

C. *His Forerunners.*

Some are seen in the Scriptures, and some out of the Scriptures.

1. *Cain.* He denied the blood and was a liar and murderer (I John 3:12).

2. *Nimrod.* His history preceded the calling of Abraham to the Promised Land. The Antichrist will precede the call of the seed of Abraham and enter into the Promised Land the second time. Nimrod means "rebel." While the Scriptures speak of him as being a mighty hunter, in reality he was not a hunter of animals, but a hunter of souls. He was "a mighty man against the Lord." So the Antichrist will be.

3. *Saul.* This king of Israel was demanded by the people, but he was against the anointed of the Lord. The Antichrist will be the choice of the people also, and he will be against God's anointed.

4. *Absalom.* Absalom means "father of peace"; yet he denied his father. He posed as a man of peace and tried to steal the kingdom. So will the Antichrist.

Absalom	*Antichrist*
1. A man of beauty.	1. The same.
2. Tried to gain the kingdom by flatteries.	2. The same.
3. Set up a pillar to himself.	3. The same.
4. Came to a violent end.	4. The same.

5. *Nebuchadnezzar.* He was the first world ruler, who became the forerunner of the last world ruler.

6. *Antiochus Epiphanes.* He was the mad man who sacked Jerusalem, killing four hundred thousand Jews. He took a sow and burned it upon the altar. The Antichrist, too, shall profane the altar.

7. *Alexander the Great.* He was known as the "Unsatisfier." He was a military genius who never suffered defeat. He sought to be worshiped as the Son of God. The same will be true of the Antichrist.

8. *Caias Caligula.* This Roman Emperor was considered mad. No doubt he was possessed by a demon. The Antichrist shall be fully possessed by the Devil.

9. *Nero.* During his life he was thought to be the Antichrist by the early Christians. Many believed that when he died he would be raised from the dead. The Antichrist shall be raised from the dead.

10. *Charlemagne.* This man was considered a great warrior and statesman. The Antichrist shall be considered the same.

11. *Napoleon.* He thought to revive the Holy Roman Empire. This figurative empire is considered to comprise those countries whose lands are washed by the waters of the Mediterranean Sea. Napoleon planned a new Jewish kingdom and Sanhedrin. The Antichrist will accomplish many of these same plans.

12. *Kaiser Wilhelm.* This leader of the German Empire had the same objective as Napoleon. It is said that every general carried a map of the Holy Roman Empire.

13. *Mussolini.* There were no doubts as to the objectives of this man. At one time he made a map of the old Roman Empire and included England in it. England protested, but the map remained. The Antichrist will not only make a map, but he will make a kingdom with all empires in it.

D. His Work.

His work shall be motivated by Satan, ruling the world and trying to destroy the Jew (Is. 10:12-27).

E. His Career.

Remember, this is the mocker and mimic of Christ. He shall claim a reincarnation. His birth shall be obscure; he will begin as a mere man in world affairs; but he will be rapidly promoted until he becomes ruler of the entire world. Daniel 9:27 states that he will "confirm the covenant" with the Jews. "Confirm" means to "recognize." What covenant is Israel interested in? The Mosaic Covenant. For the first three and one-half years of the Tribulation the Jews will be allowed to worship in their new temple. This would have been hard to believe a hundred years ago, for then only a handful of Jews lived in Palestine. But look at Israel today. She is recognized as a nation; she has a government, an army, an air force; she is doing business with the rest of the world. There are literally hundreds of thousands of Jews back in the land. Here is Israel as a nation; why do they so exist? Is this the last regathering? Are they waiting for the Messiah? No. For the most part, Israel has returned to the land in unbelief. They do not even believe the God of their fathers, much less in their rejected Messiah. What, then, is Israel waiting for? She is waiting for the rise of the Antichrist, although she knows it not. He is to confirm the covenant. Therefore, there must be a nation with which the Antichrist can confirm the covenant. Here is Israel waiting for the Antichrist.

"I saw one of his heads as it was wounded to death; and his deadly wound was healed: and all the world wondered after the beast" (Rev. 13:3). According to this Scripture and Revelation 17, we see that the Antichrist shall suffer death, that he shall die. The words "deadly wound" are better translated "death stroke." Revelation 13:12 has the phrase, "whose deadly wound was healed," which describes fully the death and resurrection of the Antichrist. See also Revelation 13:14. No wonder the world will wonder after him and say, "Who is like unto the beast? who is able to make war with him?" (Rev. 13:4).

He shall be the seventh of seven kings who shall be world rulers. When he dies and is resurrected he becomes the eighth ruler of the world. The world shall be divided into ten kingdoms, overlorded by ten rulers. "These have one mind, and shall give their power and strength unto the beast" (Rev. 17:13).

No doubt he comes to the ascendancy of world rule in the seventieth week of Daniel. He demands to be worshiped as God at this time, and thus he marks the beginning of The Day of the LORD.

F. His Time.

He has not yet been revealed, but it is *possible* in the light of present-day events, that somewhere in the world he is alive today. He will not appear as the Antichrist until the old Roman Empire is revived, composed of the ten-toed kingdom of Daniel 2 and the ten-horned beast of Revelation 13 and 17. Another thing that must come to pass before he is revealed is the Rapture of the Church.

G. His Appearance.

He shall be a Jew by birth, a Roman by citizenship, and a Syrian by nationality. "Out of one of them came forth a little horn, which waxed exceeding great, toward the south, and toward the east, and toward the pleasant land" (Dan. 8:9). He marches on to conquer the nations of the south, and the east, and the west, He does not conquer the north, for that is where he shall come from – *Syria!*

H. His End.

"Then shall that lawless one be revealed, whom the Lord shall consume with the spirit of his mouth, and shall destroy with the brightness of his coming" (II Thess. 2:8). See also Revelation 19:20.

VI. The Tribulation

There are three distinct tribulations in the Scriptures, and unless they are distinguished from each other, confusion will result. While the Word says that the Body of Christ is enduring tribulation, it also says that Israel shall have tribulation. Then there shall be three and one-half years of great tribulation, such as the world has never seen. At this point many get confused – by the combination of these three into one tribulation. They are distinctly separate, however. First, there is the Tribulation of the Church, which is for the Body of Christ and is now present. Second, there is the Tribulation known as Jacob's Trouble, which lasts seven years and is future. Finally, there is the Great Tribulation, which commences in the midst of Jacob's Trouble and lasts for three and one half years. The first Tribulation is for the Church and is brought about by Satan. The second Tribulation is upon Israel and is brought by God. The Great Tribulation is pronounced upon Israel and the world and is brought by God through Satan.

A. The Tribulation of the Body of Christ.

There is no denying that the Church is enduring tribulation. "For verily, when we were with you, we told you before that we should suffer tribulation; even as it came to pass, and ye know" (I Thess. 3:4). "Yea, and all that will live godly in Christ Jesus shall suffer persecution" (II Tim. 3:12). It is the nature of the Church to suffer. The world lieth in the hands of the wicked one; we being of heavenly origin, are bound to be persecuted by Satan and his cohorts. The Church is a Body; as it is natural for it to suffer, one member may be suffering while the others are not; yet, one member cannot be hurt without the entire body suffering.

Paul, in speaking to the Colossians, said, "[I] now rejoice in my sufferings for you, and fill up that which is behind of the *afflictions* of Christ in my flesh for his body's sake, which is the church" (Col. 1:24). Notice that the word "afflictions" is the Greek word *thlipsis,* meaning tribulation. This is the same word that is used of the Tribulation and the Great Tribulation. Also, we call attention to the words "afflictions of Christ": the definite article should appear before "Christ," making it read "the afflictions of *the* Christ." Thus, it is the Tribulation of the Christ, or the Body of Christ, the Church. As it is natural for the Body to suffer, and as the Colossians were not suffering, Paul had to make up for what was lacking on the part of the Colossians. He so states in this verse. If this were not so, how could he be suffering for the Colossians? He had never been there; he only knew a few of the Christians there; he was in Rome, hundreds of miles away from them. How could his suffering in Rome be effective for them in Colosse? The only answer is that he had to make up for the lack of suffering on the part of the Colossians. In Colossians 1:13 Paul speaks of the Church as being the kingdom of God's dear Son, and then in verse 24 he emphasizes its sufferings, or tribulation.

John states the same thing in Revelation 1:9 (R. V.): "I John, your brother and partaker in *the* tribulation and kingdom and patience which are in Jesus, was in the isle that is called Patmos, for the word of God and the testimony of Jesus." Verily, the Church is enduring tribulation – it is the Tribulation of the Christ.

B. The Tribulation of Israel.

A more familiar term is "Jacob's Trouble." "Alas! for that day is great, so that none is like it: it is even the time of Jacob's trouble, but he shall be saved out of it" (Jer. 30:7).

This period lasts for seven years, and is known as the 70th week of Daniel. "Seventy weeks are determined upon *thy people* and upon thy holy city, to finish the transgression, and to make an end of sins, and to make reconciliation for iniquity, and to bring in everlasting righteousness, and to seal up the vision and prophecy, and to anoint the most Holy. Know, therefore, and understand, that from the going forth of the commandment to restore and to build Jerusalem unto the Messiah the Prince shall be seven weeks, and threescore and two weeks: the street shall be built again, and the wall, even in troublesome times. And after three score and two weeks shall Messiah be cut off, but not for himself: and the people of the prince that shall come shall destroy the city and the sanctuary; and the end thereof shall be with a flood, and unto the end of the war desolations are determined. And he shall confirm the covenant with many for one week" (Dan. 9:24-27).

By these verses we learn that seventy weeks, four hundred and ninety years, were determined for *Daniel's people,* the Jews. From the time that the command came to rebuild Jerusalem to the time when Messiah (Christ) was cut off, was sixty-nine weeks, or four hundred and eighty-three years. Between the sixty-ninth and seventieth week is a gap, known as the Church Age, which Daniel knew nothing about, nor did any other Old Testament prophets (Eph. 3:5). We know that these seventy weeks have to do with Israel alone. The years during the Church period have, we must confess, been lean years for the Jews. It seems that God has forsaken them, but He has not. After this Church Age is completed, known as the "fulness of the Gentiles" (Rom. 11:25), the Church will be raptured, and the Lord shall give full attention to the Jews (Israel) again. This will be the seventieth week, known as the Tribulation, which lasts seven years.

The Church will not go through any part of this seven-year Tribulation. The fourth and fifth chapters of Revelation fully describe the Rapture of the Church before the Tribulation. Chapters six through nineteen then deal with the Tribulation. The Tribulation is identified when the Antichrist confirms the covenant with the Jews. It is concluded with the revelation of Christ in judgment.

C. The Great Tribulation.

While it is still Jacob's Trouble, judgment shall be intensified the last three and one-half years of the Tribulation. It is marked by the breaking of the covenant by the Antichrist, and by the revelation of the Antichrist as *the* Lie. "In the midst of the week he shall cause the sacrifice and the oblation to cease, and for the overspreading of abominations he shall make it desolate, even until the consummation, and that determined shall be poured upon the desolate" (Dan. 9:27). The Lord Jesus re-emphasized this truth when He added some details to the above quoted Scripture: "When ye therefore shall see the abomination of desolation, spoken of by Daniel the prophet, stand in the holy place, (whoso readeth, let him understand:) then let them which be in Judea flee into the mountains. . . . For then shall be *great* tribulation, such as was not since the beginning of the world to this time, no, nor ever shall be" (Matt. 24:15, 16, 21). From the words of Daniel and the Lord Jesus we learn that in the middle of the Tribulation the Antichrist breaks his covenant with the Jews, causes the revived sacrificial rites to come to an end, and places himself in the holy place, which is described as the abomination of desolation. II Thessalonians 2:4 describes this event in added detail: the Antichrist "opposeth and exalteth himself above all that is called God, or that is worshipped; so that he as God sitteth in the temple of God, showing himself that he is God."

During this last three and one-half years, when the Antichrist shall demand to be worshiped as God, man will not be able to buy or sell without his mark (Rev. 13:17).

Many times the question is asked, "Will anyone be saved during the Tribulation (including the Great Tribulation)?" Yes, people will be saved, even during the first three and one-half years of the Tribulation. The departure of the saints will convince many unbelievers of the truth of the Gospel; however, these believers will *not* be part of the Body of Christ. Some may question these statements by using the following verses: "Then shall that lawless one be revealed, whom the Lord shall consume with the spirit of his mouth, and shall destroy with the brightness of his coming: even him, whose coming is after the working of Satan with all power and signs and lying wonders, and with all deceivableness of unrighteousness in them that perish; because they received not the love of the truth, that they might be saved. And for this cause God shall send them strong delusion, that they should believe a [the] lie: that they all might be damned who believe not the truth, but had pleasure in unrighteousness" (II Thess. 2:8-12).

The above verses seem to teach that if one has rejected Christ before the Rapture he will not be able to be saved during the Tribulation. But we call attention to the fact that

God causes them to believe the *Lie,* and they will not be able to believe the Lie until the *middle* of the Tribulation period, as the Antichrist will not be revealed, as such, until then. Therefore, we are led to believe that the invitation will still be given men to be saved during the first three and one-half years of the Tribulation. But if they reject Christ during this time, God shall give them strong delusions to believe the Lie, and it will be impossible for them to be saved during the last three and one-half years of the Tribulation.

The natural question then arises, "Will anyone be saved during the last three and one-half years?" Revelation 7 declares emphatically that there shall be countless numbers of Jews and Gentiles saved during this period, known as the Great Tribulation. Those saved during the Great Tribulation will be those who have never heard the Gospel and have not taken the mark of the beast. Their salvation will be brought about by the preaching of a great evangelistic movement, which will be composed, we believe, of the 144,000 Israelites (Rev. 7:4-8).

You may ask, "How, then, will it be possible for them to be saved when the Holy Spirit has been taken up out of the world?" Let us turn to Moffatt's translation and read: "For the secret force of lawlessness is at work already; only, it cannot be revealed till he who at present restrains it is removed" (II Thess. 2:7). The Holy Spirit will not be taken up out of the earth, but will take His restraining hand off sinful man and give him up fully to his sin. The Holy Spirit will still be here, for He is omnipresent. He will not manifest Himself during the Great Tribulation as He did *before* the dispensation of grace. Again we remind you that the Great Tribulation ends with the coming of Christ to this earth.

VII. The Battle of Armageddon

Whenever a great battle is fought, people fear that it is the Battle of Armageddon. In order clearly to understand this battle, let us find out first what it is not, and then what it is.

A. *What It Is Not.*

1. *It Is Not World Wars I and II.*

2. *It Is Not the First Battle of Gog and Magog.* This battle is composed of the forces of the Northern confederacy (Russia and her allies). It is not much of a battle, but God

rains fire and brimstone upon the armies and country. This occurs at the beginning of the Tribulation.

3. *It Is Not the War in Heaven.* This battle is described in Revelation 12:7-17. It concerns the forces of Satan being defeated by Michael and his army.

4. *It Is Not the Second Battle of Gog and Magog.* This is the concluding battle of all battles, whether physical or spiritual. It is fought *after* the Millennium, when Satan is loosed for a season and deceives the Gentile peoples (Rev. 20:7-9). Fire comes down from heaven and destroys them.

B. What It Is.

1. *The Participants.* "I saw the beast, and the kings of the earth, and their armies, gathered together to make war against him that sat on the horse, and against his army" (Rev. 19:19). This is the seed of the serpent fighting against the Seed of the woman (Gen. 3:15). It is the conflict between Christ and the Antichrist.

2. *The Place.* The plain of Esdraelon is the place of this battle. It is an ancient battleground. Gideon fought there; Saul and Jonathan were killed there; Josiah was killed by Pharaoh there; the Greeks and Romans battled there; and Napoleon suffered his first defeat there.

3. *The Time.* The battle occurs at the end of the Great Tribulation, just before the Millennium begins.

4. *The End.* The end of this battle results in the complete annihilation of the Antichrist's army. The Antichrist and the False Prophet are then cast alive into Hell. "The beast was taken, and with him the false prophet that wrought miracles before him, with which he deceived them that had received the mark of the beast, and them that worshipped his image. These both were cast alive into a lake of fire burning with brimstone" (Rev. 19:20).

VIII. The Millennium

The Millennium is the thousand-year reign of Christ immediately following the Great Tribulation. Millennium is not a Scriptural word, but it is a Scriptural truth.

A. The Fact of the Millennium.

1. *The Lord Has Decreed It* (Ps. 2).
2. *Christ Taught It* (Matt. 24; Mark 13; Luke 21).
3. *The Scriptures Teach It* (Is. 2, 11).

4. *The Psalmist Described It* (Ps. 72).
5. *The Angels Declared It* (Luke 1).
6. *The Transfiguration Pictures It* (Matt. 16:28; 17:1).
7. *A Gospel Outlines It* (Mark 6:45-56).
8. *The Apostles Preached It* (Acts 2, 3).
9. *Nature Longs For It.* (Rom. 8).

B. The Description of the Millennium.

1. *The Thousand Years* (Rev. 21:1-7).
2. *The Age to Come* (Eph. 1:21).
3. *The Day of the* LORD (Rev. 6:12-17; Joel 2:10, 11, 30, 31; Hag. 2:6, 7; Matt. 24; Zech. 14:1-5).
4. *In That Day* (Is. 4:2; 2:11, 17, 20, 21; 11:11).
5. *The Restitution of All Things.* "[The Lord] shall send Jesus Christ . . . whom the heavens must receive until the times of restitution of all things, *which God hath spoken by the mouth of all his holy prophets* since the world began" (Acts 3:20, 21). Some use this verse as meaning the restitution of Christ-rejecting sinners, and even the Devil. But notice that the above verse says, "which *God hath spoken* by the mouth of all his holy prophets." The prophets say nothing of the restitution of the Devil and sinners.

   a. *Israel to the Promised Land* (Is. 11:10-12).
   b. *Repentance of the Nations to Jehovah* (Zech. 12:10-14).
   c. *The Removal of the Band of Iniquity* (Zech. 3:9).
   d. *Restoration of Rain* (Joel 2:23-29).
   e. *Re-engraving of Jehovah's Law* (Jer. 31:28-37).
   f. *Redistribution of the Land* (Ezek. 48).
   g. *Reconstruction of Jerusalem* (Is. 62; Ezek. 40).
   h. *Restitution From Bondage of Fear* (Is. 14:1-3; Jer. 33:14-16).
   i. *Restitution of Jehovah's Love* (Zeph. 3:16-20).

6. *The Regeneration of All Things* (Matt. 19:18; Is. 32).
7. *The Falling Stone* (Dan. 2).

C. The Types of the Millennium.

1. *The Year of Jubilee* (Lev. 25).
2. *The Feas of Tabernacles* (Lev. 23).
3. *The Sabbath.* It is that rest to come.
4. *The Kingdom of Israel Under Solomon's Reign.* This was an absolute reign of peace.

D. The Conditions During the Millennium.

1. *The Church.* "It is a faithful saying: For if we be dead with him we also shall live with him: if we suffer, we shall also reign with him: if we deny him, he also will deny us" (II Tim. 2:11, 12). Wherever the Lord shall be, there we shall be with Him (I Thess. 4:17). We shall reign, and we shall judge over angels and the world. I Corinthians 6:2, 3 says, "Do ye not know that the saints shall judge the world. . . . Know ye not that we shall judge angels?"

2. *Satan.* Satan shall be sealed and bound for a thousand years (Rev. 20:1-7). The Antichrist is cast into the lake of fire before that (Rev. 19:20).

3. *Israel.* She shall become the head of all nations again, and will not remain the tail as she is today (Is. 2:1-4; 11:3, 4; 61:5; Zech. 8:23; Deut. 28:13).

4. *The Nations of the World.* All nations will have to come up to Jerusalem year by year and worship Jehovah there. If they do not keep the yearly Feast of Tabernacles, God will cause no rain to fall upon that nation (Zech. 14:16; Is. 2).

5. *Mankind.*

a. *Spiritual Condition.* Some have been led to think that there will be no sin during the Millennium, but there will be. Human nature has never changed from one dispensation to another. There will be universal adoration of Christ (Heb. 8:11; 2:14; Phil. 2:10, 11), but it will be feigned obedience upon the part of many. For example, many in prison obey their warden, not because they love him, but because they must. Where will these sinners come from, as the Millennium begins with only born-again believers? They will be born of saved parents who came out of the Tribulation alive.

b. *Physical Condition.* Human life will be lengthened. Some will be able to live throughout the Millennium. There shall be death during this reign of Christ, also – death, not to the believer, but to the unbeliever. No babes or children shall die. When the sinner becomes one hundred years old and still rejects Christ, he shall be cut off by death. "There shall be no more thence an infant of days, nor an old man that hath not filled his days: for the child shall die an hundred years old; but the sinner being an hundred years old shall be accursed [cut off]" (Is. 65:20).

c. *Moral Condition.* This will not be a period of absolute perfection. However, sin will not be allowed to raise its head. Christ shall rule with a rod of iron (Ps. 46:9; Is. 2:4). Sin, nevertheless, will be committed in the hearts of men.

6. *Creation.*

a. *Physical.* When Adam fell, the earth was cursed (Rom. 8:18-23). Man has accomplished wonders with his irrigation systems, and the like, but look what God will do! "The wilderness and the solitary place shall be glad for them; and the desert shall rejoice and blossom as the rose" (Is. 35:1). See also Isaiah 55:13. Creation shall be restored completely; no more earthquakes; no more storms, famines and pestilences (Joel 2).

b. *Animal Creation.* Before man sinned, God had put the fear of man in the animals. They ate the grass of the fields. During the Millennium they shall revert back to the same order which He had intended for them (Is. 11:6-9). "And a little child shall lead them" (Is. 11:6) means that a child, during the Millennium, shall *literally* lead animals around. It is not speaking about children leading sinners to the Lord.

IX. The Judgments

The Bible does *not* teach a general judgment. Instead, it informs us that there are many judgments, some past, some present and some future. For example, there is the past judgment upon Sodom and there is the future judgment upon Babylon.

A. *Judgments of the Christian.*

1. *Judgment on Sin.* When did this occur? For the Christian this is a past judgment, for all of our sins were judged at Calvary. "Christ also hath once suffered for sins, the just for the unjust, that he might bring us to God, being put to death in the flesh, but quickened by the Spirit" (I Peter 3:18). "Who his own self bare our sins in his own body on the tree, that we, being dead to sins, should live unto righteousness: by whose stripes ye were healed" (I Peter 2:24). See also Galatians 3:13; John 3:16; Isaiah 53:5, 6.

2. *Judgment on Christian Service.* No Christian will have to be judged for his sins; they have already been judged upon the Cross of Calvary. The Christian will have to answer to God for his works. "We must all appear before the judgment seat of Christ; that everyone may receive the things done

in his body, according to that he hath done, whether it be good or bad" (II Cor. 5:10). Yes, the Christian has escaped the future judgment of the wicked ("Verily, verily, I say unto you, he that heareth my word, and believeth on him that sent me hath eternal life, and cometh not into judgment, but hath passed out of death into life"—John 5:24, R.V.), but he shall stand before the judgment seat of Christ to receive rewards for the deeds done in the body. The words, "judgment seat," are from the Greek word "Bema," better translated "Rewarding Stand." This will be set up when Christ comes. "Behold, I come quickly; and my reward is with me, to give every man according as his work shall be" (Rev. 22:12).

There are several crowns that the Christian may achieve:

a. *The Crown of Life.* "Blessed is the man that endureth temptation: for when he is tried, he shall receive the *crown of life,* which the Lord hath promised to them that love him" (Jas. 1:12). See also Revelation 2:10. This is rewarded for faithfulness, even unto death.

b. *An Incorruptible Crown.* "Every man that striveth for the mastery is temperate in all things. Now they do it to obtain a corruptible crown; but we an *incorruptible*" (I Cor. 9:25). This is a reward for those who live separated lives unto the Lord.

c. *Crown of Rejoicing.* "What is our hope, or joy, or *crown of rejoicing?* Are not even ye in the presence of our Lord Jesus Christ at his coming?" (I Thess. 2:19). This is the soul-winner's crown.

d. *Crown of Glory.* "Feed the flock of God which is among you, taking the oversight thereof, not by constraint, but willingly; not for filthy lucre, but of a ready mind; neither as being lords over God's heritage, but being ensamples to the flock. And when the chief Shepherd shall appear, ye shall receive a *crown of glory* that fadeth not away" (I Peter 5:2-4). This is the shepherds', pastors', or ministers' reward.

e. *Crown of Righteousness.* "There is laid up for me a *crown of righteousness,* which the Lord, the righteous judge shall give me at that day: and not to me only, but unto all them also that love his appearing." This crown goes to all who love His second coming. If you love His appearing, you will talk about it. All doctrines are headed up by the Second Coming.

B. Judgment of the Nations. This takes place at the beginning of the Millennium, the thousand year reign (Matt. 25:31-46). A better name for "nations" is "Gentiles." This is the judgment of all Gentiles who come out of the Tribulation alive. There are three classes of people mentioned: sheep, goats and brethren. The brethren are the Jews; the sheep are the righteous; and the goats are the unrighteous.

The righteous (sheep, Gentiles) go into the kingdom, then on to eternal life. The unrighteous (goats, Gentiles) are sent immediately to the lake of fire; therefore, they will not be judged at the Great White Throne. They go there a thousand years sooner than the wicked *dead.*

There are those who contend that this is a judgment of works and that men go to heaven or hell on the basis of their works; for, they say, the Scriptures state that this judgment is based upon the words "inasmuch as ye have done it, or inasmuch as ye did it not." However, we will show that it is still a judgment based upon faith. The Lord, here, is the judge, and He does mete out judgment on the basis of the words "inasmuch as. . . . " But let us ask, What prompted the sheep nations to minister to the brethren, the Jews, during the Tribulation? They did it because they accepted the brethren's preaching. Do you think that they would have visited, clothed, fed and ministered to the brethren during the Tribulation if they had not believed? Remember, the Tribulation is going to be a time of peril. Man will not be able to buy or sell without the mark of the beast. The sheep (Gentiles) defy this order, reject the mark of the beast, and accept what the brethren preach. We know they accept Christ, for the Lord has said, "He that receiveth you receiveth me" (Matt. 10:40). Again we emphasize that the sheep (Gentiles) are saved because of their faith in Christ, for Revelation 7:14 declares it so: "He said to me, These are they which came out of great tribulation [the Great Tribulation], and have washed their robes, and made them white in the blood of the Lamb."

The unrighteous nations (goats, Gentiles) are cast into hell because of their unbelief. They rejected the brethren, thus rejecting Christ.

C. Judgment at the Great White Throne. This great judgment is found in Revelation 20:11-15: "I saw a great white throne, and him that sat on it, from whose face the earth and the heaven fled away; and there was found no place for them. And I saw the dead, small and great, stand before God; and the books were opened: and another book was opened, which is the book of life: and the dead were judged out of those things which were written in the books according to their works." It is the judgment only of the wicked dead who have been raised at the last resurrection. No born-again believer shall appear here. The wicked dead are not to be tried as to whether they are going to heaven or hell; it has already been determined that they are going to hell, for they died condemned (John 3:18). This judgment is to determine the degrees of punishment, "according to their works" (Rev. 20:13).

There are two witnesses against them: The Book, and the Books; that is, the Book of Life, and the Book of Works. We do not know what the different degrees of punishment will be.

X. After the Millennium

"When the thousand years are expired, Satan shall be loosed out of his prison, and shall go out to deceive the nations which are in the four quarters of the earth, Gog and Magog, to gather them together to battle, the number of whom is as the sand of the sea. And they went up on the breath of the earth, and compassed the camp of the saints about, and the beloved city: and fire came down from God out of heaven, and devoured them" (Rev. 20:7-9).

This is the war that ends all war. It is the final conflict of the universe.

A. Satan Loosed.

As he is loosed for a short time, he tries one more thrust at God.

B. Nations Gathered.

We ask ourselves, Who could Satan organize among the Gentiles to fight against God? None other but those unsaved who are ninety-nine years old and younger, who have been born during the last century of the Millennium.

Notice that no army has gathered against them.

C. Army Destroyed.

Fire comes down from heaven and destroys them.

D. Satan Doomed.

He is then cast into the lake of fire prepared for him and his angels.

XI. The Future of the Wicked.

It is not hard to think of everlasting life, but it is hard to think of an eternity in hell; nevertheless, it is true.

A. *The Scriptural Teaching.*

1. *There Will Be a Day of Judgment* (Acts 17:30, 31).

2. *Every Man Will Be Judged for His Works* (Rom. 2:16; Rev. 20:12).

3. *It Is Eternal* (Mark 9:43-48). See also Matt. 13.

4. *There Will Be Degrees of Punishment* (Rev. 20:12; Rom. 2:5, 6).

5. *There Will Be a Resurrection of the Unjust As Well As of the Just* (John 5:29).

6. *Language Describes It* (Matt. 25:46; Mark 9:45-48; John 3:36).

7. *All Is Based Upon the Character of God as Righteous.*

B. *The Terms Used.*

The following are the places where wicked human beings and angels are, or shall be sent to:

1. *Sheol.* This is the Old Testament word describing the place of the departed wicked.

2. *Hades.* This is the New Testament Greek word, describing the immediate state of the wicked dead; it is the same as Sheol. There is nothing in the Bible that speaks of an eternal Hades, or Sheol.

3. *Tartarus.* This is the place where the wicked angels are chained; it is a place of darkness.

4. *Gehenna.* Gehenna was the city dump outside of Jerusalem, whose fire never went out. The Lord Himself likened hell unto it, describing the fires of hell that shall always burn: "Where their worm dieth not, and the fire is not quenched" (Mark 9:44).

5. *Tophet.* "Tophet" is the Old Testament Hebrew word meaning the same as Gehenna.

6. *Abyss.* This is the place of fallen angels, human beings are never placed here (Rom. 10:7).

7. *Lake of Fire.* This is found only in the Book of the Revelation. Its meaning is the same as Gehenna.

8. *Eternal.* Sometimes this word is translated "everlasting." The meaning is the same. The punishment of the wicked is eternal.

a. *First Interpretation.* Thayer translates it to mean "without beginning and without end."

b. *Second Interpretation.* This states that "eternal" means "without beginning."

c. *Third Interpretation.* This holds that "eternal" means "without ending." We agree with all three. We do not hold to the interpretation that it means only "age lasting." Some would have us believe that the wicked will endure hell for just an age. But the word "eternal" describing hell is the same word which describes eternal life (John 3:16), and the everlasting God (Rom. 16:26), and the everlasting kingdom of Jesus Christ (II Peter 1:11).

C. *The Theories Proposed.*

1. *Universalism.* This is the belief that all will finally be saved, including the Devil. What would the words "judge" and "judgments" mean if they did not mean judge or judgment. When God speaks about eternal judgment, He means eternal judgment (Acts 3:21-24; I Cor. 15:22; Matt. 18:9; John 3:36).

2. *Conditionalism.* This false teaching was not found in the Early Church, but it first made its appearance in the nineteenth century. It was reasoned that eternal life is based upon the acceptance of Jesus Christ. If one accepts Him, he has eternal life. If he does not accept Him, he will never live; *non-acceptance* in this life will result in *non-existence* in the future life. There is no *Scriptural* foundation for this theory.

3. *Everlasting Punishment.* This is based upon Biblical truth, which connects sin with punishment. All sins committed are committed against eternity. He who sins by rejecting Jesus Christ shall endure eternal punishment.

XII. Heaven

The Scriptures teach that there are three heavens:

A. *First Heaven.*

This is the region of the clouds where the birds fly, the atmospheric heaven.

B. *Second Heaven.*

This is the stellar heaven, where the stars are located.

C. *Third Heaven.*

This is the place where God lives; it is the place where Jesus came from.

The Lord Jesus went through the first and second heaven to get to the third heaven. "Having then a great high priest, who has passed *through the heavens,* Jesus the Son of God, let us hold fast our confession" (Heb. 4:14, R.V.).

Heaven is just as real as the clouds and stars. It is the place where Stephen saw God; the place to which John was caught up by the Spirit. The first thing he saw, was the Lord Jesus. He is the heart of heaven (Rev. 1, Heb. 9:24). Paul, too, was caught up to the third heaven (II Cor. 12:2). Where is heaven? Does the Bible make it clear? Heaven is always in the *north.* "He stretcheth out the north over the empty place, and hangeth the earth upon nothing" (Job 26:7). See also Isaiah 14:12-14; Psalm 82:1; 48:2.

Is heaven foursquare? Is it a cube? What will man have for his future home? Will it be a small cubby hole in a square city? Is heaven only fifteen hundred miles square? While the new Jerusalem (Rev. 21, 22) is foursquare, this is only a city of heaven, which descends as a present for the Bride.

Those who go there will live in perfect peace and perfect love for all time and eternity. "Ye are come unto mount Sion, and unto the city of the living God, the heavenly Jerusalem, and to an innumerable company of angels" (Heb. 12:22).

INDEX